MUSLIMS AND CHRISTIANS DEBATE
JUSTICE AND LOVE

Published

Contemporary Puritan Salafism
Susanne Olsson

Earth, Empire and Sacred Text
Muslims and Christians as Trustees of Creation
David L. Johnston

East by Mid-East
Studies in Cultural, Historical and Strategic Connectivities
Edited by Anchi Hoh and Brannon M. Wheeler

Ibn Arabi and the Contemporary West
Beshara and the Ibn Arabi Society
Isobel Jeffery-Street

Notes from the Fortune-Telling Parrot
Islam and the Struggle for Religious Pluralism in Pakistan
David Pinault

Orientalists, Islamists and the Global Public Sphere
A Genealogy of the Modern Essentialist Image of Islam
Dietrich Jung

Prolegomena to a History of Islamicate Manichaeism
John C. Reeves

Prophecy and Power
Muhammad and the Qur'an in the Light of Comparison
Marilyn Robinson Waldman
Edited by Bruce B. Lawrence, with Lindsay Jones and Robert M. Baum

The Arabs and the Scramble for Africa
John C. Wilkinson

The Qur'ān
A New Annotated Translation
A. J. Droge

Forthcoming

Words of Experience
Translating Islam with Carl W. Ernst
Edited by Ilyse R. Morgenstein Fuerst and Brannon M. Wheeler

MUSLIMS AND CHRISTIANS DEBATE JUSTICE AND LOVE

David L. Johnston

SHEFFIELD UK   BRISTOL CT

Published by Equinox Publishing Ltd.

UK: Office 415, The Workstation, 15 Paternoster Row, Sheffield, South Yorkshire S1 2BX
USA: ISD, 70 Enterprise Drive, Bristol, CT 06010

www.equinoxpub.com

First published 2020

British Library Cataloguing-in-Publication Data

A catalogue record for this book is available from the British Library.

ISBN-13   978 1 78179 934 5   (hardback)
          978 1 78179 935 2   (paperback)
          978 1 78179 936 9   (ePDF)

Library of Congress Cataloging-in-Publication Data
Names: Johnston, David L, 1952- author.
Title: Muslims and Christians debate justice and love / David L Johnston.
Description: Bristol : Equinox Publishing Ltd, 2020. | Series: Comparative
  Islamic studies | Includes bibliographical references and index. |
Summary: «This book seeks to elucidate the concept of justice, not so
  much as it is expressed in law courts (retributive and procedural
  justice) or in state budgets (distributive justice), but as primary
  justice - what it means and how it can be grounded in the inalienable
  rights that each human being possesses qua human being. It draws
  inspiration from two recent works of philosopher Nicolas Wolterstorff,
  but also from the groundbreaking Islamic initiative of 2007, the Common
  Word Letter addressed by 138 eminent Muslim scholars and clerics to the
  pope and all Christian leaders. This document affirmed that the two
  highest commandments in both Judaism and Christianity are also at the
  heart of the Islamic tradition - love of God and love of neighbor. In a
  style that lends itself to the classroom and beyond, the book's six
  chapters all begin with a case study of justice, so as to emphasize that
  justice must also be embodied in righteous social, political and
  economic practices. Along the way, leading contemporary scholars and
  activists from both traditions urge the reader - Muslim, Christian, or
  whatever - to look afresh at an age-old conundrum: how do justice and
  love interact so as to create a world in which everyone finds his or her
  rightful place?»-- Provided by publisher.
Identifiers: LCCN 2019025665 (print) | LCCN 2019025666 (ebook) | ISBN
  9781781799345 (hardback) | ISBN 9781781799352 (paperback) | ISBN
  9781781799369 (ebook)
Subjects: LCSH: Justice. | Christianity and justice. | Islam and justice.
Classification: LCC JC578 .J665 2020 (print) | LCC JC578 (ebook) | DDC
  320.01/1--dc23
LC record available at https://lccn.loc.gov/2019025665
LC ebook record available at https://lccn.loc.gov/2019025666

Typeset by S.J.I. Services, New Delhi, India

Contents

– 1 –

Introduction

Children at play seem to have an innate sense of justice. In fact, they argue and fight over it all the time: 'That isn't fair!' Look again, and that the argument implies a sense of equality. An older sibling cannot change the rules of the game just because she's older and stronger. A younger sibling cannot be left to win just because if he loses he will have a tantrum. Rules are rules and everyone playing the game should follow them. At least, that seems to be the ideal children naturally entertain, even if in reality the older and stronger ones tend to get their way.

If you widen the context just a bit, and you examine a school courtyard at recess or break time, you are likely to find instances of bullying – a stronger child taking advantage of a weaker one, either by taking something from her, or by abusing her verbally or physically. Naturally, one hopes an adult supervisor will step in, punish the offender and restore anything stolen. Then too in elementary school different groups of friends start to form. Some of those just keep to themselves and follow their own interests without interfering with others. Yet one or two of them may seek to gain power over others, often by establishing themselves as the 'popular kids' or strong athletes, and thereby excluding those who want to join them because they are found wanting. This social dynamic of course only intensifies at the middle and high school level.

At that point there is only so much a school administration can do to create harmony, quash conflicts, and deal with thefts, illegal drugs, and – heaven forbid – weapons like knives and firearms. Justice, then, is about governance, whether at the school level or at a state level. The ancient Greek philosopher Plato saw justice in two dimensions. First, it is the virtue an individual displays in being fair and kind. Second, justice is what creates a harmonious society.

For Plato, however, justice was only about Athenian middle and upper class men being able to freely pursue their interests and contribute to the good of their own society of peers. Democracy, or the power of the people to determine the shape of their society, applied only to these privileged males and not to women, foreigners, and certainly not to slaves. So his concept of a 'just society' was skewed from the start.

Every society, it turns out, suffers at least from the potential harm of conflicting groups – rich and poor, various ethnicities, political and religious identities, and this particularly in our age of increasing globalization. Even without the uncertainty and often the threat of foreign powers, governance is a challenging and enormously complex task. Justice at this level is about a nation's laws and the way they are enforced. In a democratic polity these are managed and updated by the legislative branch of government, while the judiciary takes responsibility for the mission to keep law and order, as well as making sure that both legislative and executive branches follow the principles and directives laid out in the Constitution.

Yet even when these important institutions and organs of government are in place in order to provide proper checks and balances, corruption in many forms is apt to creep in and undermine the notion that this particular government is 'just.' Human beings seem incurably vulnerable to the temptations of money and power. Good governance requires great vigilance.

This is a book specifically about Muslims and Christians discussing these complex issues, and not simply in the area of governance. This is not a prescriptive work, that is, offering solutions to social ills in the form of government policies. Yet neither is it a book simply about the theory of justice or only about a theology of love and justice. Rather, while recognizing that these issues have exercised much greater minds than my own, I want to present some of the current discussions on the topic of justice and its relation to love. But I do so on the basis of a prior work, which argues that in the light of their sacred texts both Muslims and Christians (and Jews) see themselves as empowered by God to exercise dominion on the earth as his stewards or trustees. By virtue of creation, God has equipped men and women with both reason and a moral compass, and therefore called them to manage the earth's resources as well as their own earthly community for the common good of all, including the earth itself. And for this he will call us to account on Judgment Day.[1]

This book argues that justice and love are both complimentary and inseparable. Justice is to respect and care for the rights and dignity of each fellow human being because he or she is also a special creature of the

One God. This in effect is to 'love your neighbor as yourself', as we read in Leviticus 18:18, and then in the gospels when Jesus speaks of the greatest of all commandments. The Leviticus context is telling. It includes, a) making sure to leave gleanings in the fields and grapes in the vineyards at harvest time for the poor; b) forbidding theft and lying; c) banning injustice from court proceedings, especially partiality toward the rich; d) forbidding slander, hatred, and holding grudges. Clearly both justice and love are involved in these injunctions. The poor have a right against those with means. Those who are able must help them in their need and the courts in particular must be a place where the rights of all are respected.

I embark on this project as one who lived for a decade and a half in three different Arab countries, serving as a clergyman (Algeria) and then as a teacher (Egypt and the West Bank). After that I launched into Islamic Studies and Muslim-Christian dialogue. In academia today we have come to accept that scholars do not write in a vacuum. They come to their subject manner with questions and perspectives that are specific to their own 'social location.' Theologically, I still consider myself an evangelical, although definitely not associated in any way with the 'Christian Right', that influential movement launched in the late 1970s by Jerry Falwell and Pat Robertson. I rather identify with the 39 leaders who came together in October 2018 and signed the 'Chicago Invitation' declaration, attempting 'to disrupt the narrative that evangelicals as a whole are white, right-wing Trump supporters who are indifferent about social justice.'[2]

I have long fought the stereotype that Muslims only care about justice while Christians only care about love. That simply is not true. More importantly, Muslim and Christian scholars are becoming more aware of how these two ethical norms overlap and even how inseparable they actually are. Telling that story from different angles, including my own analysis, is what I am doing in this book.

As I write, my own country (USA) is politically divided about what to do with the tens of thousands of migrants who manage to survive the perilous crossing into our territory from Mexico, mostly originating from the Central American nations of Honduras, El Salvador and Guatemala, where many face gang violence and abject poverty, precipitated in part by droughts and a changing climate. This is nothing new, of course, but the Trump administration with its 'zero tolerance' immigration policy began separating children from their parents while the latter were being tried in criminal courts. As might be expected, a chorus of protest arose both internationally and domestically against a practice described by the United Nations' high commissioner for human rights as 'arbitrary and unlawful interference in family life, and ... a serious violation of the rights of the child.'[3]

The expression 'rights of the child' is a reference to 'international law', a body of international legal instruments associated with the United Nations and traced back to its founding Charter and especially its first document on human rights, the Universal Declaration of Human Rights (UDHR, 1948). This was followed-up by two more detailed conventions in 1966, the International Covenant on Civil and Political Rights (ICCR) and the International Covenant on Economic, Social and Cultural Rights (ICESC). All three documents form 'the International Bill of Human Rights.' Whereas the ICCR concerns 'negative rights' (protection of individual liberties from state encroachment and abuse), the ICESC deals with 'positive rights', like the right to education, health care, employment, and even vacation time from work.

These United Nations conventions, signed and ratified by most nations, came into force as 'soft' international law; yet despite – or *because of* – the lack of systematic mechanisms of enforcement, it is still up to individual state parties to live up to the commitments they made as signatories of these documents. In particular, the UN Convention on the Rights of the Child (CRC, 1989) expressly forbids the forceful removal of children from their families. That said, the United States is the only country that has not ratified the CRC.

The idea of human rights comes up several times in the course of this book. Allow me to simply say here that their definition and the extent to which they apply within national boundaries have long been a subject of debate. For instance, just like the CRC, the US never ratified the ICESC or CEDAW (Convention on the Elimination of All Forms of Discrimination against Women, 1981). The US did ratify the ICCR, but only in the 1980s, and even then while registering significant reservations. To say the least, and in the words of Malcolm Evans, Dean of the University of Bristol's School of Law, 'human rights instruments are the product of varying inputs, many highly contentious, often largely political, and are the product of intense negotiation.'[4] Yet throughout these pages, I will maintain that justice in human society is tied to the respect of universal human rights. To make this argument I will draw from a number of disciplines – historical and legal studies, sociology and philosophy, and ethics in particular, but especially from theology and Religious Studies.

Justice is Central to both Islam and Christianity

Amidst the swirling political debates around the issue of migrant families to the United States, religious voices are also being heard. Christians from all denominations, Catholics and also mainline and evangelical Protestants have been speaking out. A large demonstration in Murietta, CA, which included many immigrant mothers and children, sparked a counter demonstration with participants repeatedly shouting 'Go home!' Incensed, Roman Catholic archbishop of New York, Timothy M. Dolan, went back to his guest room and posted a spirited blog characterizing the counter protests thus: 'It was un-American; it was unbiblical; it was inhumane.'[5] In Dallas, TX, over 100 religious leaders came together to find ways to help these children. Among them was Rabbi Asher Knight of Temple Emanu-El, who said that some in his congregation were comparing this wave of migrant children to the great rescue mission in the late 1930s, the Kindertransport, when Jewish children were escorted from Nazi Germany to Britain.

These protests are all in the tradition of the Hebrew prophets who ceaselessly railed against the abusive actions of kings and nobility against the poor, the immigrants and foreign residents, the widows and orphans in their midst. Martin Luther King Jr.'s civil rights movement was launched from the pulpit of churches, preaching on such Old Testament passages like this one by the prophet Amos, 'But let justice roll on like a river, righteousness like a never-failing stream!' (Amos 5:24).[6]

When the most vulnerable of human beings come under attack, people of faith speak out. The Dalai Lama voiced his great sadness and firmly rebuked the Buddhist monks of Myanmar who have been guilty of violence and oppression against the Muslim Rohingya minority in that country. In particular he said, 'All the world's major religions convey a message of peace and compassion, so it is especially saddening when we hear of violence being used in the name of religion like the very unfortunate events concerning the Muslim community in Burma [Myanmar].'[7] At least in the Dalai Lama's version of Buddhism, compassion is its central virtue. Although Muslims would echo this sentiment, they would surely have added the word 'justice' somewhere in that sentence – and rightly so.[8] The Qur'an, after all, mentions over 50 times how crucial justice is in human relations and in several hundred other verses it deplores the damage done to one's self and to others when one resorts to injustice (*ẓulm*).

Indeed most Muslims, if not all, would agree with Mohammad Hashim Kamali, a leading scholar of Islamic law, when he writes that 'justice is the overriding goal and objective of Islam.' He goes on to explain:

> Justice is ... made applicable not only in the courtroom and in respect of fair distribution of wealth in the community but also to the personal conduct of the individual in his vision of himself and his relationship with others, his family, his environment, and the world at large. Muslims are thus enjoined "to speak with justice even if be someone close to you" (al-An'am 6:152). The emphasis on impartial justice and the unqualified scope of this demand is such that justice is demanded by everyone "even if it be against yourselves, your parents and your relatives, or whether it be against the rich or poor" (al-Nisa' 4:135).[9]

The centrality of justice in Islam is well known, but why 'justice and love' here?

Why Justice and Love?

If mercy and compassion are the best values on which to base a fruitful Muslim-Buddhist dialogue, justice and love fit much better in any bid to enhance a Muslim-Christian conversation. Here I assert that inherent and inalienable rights for all human beings are the only guarantee for true justice in human society. At the same time, there are plenty of situations in which naked justice can do more harm than good, to the individual and to the wider community. Thus, British Muslim scholar Timothy J. Winter writes that 'Islam's is a God of justice but also of mercy.' He explains:

> The extent to which the latter virtue can override the former in political life can only be defined in a very limited way in books of law. In Islamic legal culture, which grants the judge more discretion than the heavily statutory jurisdictions of the West, the judge has much more room for mercy. In the religion of wisdom and compassion, which deeply trusts human beings, it is no surprise that the judge should have been given this privilege.[10]

This concept of mercy mitigating strict justice is familiar to Christians as well ('Mercy triumphs over judgment', James 2:13, NIV), but it was the concept of justice connected to rights in particular that became the topic of a Muslim-Christian conference. The former Archbishop of Canterbury, Rowan Williams, had already sponsored four Building Bridges seminars for Muslims and Christian scholars when he convened the fifth in 2006 at Georgetown University in Washington, D.C. Its theme was 'Justice and Rights – Christian and Muslim Perspectives', resulting in a book by the same title, from which I have already quoted. Michael Ipgrave, its editor and a Muslim-Christian dialogue veteran, writes in the Introduction that 'justice is recognized by Christians and Muslims as one of the defining characteristics of God and sought by them as his purpose for a world that is manifestly unjust.'[11] That said, a human rights discourse that seems to elevate the Enlightenment ideals of human autonomy and freedom rests uneasily with two religious traditions that emphasize human responsibility before God and one's fellow man. As we shall see, partly because the Enlightenment grew out of Christian intellectual roots, and partly because Christianity's founder never exercised political authority, the clash between a rights discourse and traditional Islamic thought is perhaps greater for Muslims than it is for Christians.

Still, justice as rights is central to both traditions, at least as articulated by many contemporary scholars on both sides. But what about love? I quoted Winter on the central role of mercy, which balances justice in Islam, but is mercy the same as love? That point too is discussed in greater detail in Chapter 6, but suffice it to say here that this book takes seriously the Common World letter of 2007 and the movement of interfaith dialogue that followed in its wake.

That historic letter ('A Common Word Between Us and You'), signed by an impressive global array of Muslim leaders and scholars, was triggered by a couple events but its formulation and subsequent influence should rightly be attributed to Jordan's Prince Ghazi bin Mohammad. The first event, as one might imagine, was the attacks on US soil on September 11, 2001, commonly referred to as 9/11. Besides triggering a flurry of condemnations from all manner of Muslim scholars, officials and Islamic organizations,[12] the 9/11 killings produced a movement of unity among various Muslim constituents, in part to better denounce terrorism. Surprisingly perhaps, the initiative and momentum came from the small kingdom of Jordan, which had already managed to bring together an imposing quorum of Islamic leaders and figureheads in 2005. According to the official Jordanian website of 'The Amman Message', the participants managed to issue a unified declaration on three issues that have kept Muslims divided almost from the start:

> In order to give this statement more religious authority, H.M. King Abdullah II then sent the following three questions to 24 of the most senior religious scholars from all around the world representing all the branches and schools

of Islam: (1) Who is a Muslim? (2) Is it permissible to declare someone an apostate (*takfir*)? (3) Who has the right to undertake issuing fatwas (legal rulings)?[13]

Based on their answers, the king organized an international conference of Muslim luminaries from 50 countries in Mecca in July 2005. The following 'Three Points of the Amman Message' were unanimously approved and within the next year and a half were ratified by seven other international Islamic bodies.[14] This is the context, then, that must be kept in mind when one refers to the Muslim reactions to Pope Benedict XVI's 2006 lecture at the University of Regensburg.[15] After the initial outbursts of outrage around the Muslim world, 38 Muslim authorities and scholars sent a letter to the pope, correcting what they saw as his mischaracterizations of Islam and calling for some open conversation on the matter.

One year later, Prince Ghazi bin Muhammad, King Abdullah's cousin and chief advisor, penned a letter addressed to the pope and all Christian leaders entitled, 'A Common Word Between Us and You.'[16] It was signed by 138 leading Muslim opinion leaders, but thousands of others have signed it since then.[17] It begins with the fact that Muslims and Christians form more than half of today's humanity, and therefore, unless past and present conflicts, wounds and misunderstandings are not cleared up, there will be no peace in our world. Yet the principle upon which such peace can be achieved is in plain sight. Prince Ghazi explains:

> It is part of the very foundational principles of both faiths: love of the One God, and love of the neighbour. These principles are found over and over again in the sacred texts of Islam and Christianity. The Unity of God, the necessity of love for Him, and the necessity of love of the neighbour is thus the common ground between Islam and Christianity.[18]

So clearly, justice, love, forgiveness and mercy are interconnected concepts and values. But from another perspective, justice and love must be paired. That is a long argument I have picked up from Yale philosopher Nicholas Wolterstorff.

Nicholas Wolterstorff and Justice

As mentioned above, this book grows out of the monotheistic conviction that God created humankind to be His trustees on earth.[19] God sternly reprimanded Adam's son Cain, and not just for killing his own brother Abel.

At stake was the callous, selfish attitude he harbored toward his brother and fellow human created in God's image,[20] as evidenced in his sarcastic quip, 'Am I my brother's keeper?' So human solidarity expressed in justice, mercy and love is grounded in God's creation and special vocation addressed to humankind.

Yet I write this now with anxiety in my soul. It is not just the children whose very lives are endangered by violence, famine and grinding poverty in many places; it is not just the blatant inequalities of a world in which half lives on less than two dollars a day while the richest 1% piles up more and more mansions, yachts and stocks. It is also that, given my personal attachment to the MENA region, my heart breaks at the devastation and tragedy wrought by the three wars between Israel and Hamas-led Gaza and its continued blockade, the aftermath of the brutal civil war in Syria, the catastrophic war in Yemen, and the suffering of both Iraq and Afghanistan after the ill-fated American-led invasions of the 2000s. The rise of jihadi militancy in the guise of al-Qaeda and the Islamic State in their several incarnations in North Africa, the Sinai, Somalia and elsewhere, the Taliban in Afghanistan and Pakistan, Boko Haram in West Africa and others of its type – all of these movements are to some extent responses to perceived Western neo-colonial interference in the Muslim *umma* (worldwide community).

On all sides of this violence, whether state-sponsored or initiated by self-righteous terror organizations, we see a shocking disregard for the humanity of others, a phenomenon which also points to a tendency we all have as humans to discriminate in our dealings with others. In fact, it was this kind of experience of injustice far from home that spurred philosopher Nicholas Wolterstorff to write two books on justice after he officially retired.[21]

In 1976 Wolterstorff attended a conference at a South African university founded and run by Afrikaners. These were the white South African descendants of seventeenth-century Dutch Reformed or Huguenot settlers who dominated South African politics until the fall of the Apartheid regime in 1994. Besides a few foreign scholars like himself, most of them Dutch, there were Afrikaner, 'black' and 'colored' scholars contributing to this conference. Here is how Wolterstorff describes the dynamics:

> At first the Afrikaners and the Dutch vented their fury at each other. But as the conference proceeded, the "blacks" and the "coloreds" began to speak up, not with the rage of the Dutch but with faces and voices of suffering. They told in slow quiet tones of the many ways in which they were wronged.

The Afrikaners responded by saying that it was all for the sake of the future good. Some told of the charity that they and their families had extended to blacks and coloreds: cast-off clothing given to families living in huts in the back yards, Christmas trinkets given to children, and so forth. They charged that the strategies of resistance and the words of criticism employed by some blacks and colored were hurtful and not loving. And they assured their black and colored "brothers," as they called them, that if they just behaved, they would see what a generous people the Afrikaners were at heart. I saw, as never before, the good overwhelming the just, and benevolence and the appeal to love being used as instruments of oppression.[22]

So it is possible, argues Wolterstorff, that a misplaced sense of love and mercy can trample over justice? Was this not genuine love or mercy in the first place? That much is clear. But how does he develop his argument about justice as a philosopher?

Wolterstorff writes in *Justice: Rights and Wrongs* as a philosopher in the Anglo-American analytic tradition, though with a twist. In his own words, 'The account of primary justice that I develop is a theistic account, a *Christian* theistic account; for I am a Christian believer who holds that God and justice are intimately intertwined.'[23] He explains that though there are still many philosophers for whom this is a betrayal of their craft meant to be carried out in the realm of reason, times have changed and 'rationality in belief is a far more subtle matter than it was assumed to be.' The old 'foundationalist picture', what I have called the 'modern' intellectual mindset, was inspired by Descartes who firmly believed in philosophy building its edifice on the foundation of rational certitudes.[24] Today, writes Wolterstorff, philosophers are beginning to take for granted what he calls 'dialogic pluralism.' By this he means that the goal of academic research is the search for truth, but from a variety of perspectives. So while the goal is to 'achieve agreement', this will be a dialogue and not a zero-sum game in which one voice ends up declaring victory by obliterating the others.

By the same token, Wolterstorff illustrates well the spirit that, as I see it, drives the most fruitful conversations about human rights, justice and peacebuilding now taking place in our broken world. I was recently asked by an international law review to contribute an article on Muslim and Christian views of human rights, and in browsing the literature for this purpose I came away with a similar conviction.[25] Human rights discourse has a rich and contested genealogy, a fact that actually opens the way for both secular and religious persons of various traditions to join in the ongoing collective effort to hammer out better formulations and applications of it. It is clearly a work in progress, and I want to privilege the theistic account, particularly coming from Muslim and Christian perspectives, in this project.

Book Outline

Each chapter of this book begins with a case study of injustice that needs to be righted, with the exception of the first chapter which is itself a case study of racial injustice in the United States. So two come from the United States, and the rest from Israel/Palestine, Egypt, Pakistan, and Nigeria. For one thing, I do not want the discussion to get stuck in the theory of justice and rights. We need to remind ourselves that as we read and reflect, real people are suffering, and sometimes in the throes of grief and despair. And at times too, with further reflection, it dawns on us that our silence directly adds to their plight. Another reason for these vignettes is a reminder of the complexity behind these inequalities. Structural injustice and corruption abound from local to regional to national government. Further, many nations do not have the luxury of deciding their own fates without being oppressed by the predatory practices of larger regional or global entities, whether economic or political.

The first chapter, then, is a look at the legacy of slavery in the United States, of Jim Crow laws in the south, of routine violence and discrimination against African Americans up to World War II, and even of continuing racism today as black men especially make up over a third of the prison population and are routinely killed in the streets at the hands of the police. This offers an opportunity to briefly examine the messages of Malcolm X and Martin Luther King Jr., and others as well, with the goal of presenting some themes that will be picked up later in the book.

The second chapter sets up the basic argument of the book with respect to justice. I am not primarily concerned with distributive justice (mitigating economic inequality or fostering greater political participation for those on the margins),[26] retributive justice (setting up a just penal system for those who commit crimes), or procedural justice (making sure that all parts and procedures of a state's justice system work efficiently and fairly), though talk of a 'just society' involves all of that, to be sure. This book is about *primary justice* – defining what is 'justice' is and grounding it, not in some kind of natural order or social contract ('justice as right order') but in certain rights that belong to human beings *as* human beings. I agree with Wolterstorff that a social order is 'just insofar as its members enjoy the goods to which they have rights.' Those rights fall into two categories:

rights conferred on people by the issuing of legislation or even religious rulings; and natural rights that are neither conferred by any human or divine authority, but are inherent to human beings.

This way of seeing justice (as inherent rights) conflicts with a common narrative today which faults the rights discourse as a product of the modern individualism arising from the eighteenth-century Enlightenment. It's a way of reading history, a particular narrative, which has adversely affected the way many view the human rights concept, Christians and Muslims in particular. Thus it will be important to revisit that history for the sake of this project.

In Chapters 3 and 4 I take a look at a somewhat marginal current in classical Islamic law but which has now taken center stage – the focus on the Shari'a's objectives, or 'purposive' jurisprudence, as Notre Dame University Islamicist Ebrahim Moosa has put it.[27] Although I have written about this topic in several places,[28] Chapter 3 is a reworking of an essay I had published in Malaysia as a small monograph, but to which I now added a section on Tariq Ramadan.[29]

Chapter 4 is devoted to the immensely popular and controversial Shaykh Yusuf al-Qaradawi, starting with his February 2011 Friday sermon in Tahrir Square with an audience of over a million Egyptians who came to hear him and celebrate 'Pharaoh' Mubarak's overthrow. I then scrutinize his writings in order to discern whether or not his late turn to the purposive legal theory actually changed any of his positions. Qaradawi is important, not just as the first great global media cleric, but also because of his loose Muslim Brotherhood connection over the years and his close ties to the Qatari royal family. How does he see the connection between Shari'a and justice?

Chapter 5 brings us back to the 2007 Common Word initiative. I examine the letter itself in terms of its impact on Muslim-Christian dialogue and for what it teaches us about justice and love. More importantly, I comb through Prince Ghazi's *Love in the Holy Qur'an*, for clues about how he would connect love and justice.

This leads us back to the Christian side of the issue in Chapter 6, as I peruse Wolterstorff's second book on our topic, *Justice in Love*, with an eye here and there for possible Muslim responses. In particular, I follow his critique of a movement initiated by Soren Kierkegaard, which focused theologically on love ('agapism') but which saw love as transcending (and at times contradicting) justice. Wolterstorff argues that true love is giving each person his or her due and therefore coincides perfectly with the goals of justice. Or to put it more precisely, love includes several virtues, one of which is justice – hence the title, 'Justice *in* Love.'

In the end, I will be arguing that justice is about the inherent dignity of all human persons, whether they are in possession of all their mental faculties or not. An elderly woman in her last stages of Alzheimer's disease, or any child, woman or man with severe disabilities, or anyone whatsoever regardless of her race, religion, social status or ethnicity, has a claim on other human beings to be treated with respect and have the means to live a happy and dignified life. That is what primary justice requires. Muslims, Jews and Christians, in particular, believe God has entrusted them with the mission to make this world more just, more loving and more merciful.

Endnotes

1   Johnston 2010.

2   Kuruvilla 2019, online, https://www.huffingtonpost.com/entry/diverse-evangelicals-take-back-faith_us_5bb4fdf5e4b028e1fe3a0dbd, accessed September 22, 2019. Further, I teach as an affiliate assistant professor at Fuller Theological Seminary. See our president Mark Labberton's recent edited book, Labberton 2018. The 2016 US presidential election has sparked much soul-searching in at least some evangelical circles. Two more books offer perspective on this: Kirkpatrick 2019 and Fea 2018.

3   Cumming-Bruce 2018; online, https://www.nytimes.com/2018/06/05/world/americas/us-un-migrant-children-families.html, accessed February 24, 2019.

4   See 'Human Rights and the Freedom of Religion,' in Ipgrave 2009, 109–116, at 110.

5   Paulson 2018, online, https://www.nytimes.com/2014/07/24/us/us-religious-leaders-embrace-cause-of-immigrant-children.html, accessed July 2, 2018.

6   This is from the New International Version, NIV, 1984, 2011. Unless otherwise indicated, all Bible quotations are from the New Living Translation (NLT), 2nd ed., 2004. English translations fall into two broad camps: 'formal equivalence' or 'literal' translations seek to preserve the original language's syntax and sentence structure as much as possible (for example, the NIV). The other kind of translation is called 'dynamic equivalence,' an insight taken from anthropology that language is embedded in a wider cultural system and worldview. It seeks above all to present the message of the original in a way that is readily understandable to today's readers and to produce the same kind of impact on them that it likely would have produced on the original hearers (for example, the NLT).

7   'Dalai Lama adds voice to the Pope's in calling for the persecution of Rohingya to end,' The Sydney Morning Herald 2017, online, https://www.smh.com.au/world/dalai-lama-adds-voice-to-popes-in-calling-for-the-persecution-of-rohingya-to-end-20170303-gupz06.html, accessed July 2, 2018.

8   Myanmar (formerly Burma) denied citizenship to the more than one million Muslim Rohingya people, making them stateless and exposing them to abuse

by a mostly Buddhist population. As of June 2018, more than 700,000 Rohingya refugees had fled to neighboring Bangladesh. The Human Rights chief called this unfolding situation 'a textbook example of ethnic cleansing.' See this article in particular on the UNICEF website, https://www.unicefusa.org/monsoon-season-another-deadly-threat-rohingya-children?utm_campaign=2017.html, accessed July 2, 2018.

9   'The Ruler and the Ruled in Islam: A Brief Analysis of the Sources,' in Ipgrave 2009, 3–13, at 8–9.

10   Kamali 2009, 'Seven Ahadith,' in Ipgrave 2009, 39–44, at 44.

11   'Introduction: Muslim and Christian Perspectives,' in Ipgrave 2009, ix–x, at ix.

12   See the collection of statements on Charles Kurzman's website, http://kurzman.unc.edu/islamic-statements-against-terrorism/. Kurzman is Professor of Sociology and Director of Graduate Studies at the University of North Carolina.

13   See website, http://www.ammanmessage.com/

14   These points are worth reiterating here: '1. They specifically recognized the validity of all 8 *Mathhabs* (legal schools) of *Sunni, Shi'a* and *Ibadhi* Islam; of traditional Islamic Theology *(Ash'arism)*; of Islamic Mysticism (Sufism), and of true *Salafi* thought, and came to a precise definition of who is a Muslim.
     2. Based on this definition they forbade *takfir* (declarations of apostasy) between Muslims.
     3. Based upon the *Mathahib* [plural of *mathhab*] they set forth the subjective and objective preconditions for the issuing *of fatwas*, thereby exposing ignorant and illegitimate edicts in the name of Islam' (Amman Message).

15   See Chapter 5 for more on that lecture and why it stirred up Muslim public opinion.

16   See the page devoted to 'The Common Word' on the Amman Message website, http://www.acommonword.com/. Considering the several books entirely devoted to it, the more than a dozen conference dialogues based on it, its wide acceptance (over 15,000 signatures to date) and international awards it has won, the website calls it 'The Most Successful Interfaith Initiative in History.' There is no doubt that this was an historic gesture and its momentum keeps growing.

17   The earliest and most dramatic Christian response was made by a majority of evangelical leaders, spearheaded by Miroslav Volf, Professor of Theology at Yale Divinity School and Director of the Yale Center for Faith and Culture. Several mainline Protestant scholars and leaders also signed it, including Rowan Williams, then Archbishop of Canterbury. It was published about a month after 'The Common Word' letter as a full-page advertisement in *The New York Times*. See Volf et al. 2010.

18   See Volf et al. 2010.

19   Many Muslim writers use 'vicegerent' for the Arabic word, *khalifa*. The word sounds a little archaic in English, especially the term 'vicegerency.' Christians tend to use the term 'steward' and 'stewardship.' There are other synomyms such as representative or deputy. I have found that 'trustee' is useful, because it is used in Muslim literature, and it also connects directly to the idea of the Trust given to humankind (Q. 33:72).

20   Though rarely mentioned in Muslim writings, the hadith (saying of the Prophet) 'For God created Adam in His image' (*'alā surātihi*) is mentioned in three collections

of hadith: Bukhari (once), Muslim (twice), Ahmad b. Hanbal (7 times). That said, my argument for the joint trusteeship of all human beings in *Earth, Empire and Sacred Text*, Johnston 2010, and the argument here for justice as based on the inherent rights of all are not based on the image of God in them.

21 Wolterstorff retired as Noah Porter Professor of Philosophical Theology at Yale University in 2002. The two books are: *Justice: Rights and Wrongs*, Wolterstorff 2008; and *Justice in Love*, Wolterstorff 2011.

22 'Preface,' in Wolterstorff 2008, vii, emphasis his.

23 Wolterstorff 2008, x.

24 See chapters 2–4 in Johnston 2010 for the impact of postmodernism on many aspects of contemporary thought. Although he would not put it in these terms, I believe his use of the term (and concept) of 'dialogic pluralism' is exactly that impact of postmodern thought to which many have pointed in their writing. This is indeed a post-foundational perspective.

25 This was published under the title, 'A Muslim and Christian Orientation to Human Rights: Human Dignity and Solidarity,' Johnston 2014a, 899–920.

26 On this see the damning 2018 United Nations' report by Philip Alston, 'Report of the Special Rapporteur on extreme poverty in his mission to the United States' (United Nations 2018). Elise Gould comments on it for *The Hill* with this title, 'UN report on US poverty: dystopian future or devastating reality?' Online, http://thehill.com/opinion/finance/395076-un-report-on-us-poverty-dystopian-future-or-devastating-reality, accessed July 30, 2018. Notice the use of 'human rights': 'A recent piece of literature describes a society of extreme poverty and human rights violations. Across the country, in urban as well as rural areas, in the North and South, the East and West, it tells a story of a United States where vast wealth and great innovation exist side by side with shocking and abject poverty, where millions have little hope to improve the circumstances for themselves or their children.' Much of the blame, the report says, goes to a cultural myth of 'winners and losers, those worthy and those not, and how this ideology gets reinforced and is used to justify the actions of our policymakers.'

27 Among other places, see his chapter 'The Debts and Burdens of Critical Islam,' in Safi 2003, 118–27, at 23.

28 First, I traced a move in this direction in twentieth-century Islamic legal theory: 'An Epistemological and Hermeneutical Turn in Twentieth-Century *Usul al-Fiqh*,' Johnston 2004, 233–82; then I spelled it out more clearly in the works of several scholars, both islamists and progressives, on the issue of human rights: '*Maqasid al-Shari'a*: Epistemology and Hermeneutics of Muslim Theologies of Human Rights,' Johnston 2007a): 149–187. Then more recently as a chapter in an edited book devoted to this topic: 'Yusuf al-Qaradawi's Purposeful *Fiqh*: Promoting or Demoting the Future Role of the Ulama?' in Duderija 2014.

29 This was published under the title, *Evolving Muslim Theologies of Justice: Jamal al-Banna, Mohammad Hashim Kamali and Khaled Abou El Fadl*, Johnston, 2020b. It went out of print when Muzaffar left his academic post as the Noordin Sopiee Professor of Global Studies at the Universiti Sains Malaysia (USM) in Penang in 2012.

2

Racial Justice in the United States

This is a case-study chapter and the accompanying material by both Muslims and Christians will introduce themes discussed further in the coming chapters. I will frame the commentary on racial injustice by slavery narratives on the front end, by the story of my own experience near the middle, and by a hopeful narrative on the back end. Indeed, by confessing past injustices, we seek to move toward healing our national wounds.

Slavery Narratives

Among the appalling crimes committed by humans against one another from time immemorial, slavery must rank in the top tier, along with war itself and the systematic rape of enemy women. Elikia M'Bokolo, a Congolese historian who has taught both in Paris and in Kinshasa, has done extensive research on slavery in relation to Africa. Writing in the prestigious Le Monde Diplomatique in 1998, the year marking the 150th anniversary of the French abolition of slavery, he lamented the staggering numbers of slaves extracted from his continent over the centuries. 'A tragedy of such dimensions has no parallel in any other part of the world.' He then explains,

> The African continent was bled of its human resources via all possible routes. Across the Sahara, through the Red Sea, from the Indian Ocean ports and across the Atlantic. At least ten centuries of slavery for the benefit of the Muslim countries (from the ninth to the nineteenth). Then more than four centuries (from the end of the fifteenth to the nineteenth) of a regular slave trade to build the Americas and the prosperity of the Christian states of Europe. The figures, even where hotly disputed, make your head spin. Four million slaves exported via the Red Sea, another four million through

the Swahili ports of the Indian Ocean, perhaps as many as nine million along the trans-Saharan caravan route, and eleven to twenty million (depending on the author) across the Atlantic Ocean.[1]

M'Bokolo believes the Arab slave trade was a complement to its importation of African gold, ivory, hardwoods and other products and that slaves were used for 'domestic' purposes, not as in the European Atlantic slave trade, which used its slaves as 'the workforce for the colonial plantations and mines (gold, silver, and above all, sugar, cocoa, cotton, tobacco and coffee)'[2] Muslim states historically enslaved a variety of white populations as well and some of these populations climbed the social ladder over generations.[3] M'Bokolo's contention in this article is that it was the European slave trade from the seventeenth to the nineteenth centuries that devastated Africa politically and economically, while injecting a racist sentiment in its people that still lives today.

Both Western and Middle Eastern systems of slavery shared a racist ideology coated with a religious veneer. M'Bokolo explains: 'In both cases, we find the same fallacious interpretation of Genesis, according to which the Blacks of Africa, as the alleged descendants of Ham, are cursed and condemned to slavery.'

The transatlantic slave trade, argues M'Bokolo, was the Trojan horse used by the Europeans to subjugate the continent under their colonial rule. From the second half of the seventeenth century, just about all the European powers held on to territories, from Senegal in the west to Mozambique in the east, from which they could extract slaves in return for weapons. It was a trap, he contends. 'Trade, or go under.' This also meant European intervention and manipulation of African tribal conflicts to their advantage, under the old adage, 'divide and conquer.'

M'Bokolo's final point is that all of this exploitation was consistently packaged at home using the racist trope of Africa as 'a continent of savages.' He then quotes several historians who have demonstrated that again and again, it was the Africans themselves who mounted spirited and often powerful resistance to the slave trade. American and European narratives mostly attribute the abolitionist movement to white abolitionists, but thereby completely erasing the agency of African activists and leaders like Félix Houphouët-Boigny and Léopold Sédar Senghor.[4]

Fortunately, one amazing story of an African slave was unearthed by Terry Alford, a history PhD graduate who was poking around in the archives of the courthouse in Natchez, Mississippi. The story, which took Terry Alford from Natchez to Washington, DC, and then from England to

Senegal, was published in 1977 under the title, *Prince Among Slaves*.[5] This story is remarkable in at least two ways. First, Ibrahima Abdul Rahman represents the tens of thousands (scholars disagree as to their numbers) of Muslim slaves forcibly brought to America. In Ibrahima Abdul Rahman's case, he was the well-educated son of an Islamic scholar and influential leader of the Fulbe people in the Senegambia (today's Senegal, Gambia, and the two Guineas). He was captured in an ambush by an enemy tribe and sold to European slavers. We now know that despite the great pressures on educated, pious Muslim slaves in America to convert to Christianity or simply to hide their religious practices, many left behind artifacts and traces of their devotion to Islam.[6]

Second, like many Muslim slaves who could read and write Ibrahima Abdul Rahman's master entrusted him with the responsibility of overseeing the other slaves. But then an astonishing coincidence happened one day when in town he happened to see an Irishman whose life his father had saved and who had lived among them for a period of time. This led to Ibrahima Abdul Rahman's manumission, and improbably, to a White House visit with President John Quincy Adams. He then embarked on a speaking tour and managed to raise enough money to free two of his children. After 40 years in the United States he finally returned to Africa where soon after he died.[7]

Americans have only reluctantly come to terms with the devastation slavery has visited on the African American community. Two notable narratives have helped to bring this tragic legacy to the public's attention. The first was Alex Haley's wildly popular novel, *Roots*, first published in 1976 and followed by a TV show the next year.[8] More recently, American slavery came back into public discussion with the celebrated film '12 Years a Slave.' It was the first film written and directed by black artists to win the Academy Award for Best Motion Picture of the Year in 2014.[9] I finally watched the movie before writing this chapter and what struck me most was the callous inhumanity of people treating others as mere chattel. It wasn't just the raw violence, but especially the sexual violence so central to the institution of slavery that overwhelmed me, while at the same time slave owners presided over Sunday worship in their respective plantations with their slaves in attendance.

Yet today, perhaps more than ever, we cannot escape the tragic legacy of American slavery. As I write, the top two officials of the state of Virginia, where arguably the first Africans were sold into slavery and which later became the capital of the Confederacy, are facing massive pressure to step down for wearing 'blackface' disguise when they were in their twenties.

The governor especially, Ralph Northam, has yet to take full responsibility for his medical school yearbook page, which had an image of a man wearing blackface and another in a Ku Klux Klan hood. One helpful article in the newspaper *USA Today* explains that wearing blackface is 'a relic of entertainment from the nineteenth century rooted in mimicry and mocking of slaves.'[10] The Ku Klux Klan hood is an even more egregious symbol of white hate and supremacy.

Ironically, an act of Congress established the '400 Years of African-American History Commission' which was celebrated in 2019 in reference to the landing of an English pirate vessel, The White Lion, at Point Comfort, Virginia in 1619, a year before the famous landing of the Pilgrims in Plymouth, MA. The pirates had stolen from a Portuguese slave ship 'twenty and odd negroes' and the first thing they did upon arrival was to sell the slaves in exchange for food. Although definitely not the first arrival of African slaves in the Americas, it does mark the beginning of a wretched thread in American history that included terrible suffering for the slaves and their descendants, and the deaths of at least half a million young men in a horrific Civil War.

As an American, therefore, I have to be honest about the grave injustices and crimes committed by white Americans against the native population and the African people forced into slavery. But even after the latter were officially declared 'emancipated', their struggles and suffering continue to this day. There were the long oppressive years of Jim Crow in the south, but also more generally the thousands of public lynchings of African-Americans and Mexicans in the United States between the Civil War and World War II.[11] These were public events that drew crowds of white men, women and children and garnered at least the tacit agreement of local authorities. These were mostly crimes (lynchings and burnings) committed at night against African-Americans and their sympathizers – all scenes illuminated by the burning crosses of the Ku Klux Klan.

Johan Galtung and the Study of Structural and Cultural Violence

To mention the many decades when African Americans were subjected to horrific crimes like lynchings and rape, randomly and with impunity, and more generally to routine discrimination and continuous insults and abuse, is to point to a vast reservoir of violence. Norwegian sociologist Johan Galtung (b. 1930), widely seen as the founder of peace and conflict studies, published a seminal article on structural violence in 1969.[12] In it, he defined violence as '*the cause of the difference between the potential and the actual*, between what could have been and what is.'[13] Violence, then, is that which widens the gap between the potential and the actual, as for example, when a child performs poorly in school because of chronic food insecurity at home. The parents, or single mother as is often the case, are not directly to blame, and particularly if they belong to a minority that for economic reasons has to live in a poor area with no supermarkets, high crime, high unemployment. That is structural violence, which Galtung also calls 'social injustice.'

Twenty-one years later, Galtung published another seminal article, this time on cultural violence. Galtung began the article with this definition:

> By "cultural violence" we mean those aspects of culture, the symbolic sphere of our existence – exemplified by religion and ideology, language and art, empirical science and formal science (logic, mathematics) – that can be used to justify or legitimize direct or structural violence. Stars, crosses and crescents; flags, anthems and military parades; the ubiquitous portrait of the Leader; inflammatory speeches and posters – all these come to mind.[14]

Cultural violence, then, is the system by which acts of direct and structural violence are 'legitimized and thus rendered acceptable in society.' It is the context that unleashes violence against the mind and the spirit of the 'underdogs' and in that process four terms are particularly important to bear in mind:

> They function by impeding consciousness formation and mobilization, two conditions for effective struggle against exploitation. *Penetration*, implanting the topdog inside the underdog so to speak, combined with *segmentation*, giving the underdog only a very partial view of what goes on, will do the first job. And *marginalization*, keeping the underdogs on the outside, combined with *fragmentation*, keeping the underdogs away from each other, will do the second job.[15]

Galtung gives patriarchy as an example of gender oppression, but he later offers the example of the United States. He writes about 'the massive direct violence over centuries' perpetrated against Africans through the institution of slavery. In turn, that direct violence 'seeps down and sediments as massive structural violence, with whites as the master topdogs and blacks as the slave underdogs, producing and reproducing massive cultural violence with racist ideas everywhere.' Long after slavery and its attendant direct violence is mostly forgotten, just two terms are left, 'pale enough for college textbooks': "'discrimination" for massive structural violence and "prejudice" for massive cultural violence. Sanitation of language: itself cultural violence.'[16]

So much more could be said here, particularly as the field of peace and conflict studies has increased rapidly over the last three decades.[17] Nevertheless, I brought Johan Galtung into the discussion in order to highlight the terrible trauma white American society has visited on the African American community over the centuries. Healing is desperately needed.

Malcolm X and the Black Muslim Hunger for Healing

These are all grim realities of our American past and there are plenty of signs that this past still festers and poisons our collective psyche today. For that reason, we should also highlight efforts on many sides to tackle these problems. Protest movements are often signs that people no longer accept the status quo and are seeing a way for justice to shine through the darkness. As of this writing, the loosely organized but highly influential Black Lives Matter movement (BLM) is about to celebrate its sixth anniversary. It began as a Twitter hashtag (#BlackLivesMatter) on July 13, 2013, when the case against George Zimmerman was dropped. Zimmerman had been on trial for shooting 17 year-old black teen Trayvon Martin. BLM was started by three 'queer Black women', Patrice Khan-Cullors, Alicia Garza, and Opal Tometi, who are all 'trained radical Black organizers' but whose 'mentors were queer and trans people whose labor had been erased and replaced with an uncontested narrative of male leadership.'[18] The BLM network now counts over 30 chapters in the US, and several others in Australia, South Africa, and elsewhere. They are clear that they stand in a long line of Black activism: 'Its roots lie in the Black organizers of centuries ago, our ancestors who, in the face of violence like chattel slavery, lynching, whipping, rape, theft and separation of our families fought for freedom from the state.'[19]

As seen from its website at https://blacklivesmatter.com, one of the values that animates this movement is 'healing justice,' which is in response to 'the persistent and historical trauma Black people have endured the hands of the State.' BLM explains it this way:

> Since the inception of BLM, organizers and healers have taken this understanding of historical and generational trauma and made it the foundation

of our healing circles, of creative and liberatory space held amidst actions, of our attempts to resolve conflict and division in ways that don't replicate harm or rely on carceral ways of being with one another.[20]

In reading through https://blacklivesmatter.com, you will not find any reference to religion but only some oblique indications of spirituality. Yet it is clear that their attempt to create 'healing circles' and 'liberatory spaces' not only makes room for the spirituality of African American Christians and Muslims but also drinks liberally from the wellspring of African spirituality more generally.

Malcolm X (1925–1965) is arguably the first African American Muslim leader to inspire and unite his battered community under the banner of Islam. Drawn to faith in prison through preachers of the Nation of Islam (NOI), Malcolm X joined the NOI as soon as he was released in 1952. The NOI is a heterodox version of Islam, which in reaction to the reigning paradigm of white supremacy in the United States developed a form of black supremacy using certain Islamic symbols.[21] After rising to the pinnacle of NOI's leadership, however, even to the point that rumors had him supplanting the founder Elijah Muhammad's son, Malcolm X grew disillusioned with it, particularly with its hostility to the civil rights movement and its skewed version of Islam. Within a month of leaving the NOI he embraced Sunni Islam and promptly flew to Jeddah, Saudi Arabia, to begin the Hajj pilgrimage. As we read in his *Autobiography*, that was where his epiphany occurred. Witnessing people from all races and ethnicities, rich and poor, all united and equal before God, led him to widen the scope of his spiritual vision.[22]

By 1959, Malcolm X had traveled extensively in Africa to prepare for a trip Elijah Muhammad was planning to make. Both after the Hajj and later again that year in July he was invited to speak in over a dozen countries giving interviews and meeting officials. Writing from Lagos, Nigeria, he asserted that the struggle American blacks had to face each day transcended religious affiliations. He appealed to African leaders to see this state oppression as 'a violation of the "human rights" of persons of African descent.'[23] In the same way, these leaders should support pan-Africanism, he urged, not as blacks or Muslims but as fellow human beings. Malcolm X had plainly made a paradigm shift from civil rights as a way to lift an aggrieved community to a view of civil rights as a fight for human rights, plain and simple. His view of justice had expanded, now encompassing all of humanity.

Abbas Barzegar claims that the great diversity of the American Islamic community is best studied, not through the lens of identity or ideology, but rather 'in terms of competing Islamic discourses in constant articulation and contest with one another.'[24] In the same vein, Edward E. Curtis IV in his 2002 book, *Islam in Black America*, had noted that even though African Americans all seek some kind of liberation from oppression, 'their understandings of oppression and their strategies for liberation from it have been incredibly diverse and complex.'[25] So the 'discourse centered approach' Barzegar recommends focuses on how various groups use the 'primary discourses of Islam' to 'authorize' particular norms, practices, and ways of being 'Muslim' in a specific context. For example, Barzegar in his ethnographic work came to distinguish six 'discursive themes' employed by American Muslims.[26]

Not coincidentally, I would surmise, one of these six discourses, the 'rehabilitative social activism' orientation, is the one mostly embraced by African American Muslims. Barzegar describes this orientation as focused 'on community building and employing Islam as a social and religious force of collective empowerment which seeks the holistic betterment of the African American community in particular, the redressing of socio-historical inequalities, and thereby, the healing of American society in general.'[27] It is difficult not to notice how close this comes to BLM's emphasis on 'healing justice.' Then too, we can easily imagine how Malcolm X's later focus on justice as the effort to regain for all, and especially the poor and marginalized, their basic human rights also taps into this discursive theme. Another example would be second generation Palestinian, Rami Nashashibi, who founded Inner-City Muslim Action Network (IMAN) and endeavors to 'make activism and the plight of America's poor a natural concern of American Muslims.'[28]

IMAN began in Chicago's South Side in 1997 with a community health center and progressively developed a re-entry program for formerly incarcerated young men, which includes both transitional housing and job training. IMAN's second office opened in Atlanta in 2016. IMAN is a great example of this 'rehabilitative social activism,' as it leverages Islamic values to bring healing and restoration to a variety of people who are at risk. IMAN's mission statement includes the idea of 'inspiring others towards critical civic engagement exemplifying prophetic compassion in the work for social justice and human dignity beyond the barriers of religion, ethnicity, and nationality.'[29]

Martin Luther King Jr., the Beloved Community and Healing

Allow me to begin this section with a personal experience of structural injustice in January of 2014. This experience concerns a victim of rampant gun violence in a predominantly African American community – Chester, Pennsylvania, to be exact, less than four miles from our house. My 88 year-old mother-in-law lived with us and had a health aide visit every night to care for her, so as to give my wife who is a full-time nurse some respite. One of the night aides is an African American woman living in Chester. Early in January 2014 the home care company called us to say she would not be coming for several weeks due to a death in her family. We later discovered that during the night her 20 year-old son had been shot dead in the street and her family had no idea who had murdered him. He was not part of a gang, did not take or sell drugs. He was actually a talented local rapper who still lived at home. Six years later, the police still had no clues about this killing, and indeed, on most of the shootings that happen so frequently in this town of 34,000 people on the Delaware river, some 15 minutes south of Philadelphia.[30]

Apparently, 2014 was a particularly bad year for crime. In May of that year the county District Attorney, Jack Whelan, joined by representatives of the FBI and state police, gave an alarming press conference during which he announced that Chester's murder rate exceeded Philadelphia's, one of the most violent cities in the United States. He pointed to one factor in particular: 'Gun violence in the city of Chester has now reached epidemic proportions. So it's now time to address illegal guns.'[31] And that was how, in my own little way, I got involved.

Our aide told me there was going to be an organized protest against illegal weapons' possession that would march that Saturday from Chester to Media, the county seat. The protest was organized by the nonprofit organization, Delaware County United for Sensible Gun Policy. I told her I would go. As promised, I arrived on June 28, 2014 at the meeting place by the Martin Luther King, Jr., historical marker. This was the church in which King had served as assistant pastor while pursuing his theological studies in Chester.[32] After a couple of speeches and instructions about the march, over 100 of us made our way through Chester to the Chester East Side Ministries property. There on the lawn by the street were planted over 60 crosses with T-shirts on each one with the name of the youth killed by gun violence, the date of the murder and the age of the victim.[33] Unfortunately, my friend had not come to the march and there was not enough time to find her son's cross. Still, she was very grateful I had made the effort to be part of this protest.

What I did learn in talking with some of the veterans of this movement is that just outside of Chester's city limits, there is a gun store with a wide assortment of firearms, including assault weapons, and that 'straw purchases' (buying a weapon then selling it to a third-party) can be made there at all times with virtually no questions asked. Is it the only factor leading to the high rate of violent crime in places like Chester? Certainly not. The Chester Upland School District has been rated lowest in the state of Pennsylvania for the last several years and there doesn't seem to be any relief in sight from its chronic mismanagement and dismal performance. An abysmal school system, grinding poverty, and drug gangs must certainly rank high as factors leading to its exceptionally high crime rate.[34]

So then, what does gun violence in a poor, depressed and dysfunctional community have to do with our theme of justice and love? An awful lot. The evangelical journal (and community) *Sojourners* founded by Jim Wallis published an article in 2014 on gun violence.[35] The author, Kaeley McEvoy, wrote that 'in 2011 alone, 19,403 children were shot and 2,703 lost their lives to guns.'[36] Further, whereas .95 percent of white youth are murdered, the homicide rate for black youth is 6.72 percent. She then offers this call to action:

> There are many other factors that influence the statistics behind the high rate of gun violence among children: the systemic racism of our justice system, the lack of proper mental health support, the militarization of police. The list can go on.

> Yet how much longer can we silently watch as children die from gun-related deaths? How many more Michael Browns? How many more Sandy Hooks? These names cannot just be memories that make our hearts ache. They must be catalysts for action.

The meaning here is clear. Injustice has crippled many different sectors of American society, including at least the justice system, the mental health system, and law enforcement. Laws themselves are unjust, and this must change, because each person, young or old, black or white is just as deserving of a dignified and peaceful life as any other.[37]

I just related my own eye-opening march, which began at the church where Martin Luther King, Jr., spent three years as an apprentice theologian and pastor under Rev. J. Pius Barbour. What would King have thought of the current state of Chester? He most likely would have been appalled.

In another book Wallis quotes from a King biography that focused more on his theology than on his politics.[38] He notes that one central emphasis throughout King's speeches and writings was 'the beloved community' which for him was a concept 'always more theological than political.'[39]

Wallis then mentions an article written by the authors of that biography, Kenneth L. Smith and Ira G. Zepp, Jr., in which they maintained that 'the ultimate aim of SCLC [the Southern Christian Leadership Conference] is to foster and create the 'beloved community' in America where brotherhood is a reality.' In fact, the goal of his battle against the negative effects of segregation was not just 'equal access to all public facilities and services', but integration and true social reconciliation. As I perused their article myself, I found Smith and Zepp saying that King often spoke of 'the solidarity of the human family.' This solidarity, in turn, spoke to the inherent value of each human person, a person bearing inalienable rights, so that 'injustice anywhere is a threat to justice everywhere.' In America, King wrote, this means concretely that '[d]iscrimination against 10 per cent of our population weakens the whole social fabric. Race and poverty are not merely sectional problems but American problems. It follows that the liberation of black people will also mean the emancipation of white people.'[40]

Plainly, this vision of the 'beloved community' for King was about God calling all of us to love our neighbor so that our society would be more just. Jim Wallis returns to this theme in *America's Original Sin: Racism, White Privilege, and the Bridge to a New America*.[41] One of the main themes of this book is the pervasiveness of racism in the United States. Social science research has now demonstrated the reality of implicit biases in this regard. Cheryl Staats of the Kirwan Institute for the Study of Race and Ethnicity at Ohio State University explains that '[i]mplicit bias refers to the attitudes or stereotypes that affect our understanding, actions, and decisions in an unconscious manner.' She adds, 'Residing deep in the subconscious, these biases are different from known biases that individuals may choose to conceal for the purpose of social and/or political correctness. Rather, implicit biases are not accessible through introspection.'[42]

On the hopeful side, however, these biases can be unlearned over time. At both institutions where I currently teach – St. Joseph's University in Philadelphia and Fuller Theological Seminary in Pasadena, CA – there have been ugly racial incidents in 2019 that have forced the institutions to take some drastic measures. Part of those has to do with specialized training for both faculty and staff in diversity awareness.

Wallis also quotes Paul Alexander, the president of Evangelicals for Social Action, in a landmark article entitled, 'Raced as White.'[43] Alexander argues that immigrants from many European countries who never would have thought of themselves as 'white' were gradually socialized to consider themselves 'white', which taps into an ideology set up in early America to justify slavery. People 'raced' in this way grow up with the expectation that they will benefit from a variety of privileges because they are 'white.' If that is our heritage, urges Alexander, we should first confess that these are both 'historical and theological realities' which we must now reject. Instead we must 'discover how the Spirit can disempower us in our Whiteness and help us become different and better.'[44] Wallis agrees. 'White privilege becomes the ideology and the idol that must be debunked, cast away, and repented of if we are to move into that new world of respecting the image of God in all God's children.'[45]

As a white American, I need to recognize that white privilege comes as a result of several centuries of deliberate, intentional policies to enhance our own economic and political status to the detriment of black and brown people. In today's parlance we call this 'affirmative action.' My own father served in the second world war (WWII) and like 7.8 million other veterans until 1956 the GI Bill paid for his college education. Although my parents moved to France in 1953 that same GI Bill would have given them a generous interest-free loan to buy a house. By contrast, African Americans benefited very little from these statutes. Historical research demonstrates that congressional leaders in the North and South ensured that these programs were carried out by local officials and not by the federal government. 'As a result, thousands of black veterans in the South – and the North as well – were denied housing and business loans, as well as admission to whites-only colleges and universities.'[46]

This is the structural violence mentioned above, which is also behind the fact that 'there are more African-American adults under correctional control today – in prison or jail, on probation or parole – than were enslaved in 1850, a decade before the Civil War began.'[47] Wallis makes this remark in a chapter devoted to reforming the American system of justice, 'The New Jim Crow and Restorative Justice.' Two other chapters touch on the legacy of this history of racial injustice: the scandalous segregation of American churches and the urgent need to reform the police force ('From Warriors to Guardians').

But just as we began this chapter with slavery narratives, Wallis offers us a new narrative – both symbolic and practical – of healing and hope. The symbol of that hope is the picture on the cover of his 2017 *America's Original Sin*. The picture is of the Edmund Pettus Bridge in Selma, Alabama. Against a blue sky, we witness a massive crowd of people marching over this bridge

– a bridge over which a few hundred black young people crossed in protest in 1965. But as they made their way across the bridge, they were badly assaulted and beaten by the forces of sheriff Jim Clark. This event became one of the symbols of the rising consciousness and courage of the black community to take its destiny in its own hands. Indeed, the bridge's name-sake, Edmund Pettus, had been a Confederate general who later became a Grand Dragon of the KKK. Yet 50 years later, as seen on that cover picture, one of the young men who had been badly injured that day by the police was now one of the main officials crossing that bridge, US Representative John Lewis. President Barack Obama joined Lewis, Jim Wallis, and other 'civil rights and faith leaders who had been part of the struggle for many years' for a symbolic re-crossing of that bridge followed by an official com-memorative ceremony.[48]

Thus Wallis's last chapter challenges his readers to 'cross the bridge to the new America' and 'make justice more possible' through reforms in the educational system, in the police force, in immigration policies, and in the criminal justice system. As the present book seeks to show, justice is intricately woven into the fabric of love. It is because King believed in the beloved community that he fought for and achieved the Civil Rights Act and the Voting Act.

Whatever one concludes about the exact causes or possible remedies for the injustice of Chester's gun victims, or of the manifold other symp-toms of the structural and cultural violence suffered by the black commu-nity, it is certainly a breakdown of love and justice – between people in that community, and between the American people as a whole who allow such unjust social policies to continue. From the wide-angled case study in this chapter, we next turn to Wolterstorff's contention that justice is both about a right legal order and about the rights of human persons. In many ways it confirms the findings of this chapter that violence in all three modes is fundamentally an affront to the inalienable rights and dignity of fellow human beings.

Endnotes

1   M'Bokolo 1998, https://mondediplo.com/1998/04/02africa; accessed February 8, 2019.
2   The Abbasid Caliphate attempted to import a large number of slaves for pro-duction in the ninth century, but the venture ended in disaster after several violent uprisings. The only modern example of black slaves working on planta-tions in a Muslim context was in Zanzibar in the late eighteenth and nineteenth

century. Some of the cloves and coconuts were exported to Europe. An Omani dynasty ruled Zanzibar for two centuries until it was integrated to Tanzania in 1964. Slavery was not abolished there until 1970, whereas the Kingdom of Saudi Arabia outlawed slavery in 1962. Mauritania did so in 1981, but there was no effective legal enforcement until 2007. After the overthrow of Muammar Qaddafi's regime in 2011, law and order broke down and in the ensuing chaos African migrants are reportedly being sold in slave markets (Nebehay 2018, available online, https://www.reuters.com/article/us-libya-security-rights/ executions-torture-and-slave-markets-persist-in-libya-u-n-idUSKBN1GX1JY).

3   The four years that the Islamic State ruled large swaths of Syria and Iraq raised again the historical issue of slavery in Muslim areas. Kecia Ali, a Boston University scholar who specializes in early Islamic law, wrote an excellent piece showing the complexity of issues. The Late Antique and Medieval worlds shared a worldview in which Christians, Muslims, and all others assumed it was permissible to enslave other human beings. In particular Ali writes, "'Islamic slavery" included conscript-convert Janissary troops, cooks, nannies, Mamluk military rulers, salt miners, pearl divers, craftsmen allowed to keep part of their wages, mothers of Ottoman sultans and the drudges who cleaned the royal harem quarters. Slavery was hierarchical and slaves were, in some times and places, assigned specific work based on ethnic origins. Slavery was not entirely racialized, however, and slaves were captured or bought from Europe, Asia and the Caucasus as well as Africa' (Ali 2015, available online, http://www.huffingtonpost.com/kecia-ali/islam-sex-slavery_b_8004824.html).

4   Félix Houphouët-Boigny ruled the Ivory Coast from independence (1960) until his death in 1993. UNESCO established the Félix Houphouët-Boigny Peace Prize in 1990 (Nelson Mandela was the first recipient). Léopold Sédar Senghor (1906–2001) served as President of Senegal from 1960 to 1980. He was also a celebrated poet and a cultural theorist. He was also the first African to be elected to the prestigious Académie Française.

5   The book is now available as a 30th anniversary edition (New York and Oxford: Oxford University Press, 2007).

6   See the Smithsonian Museum's website on African American History and Culture, and its fascinating page devoted to African Muslims in Early America: Religion, Literacy, and Liberty: https://nmaahc.si.edu/explore/stories/collection/ african-muslims-early-america.

7   A Public Broadcasting Service (PBS) documentary from 2008 tells his story, 'Prince Among Slaves' (https://www.amazon.com/Prince-Among-Slaves/dp/ B0012M1KXG). See also Johnston 2013, online, http://www.humantrustees.org/ blogs/muslim-christian-dialog/item/105-princeamongslaves, accessed September, 28 2019.

8   *Roots: The Saga of an American Family* spent 46 weeks on *The New York Times* best seller list, and the TV series was just as popular.

9   Both actors in the leading and supporting roles were born in Africa and won several awards, Chiwetel Ajiofor and Lupita Nyong'o, with recent roots in Nigeria and Kenya respectively. A third film should be mentioned, which was nominated for Best Film 2019 in the Oscar Awards: BlacKkKlansman. I watched it in the theater

and marveled at how a both dark and humorous description of the Ku Klux Klan could so eloquently paint the disturbing reality of ingrained American racism and its attendant violence – direct violence and cultural violence.

10   Guynn and Rhor 2019, 3A.

11   The Equal Justice Initiative published a landmark study on this issue in February 2015 under that title, 'Lynching in America: Confronting the Legacy of Racial Terror' (available as a pdf document, http://www.eji.org/files/EJI%20Lynching%20in%20 America%20SUMMARY.pdf). From the opening paragraph: '"Terror lynchings" peaked between 1880 and 1940 and claimed the lives of African American men, women and children who were forced to endure the fear, humiliation and barbarity of this widespread phenomenon unaided.'

12   Galtung 1969, 167–191.

13   Galtung 1969, 167–191, at 168, emphasis his.

14   Galtung 1990, 291–305, at 291.

15   Galtung 1990, 294, his emphasis.

16   Galtung 1990, 295.

17   An example is this recent article by a veteran of the sociology of violence, gender and religion, see Kurz 2017, Art. 6. Here he extends Galtung's famous violence triangle to a violence diamond, thereby adding 'ecoviolence,' which includes two domains, climate change and extinction of biological species, or reduced biodiversity.

18   Patrisse Khan-Cullors, 'We didn't start a movement. We started a network,' Khan-Cullors 2016, online, https://medium.com/@patrissemariecullorsbrignac/ we-didn-t-start-a-movement-we-started-a-network-90f9b5717668, accessed July 18, 2018.

19   Khan-Cullors 2016. See the impressive Wikipedia article on the movement at https://en.wikipedia.org/wiki/Black_Lives_Matter#Internet_and_social_media, accessed July 18, 2018.

20   'Healing Justice,' Black Lives Matter website, https://blacklivesmatter.com/ healing-justice/, accessed March 5, 2019

21   On the Nation of Islam (NOI) see Curtis 2002. See also Jackson 2011. The followers of the NOI called their experience until the death of the founder, Elijah Muhammad (d. 1975) the 'first resurrection,' as these Muslims were able to shed their slavery mentality thanks to Islam; the majority of these followed his son Warith Deen Muhammad out of the NOI movement into the fold of Sunni Islam. That was 'the second resurrection.' Jackson argues that African American Muslims are learning to master the sources and methodology of Sunni Islam as brought into the US by the Muslim immigrant community and appropriate it for their needs so tailoring it to their own unique identity.

22   Haley and Atallah Shabazz 1987, 388–393.

23   Curtis, *Islam in Blackamerica*, 98.

24   Barzegar 2011, 511–538, at 520.

25   Curtis 2002, 15; quoted in Barzegar 2011, 519.

26   They are: 1) the Abrahamic-American (fusing Islamic concepts with American civic discourses of 'citizenship, constitutionalism, and pluralism'); 2) rehabilitative social activism (see below); 3) Salafi-Sunni (American Salafi communities);

4) neo-Traditionalism (Hamza Yusuf Hanson and Zaid Shakir's Zaytuna College in Berkeley, CA, is a good example); 5) progressive reformism (contributors to Omid Safi's 2003 book, *Progressive Muslims*, illustrate this trend); 6) the 'homeland home-sick,' or 'the innumerable Muslim communities around the United States that serve primarily as cultural enclaves of specific ethnic immigrant communities' (Barzegar 2011, 536). Keep in mind that these are not air-tight categories, and that in practice they often overlap.

27   Barzegar 2011, 529. One organization that exemplifies this discourse on a national level is the Muslim Alliance of North America (MANA), which has effectively networked with a number of Muslim American organizations for the purpose of improving people's mental health, the integrity of marriages and families, and provides a range of social services in a wide range of communities. See their website, http://www.mana-net.org/. Their slogan is 'networking to empower the Muslim community.' Although predominantly African American, the executive board has other backgrounds represented, including the Indian American Altaf Hussain who earned a PhD in social work from Howard University.

28   http://www.mana-net.org/.

29   Online, https://www.imancentral.org/about/.

30   From what I can gather from city-data.com, violent crime has decreased from its high in 2008 (1566.7) to 930.8 in 2016 (compared to a 216.0 US average). That still means that the crime index in Chester, PA, is higher than 97.7 of American cities. See http://www.city-data.com/crime/crime-Chester-Pennsylvania.html, accessed February 16, 2019.

31   Madden 2014. See http://philadelphia.cbslocal.com/2014/05/06/as-murder-rate-skyrockets-in-chester-officials-promise-crime-crackdown/, accessed February 16, 2019.

32   This marker reads, 'King lived three years in this community and ministered under the mentorship of J. Pius Barbour. He graduated from Crozer Theological Seminary, 1961. A leader of the 1963 March on Washington, King won a Nobel Prize, 1964.' It is in front of the Calvary Baptist Church where King served as student pastor under Rev. Barbour who like King had attended Morehouse College in Atlanta and was the first black graduate of Crozer Seminary. For more details, see the following page explaining the marker in its historical context: http://explorepahistory.com/hmarker.php?markerId=1-A-367, accessed February 16, 2019.

33   For a view of this lawn with crosses, see the bottom photo on the following page: http://heedinggodscall.org/content/heeding-gods-call-memorials-lost, accessed February 16, 2019.

34   Indeed, 44.3 percent of Chester residents are below the federal poverty level, compared to 16.4 percent for the state of Pennsylvania as a whole; 19.6 percent are below 50 percent of the poverty level, compared to 5.7 in the state. See Chester, PA Poverty Rate Data, online, http://www.city-data.com/poverty/poverty-Chester-Pennsylvania.html, accessed July 24, 2018. Andrew van Dam confirms the correlation between poverty and crime: 'Harvard University sociologist Robert Sampson, who studies urban violence and the factors that cause it, has found that concentrated poverty, inequality and racial segregation are strongly related

to higher rates of violent crime in cities.' See https://www.washingtonpost. com/news/wonk/wp/2018/05/31/the-surprising-way-gun-violence-is-dividing-america/?noredirect=on&utm_term=.19b088790134, accessed July 24, 2018.

35   Wallis is an influential public intellectual. Besides being a New York Times best-selling author, the biography on the *Sojourner* website adds, 'He recently served on the White House Advisory Council on Faith-based and Neighborhood Partnerships and was former vice chair of and currently serves on the Global Agenda Council on Values of the World Economic Forum'; see http://sojo.net/jim-wallis.

36   McEvoy 2014, http://sojo.net/blogs/2014/10/20/protecting-god%E2%80%99s-children-how-gun-violence-impacts-america%E2%80%99s-youth, accessed July 30, 2018.

37   I think here of Paul's words to Timothy: 'I urge you, first of all, to pray for all people ... Pray this way for kings and all who are in authority so that we can live peaceful and quiet lives marked by godliness and dignity' (I Tim. 2:3-4).

38   Wallis, *On God's Side: What Religion Forgets and Politics Hasn't Learned about Serving the Common Good* (Grand Rapids, MI: BrazosPress, 2013). Wallis is not quoting directly from the biography (Smith and Zepp 1974) but from an article that the authors wrote originally for *The Christian Century* (April 3, 1974): 361–363, and available online at http://www.religion-online.org/showarticle.asp?title=1603.

39   Wallis, *On God's Side*, 120.

40   Smith and Zepp, 'Martin Luther King's Vision of the Beloved Community.'

41   Wallis 2016. Other noteworthy books by evangelicals in this vein include: Wilson-Hartgrove 2018; Cross 2014; Meredith 2019; Mulder 2015; and Loritts and Ortberg 2018.

42   Quoted in Wallis 2017, 84.

43   Alexander 2013, online http://prismmagazine.org/raced-as-white, accessed February 14, 2019.

44   Quoted in Wallis 2017, 94–95.

45   Wallis 2017, 95. I delved into this theme in more detail and related how I attempted to put this into practice during an interchurch Martin Luther King prayer vigil in January 2019, see http://www.humantrustees.org/blogs/religion-and-human-rights/item/182-america-s-original-sin.

46   Wallis 2017, 89.

47   Wallis 2017, 156.

48   Wallis 2017, 191.

3

Justice as Respect for Human Rights

God, who is the God of justice, is also the God of power and might. In God, justice and power are harmonized completely as God's justice and love. God, the source of all power, gives power to humans in order to fulfill the divine purpose of justice and peace in the world. Power is, therefore, entrusted by God to people; but like all other trusts, it can be used responsibly or abused terribly. It can carry with it a blessing or it can become a curse.[1]

Naim Ateek, a Palestinian Anglican priest, penned these words barely a year after the outbreak of the First Intifada.[2] I had the privilege of knowing him well, since I not only attended his church in East Jerusalem for three years (he was Canon of the St. George's Cathedral), but I also helped with the Arabic services he led and occasionally replaced him when he was traveling. His book *Justice and Only Justice* grew out of a pastoral concern for all the Palestinian Christians of many denominations and rites who because of the injustice and daily humiliations of Israeli military occupation could not bear to read the Old Testament and inwardly questioned whether the Jesus of the New Testament cared about their suffering. On several occasions I heard him say something like this: 'I wanted Palestinians to understand the whole Bible, to know that God cares about all the oppressed and downtrodden, and that Jesus personally endured the injustice of the Roman occupation and the hatred and treachery of the Jewish religious leaders for our sakes. He wants to walk them through their pain and give them the strength to forgive their enemies.'[3]

That said, forgiving does not mean you don't seek justice, Ateek would add. You just go about it nonviolently, and with the goal, if possible, to achieve reconciliation.[4] With regard to the Israeli-Palestinian conflict, two peoples find themselves on the same territory they both claim as their own. Above all, it's a clash of two nationalisms. Somehow they will both need to find a way to share that land. International law, Ateek remarks, can play a constructive role. For instance, in December 1979, the General Assembly of the United Nations reiterated in clear terms the Palestinian right to self-determination:

> Bearing in mind the principles of equal rights and self-determination of peoples enshrined in Articles 1 and 55 of the Charter of the United Nations and more recently reaffirmed in the Declaration of Principles of International Law Concerning Friendly Relations and Cooperation Among Nations, [the United Nations General Assembly] recognizes that the people of Palestine are entitled to equal rights and self-determination, in accordance with the Charter of the United Nations.[5]

Growing out of this book, Ateek started the Center for Palestinian Liberation Theology, called 'Sabeel,' with the goal of helping Palestinian Christians read the Bible, discuss it, and learn how God can enable them to live out their faithfulness to him in a cauldron of injustice.

On the Israeli side, a group of civil society leaders founded The Israeli Information Center for Human Rights in the Occupied Territories in 1989, better known as B'Tselem, Hebrew for 'in the image.' This had been the wish of the late Knesset member Yossi Sarid who saw this organization emanating from the creation story on the first page of the Torah, 'And God created humankind in his image' (Gen. 1:27). Its mission is clearly formulated in terms of human rights: 'Israel's regime of occupation is inextricably bound up in human rights violations. B'Tselem strives to end the occupation, as that is the only way forward to a future in which human rights, democracy, liberty and equality are ensured to all people, both Palestinian and Israeli, living between the Jordan River and the Mediterranean Sea.'[6]

A recent B'Tselem report on home demolitions carried out by the Israeli army in the occupied West Bank puts the blame directly on Israel's High Court.[7] First, in graphic form they offer the figures: 1,401 homes demolished since 2006; 6,207 people rendered homeless, of which 3,134 are minors. According to the IDF (Israeli Defense Forces), these homes are destroyed because they were built without a permit. However, out of 5,475 applications for home construction by Palestinians since 2000, only 226 were accepted (4 percent), and not one petition against home demolition was granted. As B'Tselem sees it, this is the rationale of Israeli planning in the Occupied Territories:

> The planning apparatus Israel has instituted in the West Bank serves its policy of promoting and expanding Israeli takeover of land across the West Bank. When planning for Palestinians, the Israeli Civil Administration endeavors

to obstruct development, minimize the size of communities and increase construction density, with a view to keeping as many land reserves as possible for the benefit of Israeli interests, first and foremost for the expansion of settlements. Yet when planning for settlements, whose very establishment is unlawful in the first place, the Civil Administration's actions are the very reverse: planning reflects settlements' present and future needs, aiming to include as much land as possible in the outline plan so as to take over as many land resources as possible. Such planning leads to wasteful infrastructure development, loss of natural countryside and relinquishing open areas.[8]

The text characterizes the building of settlements as 'unlawful,' that is, a violation of international law, the Fourth Geneva Convention in particular, which forbids the building of settlements in militarily conquered territory. Notice too, the obvious double standard of how the law works for Palestinians on the one hand, and for the Israelis on the other. While everything is done to favor the expansion of Jewish Israeli settlements in the West Bank, Palestinian growth is intentionally impeded by denying the right to build 'homes or public buildings, connect to infrastructure or make repairs – even essential ones – to existing buildings, and thus consigning them to a prolonged state of limbo and uncertainty as to their future.' Justice is tied to human rights, which in this case are systematically denied.

I begin this chapter with the Israeli-Palestinian conflict especially because it is one of the causes Muslims care most about worldwide. On the other hand most American Christians, and evangelicals in particular, have been influenced by the ideology of Christian Zionism and tend to focus almost entirely on the Israeli narrative of victimization – Israel is fighting for its very existence, surrounded as it is by Arab nations bent on destroying her.[9] True, there has been a good deal of anti-Semitism among Muslims over the years – and not just Arabs – along with some Holocaust-denying. That is plainly wrong. On the other hand, since the 1967 war and the military occupation of Gaza, the West Bank and the Golan Heights, dozens of UN resolutions have called Israel to withdraw from those territories and refrain from transferring their own population to them, starting with Resolutions 242 and 348 (1967 and 1973 respectively).[10] This is an obvious case of injustice in which a powerful state, backed by the world's superpower, has held a whole population in subjection for over half a century. And this brings me to Gaza, where the latest war between Hamas and Israel left over 2,200 people dead, mostly Palestinian and mostly civilian.[11] The Palestinian Authority about a week after the signing of the ceasefire (August 26, 2014) that in almost two months of fighting 20,000 homes had been flattened and most of Gaza's infrastructure had been destroyed, including its only power plant. It figured reconstruction would cost almost $8 billion.[12]

Ateek asserted that as many see it, justice means 'an impartially administered system of settling grievances under law.'[13] Others might put it simply, 'the rule of law.' Yet that is surely problematic in view of the fact that law is established by those in power. This is the topic I would like to explore in the next section before examining Wolterstorff's view of justice as rights.

Justice and the Law

No doubt, law upholds human society, protecting people's rights and providing the framework that guides every human endeavor, from the enforcement of contracts to the regulation of industry and commerce, and from the punishment of crime to the compensation of those wronged. Thus it aspires to fulfill justice. But what is justice? Is it simply what the law says, or is the law meant to approximate what people consider 'just'? The latter seems intuitively right. Furthermore, we do expect that the law will seek to apply justice, in the sense that it conforms to an ethical standard to which all 'reasonable' people could subscribe. This idea, writes Professor of Law and Legal Theory Raymond Wacks, is at the heart of natural law theory, which has made a comeback in the second half of the twentieth century.[14] This was likely not a coincidence, since it was WWII that precipitated the international consensus that led to the UDHR and the paradigm of human rights as the best framework for a just international human society.

But before commenting on that great paradigm shift, allow me to explain what other theories vie for preeminence. Wacks begins his summary of the history of legal theory with the oldest one, natural law, which goes back to the Greek Stoic philosophers. In turn, they inspired the Roman lawyer Cicero to formulate the three pillars of natural law – 'universality and immutability, its standing as 'higher' law, and its discoverability by reason': 'True law is right reason in agreement with Nature; it is of universal application, unchanging and everlasting.... It is a sin to try to alter this law, nor is it allowable to attempt to repeal any part of it, and it is impossible to abolish it entirely.... [God] is the author of this law, its promulgator, and its enforcing judge.'[15]

Much later, in the Christian context, the great North African thinker St. Augustine offered this rhetorical question, 'What are states without justice, but robber bands enlarged?.' Yet it was thirteenth-century thinker and the great doctor of the Catholic tradition, Thomas Aquinas, who distinguished four categories of law: 'the eternal law (divine reason known only to God), natural law (the participation of the eternal law in rational creatures, discoverable by reason), divine law (revealed in the scriptures), and human law (supported by reason, and enacted for the common good).'[16] Because God created human beings with the capacity for reason, their effort to enact laws aimed at the common good of society qualify as 'laws' and participate in that sense in God's eternal law.

Note too that this view presupposes the existence of objective moral truth. Justice and goodness exist in and of themselves, as do evil and corruption. This is the ethical objectivism I alluded to in the Introduction, and according to Aquinas, humans can access it through reason – an epistemological statement (how we come to know what we know). I will be arguing in this book, as I have elsewhere,[17] the divide between ethical objectivism and ethical voluntarism represents the watershed between Muslims favoring a recourse to democracy and human rights and those who do not. Though most do not use the term 'natural law,' as this might seem to diminish God's role in their eyes, the popular focus on the 'Shari'a's objectives' plays a similar function. The central objective being human welfare (*maṣlaḥa*), or even 'the common good,' the assumption is that people can discern what that is through their God–given rational ability.

This is roughly what happened in post–Renaissance Europe when Hugo Grotius (d. 1645) developed a framework for public international law arguably founded on natural law. A century later Blackstone (d. 1780) taught that English law had its source in natural law. This was the time too when the Enlightenment ideals most obviously shone through the American and French revolutionary movements with the concept of 'natural rights.' In the words of the Declaration of Independence, 'We hold these truths to be self-evident, that all men are created equal, that they are endowed by their Creator with certain inalienable rights.'

Though Thomas Hobbes (d. 1679) and John Locke (d. 1704) disagreed about the natural state of human society before the social contract, they and Jean-Jacques Rousseau (d. 1778) all agreed that humans were endowed with natural rights and that some kind of social agreement had to take place for the rule of law to triumph in society. Hobbes stipulated that for reasons of self-preservation people had to give up many rights so as to live in peace. Otherwise, humans are prone to competition, mutual distrust, and the pursuit of their own glory at the expense of others – all of which leads to discord and chaos. Locke was more sanguine about human nature, but for him the social contract was especially necessary to protect private property. So in a sense, the right to own property was a central human right in his estimation. Rousseau's view was more focused on society as a whole – how the individual merges with the whole by electing a legislative body that embodies 'the general will' in pursuit of the common good. Yet the potentially authoritarian power of the legislature in his system is somewhat tempered by the natural rights of all citizens to equality and liberty.

Not surprisingly, natural law reasoning was still widespread among the intelligentsia in the early nineteenth century, though it waned in the decades that followed. From the early nineteenth century to the first half of the twentieth century it faced the headwinds of legal positivism (law is what people make it out to be). But then natural law experienced a dramatic renaissance in the mid twentieth century by asserting the following claims: 1) law and morality are interconnected; and 2) 'that law exists independently of human enactment.'[18] No, replied the legal positivists, law is laid down by people; it is 'posited' (from the Latin *positum*). This, of course, leads to the expression 'positive law,' which for its first greatest proponent, Jeremy Bentham (d. 1832), means that the body of accumulated legal precedents (common law) must be constantly questioned and reformed on the basis of reason. Yet for him the common law system in the UK gave too much power to the judges. Better to transform common law into legal codes, said Bentham – codification would put the priority of the legal professional where it belonged, that is, to administer the law and not to interpret it.

For Bentham and his disciple John Austin (d. 1859), lawyers do not look backwards to some source of law outside of them (like 'nature'), but rather look forward by asking, 'What good will this accomplish for society?' This is a utilitarian approach, which seeks to demystify the law as if it were something sacred. This is exactly how H. L. A. Hart (d. 1992) approached the task of explaining the law. As for this 'father of modern legal positivism,' analytical philosophy and linguistics were the best tools for this purpose. His classic work, *The Concept of Law*,[19] leaves behind the utilitarianism and 'command theory of law' used by Bentham and Austin[20] and defines 'law' as a system of rules. Because human beings tend to be vulnerable, selfish and needy, they need rules in order to protect their collective existence. Primary rules forbid killing, stealing from, or willfully deceiving one's fellow citizen. Secondary rules are of three kinds: 1) rules of change confer power on individuals to draw up contracts or wills, or on legislatures to enact new laws (even relative to primary rules); 2) rules of adjudication give judges the authority to punish criminals or compensate victims; 3) the rule of recognition, a key component of Hart's theory, is what defines the criteria a society accepts for making rules 'valid.'

Legal positivism continues to guide many legal scholars today, but within two distinct camps. The 'hard positivists' consider the validity of any rule to derive exclusively from society and its own internal dynamics. For the 'soft positivists' by contrast, 'the law may sometimes rest on moral considerations.'. Wacks explains:

> For example, where a constitution (or a bill of rights) requires a court to decide a case by reference to considerations of justice and fairness, he or she will be expected to determine the outcome by evaluating these moral values. Adjudication is no longer confined to the exclusive application of *legal* rules. Hard positivists insist that the validity of a purported legal norm (its membership in the legal system) cannot turn on the moral merits of the norm in question. They therefore acknowledge that occasionally the law may incorporate moral criteria for ascertaining what the law is.[21]

Interestingly, the man who succeeded Hart as Professor of Jurisprudence at Oxford University in the 1970s was his fiercest critic, Ronald Dworkin (d. 2013).[22] Contra the positivists, Dworkin insisted that a judge, when confronted with a difficult case, need only *interpret* the law, even if there is no legal precedent and no relevant statute can be found. In other words, law is a 'gapless system.' Take the case of a will's beneficiary who in his impatience murders the testator. Should he still be able to inherit according to the law? In a specific case of this sort a New York court decided that he could not inherit, stating 'that the application of the rules was subject to the principle that no person should profit from his own wrong.'[23] Dworkin concludes that the court was right: besides rules there are also moral principles. And this is precisely what is wrong about Hart's 'rule of recognition.' It cannot distinguish between legal norms and moral principles.

Besides the fact that Dworkin calls for the necessity of interpreting the law (and then of *evaluating* one's interpretation of it in light of moral principles), his attack on legal positivism also incorporates the rights of individuals within the scope of law. As Wacks puts it,

> Rights trump other considerations such as community welfare. Individual rights are seriously compromised if, as Hart claims, the result of a hard case depends on the judge's personal opinion, intuition, or the exercise of his or her strong discretion. My rights may then simply be subordinated to

the interests of community.... His theory thus provides more muscle to the defense of individual rights and liberty than legal positivism can deliver.[24]

For the same reason Dworkin opposed legal conventionalism, which sees law as no more than social conventions – lower courts are bound to follow the decisions of higher courts on particular issues, and because law is incomplete, judges are given wide latitude to adjudicate (and 'fill the gaps') on the basis of their own preferences.[25] He also castigates the legal pragmatists, who doubt whether past decisions warrant state coercion. That use of force to make sure they are applied can only be justified by the quality of the judge's administration of justice. But, objects Dworkin, this is to treat rights instrumentally – they only count insofar as they achieve some other good but are not therefore 'inherent rights.' Legal pragmatism rejects the virtue of consistency with the past and instead posits the ideal of a judge making decisions that secure the best possible future for his or her community. Indeed, pragmatism leads to a utilitarian approach to law.

All three theories (positivism, conventionalism, and pragmatism), argues Dworkin, fall short of being able to explain the *substance* of the law. At best they can explain the linguistic usage, social functionality or instrumental value of particular rules, but in the case of Nazi law in the 1930s for instance, they could not offer a good reason why those rules were not 'law' – at least using the resources from within their respective theories. This is why he posits two crucial elements that make particular rules 'the law.' The first is his concept of 'law as integrity.' By this he means that the judge always seeks the best interpretation of the law, one that 'could form part of a coherent theory justifying the whole legal system.' Below he explains what this integrity means in practice. Notice too the role played by rights; and, additionally, you will catch a glimpse of his second cardinal rule – human dignity:

> [L]aw as integrity accepts law and legal rights wholeheartedly ... It supposes that law's constraints benefit society not just by providing predictability or procedural fairness, or in some other instrumental way, but *by securing a kind of equality among citizens that makes their community more genuine and improves its moral justification for exercising the political power it does....* It argues that rights and responsibilities flow from past decisions and so count as legal, not just when they are explicit in these decisions but also when they follow from the principles of personal and political morality the explicit decisions presuppose by way of justification.[26]

I will make one last remark about Dworkin. In his last book, *Justice for Hedgehogs*,[27] Dworkin took a stand against all the currents of thought over the last century that call into question the reliability of moral reasoning. For him – and people of faith generally, moral values like justice, goodness and truth are objective principles, independent from personal or even cultural preferences. Honest people can disagree about particular cases and how they might be evaluated, but they all refer to ethical principles that human beings generally recognize as valid. I have touched on the issue of cultural relativism as it relates to human rights elsewhere,[28] but suffice it to say here that for Dworkin people 'live well' when their own self-respect is well established enough that they want to make sure everyone else enjoys the same dignity as fellow human beings. A life well lived entails an ethical responsibility to care for others. As Wacks puts it, 'By acknowledging the significance of self-respect, we are obliged – if we are to be logically consistent – to recognize its importance in the lives of others.'[29]

I just mentioned the headwinds of moral relativism pushing hard and fast against the kind of moral certitude Dworkin upheld. Wacks devotes his Chapter 5 ('Law and Society') to thinkers who focused on the sociology of law, like Emile Durkheim (d. 1917), often dubbed 'the father of sociology,' Max Weber (d. 1920), Karl Marx (d. 1883), Jürgen Habermas (b. 1929) and Michel Foucault (d. 1984). All of these, each in his own way and from his own perspective, illuminate different ways law and legal institutions function in modern human society, and particularly how capitalism has impacted the nature of social dynamics.

Further, none of the above men, despite their vast knowledge of legal affairs, was a legal scholar per se, but rather they critiqued legal theory and practice from their own vantage points. Then Wack's Chapter 6 ('Critical Legal Theory') highlights legal theorists who, from the inside of the legal profession, spurn 'several of the enterprises that have long been assumed to be at the heart of jurisprudence.'[30] Thus different branches of legal theory take aim at a particular aspect of society, which traditionally had been justified on rational grounds but which for them is deeply problematic: patriarchy as seen by feminist jurisprudence, the construct of 'race' in critical race theory, the free market as it is unpacked by critical legal studies, and even the modern notion of 'progress,' as deconstructed by postmodern legal studies.

In the first three cases, legal theorists only seek to redress the injustices committed against women, people of color, and the poor. In *Earth, Empire and Sacred Text*, I show how Martin Luther King, Jr., and Malcolm X at about the same time realized how the principles that propelled them forward

in the civil rights movement became enlarged – King as he grappled with
the injustice of the Vietnam War, and Malcolm X as he awoke to the rights
of all human beings through his own epiphany as a first-time pilgrim at
the Hajj. But this was only a useful Christian and Muslim illustration of a
wider point I was making about the postmodern movement (cf. chapters 2
to 4). The impatience that postmodernist theory has with all modern 'met-
anarratives,' including utopianism, nationalism, statism and even democracy, pronounces in extreme cases the death of the modern autonomous
self, the death of history (certainly in progressive terms), and the death of
metaphysics.[31]

That is why I chose to side with Yale political philosopher Seyla Benhabib
who advocates for a weaker version of postmodernism.[32] After all, are not
these 'critical' movements actually calling for a redress of the injustices
committed against the weak and marginalized? Are they not assuming,
at least in part, the notion that all human beings have inalienable rights
qua human beings? The strong version of postmodernism undercuts any
notion of social justice or the very existence of common moral principles;
whereas its weaker version, while keeping its necessary critical edge, can
still promote a conversation between people of different cultures, races,
faiths, and ideologies. How can we together create a better world?

So we come back again to the notion of justice as respect for the rights
of all people. But the idea still remains fuzzy. I have found Walterstorff's
exposition of it very helpful, and to that I now turn.

Justice as Rights

By far the most influential scholar in political philosophy in the second
half of the twentieth century was the Harvard and Oxford professor John
Rawls (d. 2002). His classic book, *A Theory of Justice* (1971), set the tone
for all future discussions. Still, his many critics had mounted such good
arguments that he responded to several of them in his 1993 book, *Political
Liberalism*. One cannot write about justice today and ignore Rawls' theory.
Hence Wolterstorff in his Introduction acknowledges that 'almost everyone who picks up this book will want to know what I have to say about
Rawls.'[33]

His answer is simple: 'Though Rawls's theory of justice is an inherent
natural rights theory, he does nothing at all to develop an account of such
rights. He simply assumes their existence.'[34] Wolterstorff's ambition is to
fill in the gap – 'develop an account of such rights,' drawing on analytic

philosophy as well as the Bible, mostly because he is convinced that those who malign rights theory as self-centered modern claims antithetical to the functioning of a healthy society have bought into the wrong narrative about how they developed historically. But before I get to that point, I do have to touch on Rawls' theory, only because one particular aspect of it will serve us well when we talk about how people with different worldviews can contribute to a common democratic civil society.

Rawls is famous for defining justice as 'fairness.' A state makes a covenant, or a compact with its citizens to treat them as equally and fairly as possible. This is a social contract approach, meant to bring about the good of all citizens. To achieve this, Rawls posits the idea of a *'veil of ignorance'*: let's suppose a group of citizens who somehow are able to forget their own class, religious and ethnic condition and values, and make together objective, rational decisions about the good of the whole. This hypothetical condition then enables them to define together in a disinterested way what the 'good life' might be for their society. He then argues that they would agree to this two-fold proposition:

(1) Each person is to have an equal right to the most extensive basic liberty compatible with a similar liberty for others.[35]

(2) Social and economic inequalities are to be arranged so that they are both (a) to the greatest benefit of the least advantaged and (b) attached to offices and positions open to all under conditions of fair equality of opportunity.

This 'basic liberty,' as he defines it, includes 'freedom of thought and conscience, freedom of association, the right to representative government, the right to form and join political parties, the right to personal property, and the rights and liberties necessary to secure the rule of law.' But it excludes economic rights, unlike what is stipulated in one of the two UN covenants that form the International Bill of Rights I mentioned earlier, the *International Covenant on Economic, Social and Cultural Rights* (ICESC). Yet both communism and pure laissez-faire capitalism are unjust too, Rawls recognizes, in that they either rob people of their freedoms or leave whole swaths of the population without equal access to society's resources (starting with education), and thus deprive them of the means to compete fairly for the positions they may aspire to.

Notice too that in the second proposition Rawls takes socioeconomic disparities, and hence injustice, for granted. Therefore the system has to be tweaked, he contends, in favor of the weakest and most vulnerable in human society. The second sub-point (b) is a stab at redressing that balance of power. In a democratic society one way to level the playing field for all is to make sure that positions of power are truly open to those most left behind. Naturally this ideal is difficult to achieve in practice, and the means we choose to accomplish this will vary from one context to another.

In a series of lectures published in 1993 under the title *Political Liberalism*, Rawls sets out to answer several of his critics' reservations, and especially this one: How can a modern liberal democracy function over time with relative stability when in fact it is composed of free and equal citizens who hold to vastly different religious, philosophical, and moral doctrines? So Rawls, years after offering a basic framework for looking at justice as fairness (*A Theory of Justice*), reworked his idea of justice, this time specifically tailored to a pluralistic democratic political context. He now recognized that the gulf between holders of different religious convictions and political ideologies is wider than he once thought. One of the concepts he used to solve this dilemma turns out to be very relevant for seeing how more traditional Muslims might function in a liberal state – the idea of an 'overlapping consensus,' that is, though subscribing to different 'comprehensive doctrines,' citizens can still agree on some common values.[36]

Now, coming to Wolterstorff's theory of rights, I want to present it in three steps: justice as inherent rights, not right order; the contest of narratives; and justice in the Hebrew Bible.

Inherent Rights versus Right Order

Within the Justinian codification of Roman law, *The Digest*, is a passage Emperor Justinian I took from third-century Roman jurist Ulpian.[37] A recent translation renders his definition of justice thus: 'Justice is a steady and enduring will to render unto everyone his right. The basic principles of right are: to live honorably, not to harm any other person, to render to each his own.'[38] Wolterstorff explains how his own approach is slightly different from Ulpian's: he is not interested so much in justice as a virtue as he is in how this virtue impacts society as a whole. A just society is one in which each person can *enjoy* the goods to which he or she has a right. 'If speaking my mind freely is something I have a right to, then speaking my mind freely is a good in my life; if receiving a monthly Social Security payment is something I have a right to, then it is a good in my life.'[39]

Since Wolterstorff is concerned about primary justice, his focus here is on *moral* rights as opposed to *legal* rights, though much of what applies to the former also applies to the latter. A right is something *due* someone. To deprive that person of that right is to *wrong* him or her. He explains:

Being deprived of that to which she has a right constitutes an alteration in her moral condition. She is then *wronged*. When Union Carbide's chemical plant in Bhopal, India, spewed poisonous fumes into the air, it deprived the residents of the valley of a good to which they had a right, namely, the good of having non-noxious air to breathe; thereby the residents were *wronged*.[40]

Keep in mind too, he reminds us, that acts of injustice may have multiple agents. Anytime we investigate issues of social injustice we are likely to uncover a web of culprits, from individuals in politics, to social entities in the past who used their power to trample the rights of those who were weaker than they, and to multinational corporations annihilating small businesses in the developing world today, as the above case in India. Social groups have a life and power of their own over and beyond individuals who might seem to pull their strings as leaders. The same can be said of the recipients of injustice. When for instance a pedestrian is run over by a speeding or simply careless driver, that person's whole family will be affected by the tragedy in multiple ways.

As a consequence of such a traffic accident the issue of retributive justice kicks in – the wronged party can choose to seek punishment for the guilty person. Yet although the wronged party has permission to do so – in the sense that it is a 'right' – it is not *obligated* to do so. As Wolterstorff has it, 'nobody is wronged if it does not happen.' In some cases the exercise of retributive justice is mandatory, but usually it is not. He adds, 'forgiveness is not a violation of the moral order.' This would be just as true for Muslims as it is for Christians.[41] That said, Wolterstorff is interested not in retributive justice but in primary justice. Still, we have touched here on a crucial difference between a retributive right that can be waived on the part of the wronged person without harming the agent of that wrong and an inherent or moral right that cannot be waived. To prevent someone from enjoying his or her right is to harm that person, because it's an inherent right. This distinction also highlights the difference between justice as inherent rights and justice as right order.

Justice as right order is a concept that Greek philosophers all assumed; the gods had established an order for human beings they called *dikè*, or justice. To swerve from that divinely established cosmic order was to commit injustice, or to render society unjust. In a sense, Plato only substituted the ideal Form Justice for the gods, but the result was the same. Justice is defined by the way society is ordered. Individual rights have no role to play in this conception of justice. According to Wolterstorff, 'There is objective right; but nobody has rights.'[42] None of the right order theorists today refer to any transcendent standard that determines whether society is just or not. And although they believe a just social order confers on its members certain rights via legislation or social practices, they do not hold to any natural rights that people have by simply being *human.*

Wolterstorff quotes two leading proponents of the right order theory of justice. Oliver O'Donovan concedes, for example, that '[t]he language of subjective rights (i.e., rights which adhere to a particular subject) has, of course, a perfectly appropriate and necessary place within a discourse founded on law.'[43] But the modern rights discourse insists that those rights are 'original, not derived.' According to him, there is no 'primitive endowment of power with which the subject first engages in society.' Rights flow out of a particular kind of social contract; they are not attached to humans *qua* humans.

The other philosopher who works from a definition of justice as right order is Alasdair MacIntyre in his influential book, *After Virtue.*[44] The idea that humans have rights appears for the first time at the end of the Middle Ages, notes MacIntyre. Indeed, there was no vocabulary in any language before this time to express this idea – which does not prove, he adds, that there is no such thing as natural rights. But in fact, when today we talk about 'natural rights,' he argues,

> it is always in virtue of the existence in that time and place of some particular set of institutional arrangements requiring description in those terms, and the rights in question therefore will always be institutionally conferred, institutionally recognized and institutionally enforced rights; and all such rights of course are either rights conferred by positive law or custom or rights exercised in practices or rights arising from promises. They will not be and cannot be natural rights possessed independently of specific institutional arrangements.[45]

Wolterstorff disagrees with these justice-as-right-order theorists for two reasons. First, they are distorting the natural rights position. By pitting the two ways of understanding justice against each other as if they are logically incompatible they are attacking a straw man they have set up themselves. Critics of natural rights imply that their opponents are artificially dividing a person's socially conferred rights from these alleged 'natural rights' in a way that strips individuals of their social identity. It is as if there is a 'natural' part of the human person that is untainted by her social relations. But this is a nonsensical distinction that proponents of natural rights have never made, nor could they, he says. There is no dichotomy within us as persons, because we have both natural and socially conferred rights. Simply put, our natural rights are those we possess but were not conferred on us by society. Put another way,

> In identifying certain of the rights of a member of the social order as *natural* rights, one is not engaged in the impossible project of imagining this entity as a purely natural, asocial being. One is simply taking note of what does and does not account for having these rights. Natural rights are not the rights of asocial beings but the rights of social beings that have not been socially conferred on them.[46]

The second bone Wolterstorff picks with the right order advocates is that both views of justice are not incompatible. To believe in justice as a just social order is not incompatible with a belief in inalienable rights. Indeed, to posit an 'objective standard as a matrix of principles of natural obligation, one must concede that there are natural rights.'[47] This is because obligation and right are correlatives. This he calls the principle of correlatives:

> If Y belongs to the sort of entity that can have rights, then X has an obligation toward Y to do or refrain from doing A if and only if Y has a right against X to X's doing or refraining from doing A.

> For example, John has an obligation toward Mary to refrain from insulting her if and only if Mary has a right against John to John's refraining from insulting her.[48]

Wolterstorff sees that subjective right of not being insulted as a natural right. If that is the case, then its correlative obligation of not insulting others is natural too. As right order theorists, O'Donovan and MacIntyre claim the existence of natural subjective obligations. For Wolterstorff, one cannot posit the one without positing the other. If there are natural subjective obligations, then there are necessarily corresponding natural subjective rights.

Still, declares Wolterstorff, we have not solved the basic issue at the root of all this talk about rights. It is more fundamental than whether human beings have natural rights or not. How is the moral universe actually structured? If my government enacted a particular law about people of my status and situation being due a monthly social security check, then I have the right against the government to collect that check on a monthly basis. A right order theorist tends to see all rights in this vein. They are conferred by some outside source, be it legislation, human agreement, verbal promises, and the like. The inherent rights theorist agrees that many rights are conferred in such a manner, but that additionally there are other rights that are not conferred but inherent to the person. Wolterstorff uses the verb 'supervene' to describe how the right comes to be ascribed to each person:

> On account of possessing certain properties, standing in certain relation-ships, performing certain actions, each of us has a certain worth. The worth supervenes on being of that sort: have those properties, standing in those relationships, performing those actions. And having that worth is sufficient for having the rights. There does not have to be something else that confers those rights on entities of this sort.[49]

Most people will agree that it is morally wrong to torture another person, and therefore will assent to this 'natural law of objective obliga-tion': 'every human being is obligated not to torture any human being.' Wolterstorff argues quite consistently, it seems to me, that this general rule (this natural law of objective obligation) flows out of the inherent worth of every individual human being, which then dictates that everyone has the subjective right not to be tortured – and not the other way around. Put otherwise, inherent rights are ontologically prior to objective obliga-tions. This is a very different moral universe from the one painted by the right order theorists. Add to that a theistic perspective from which God commands people not to torture their fellow human being, and we wrong two parties by torturing another human being: the victim and God himself, who has a right to our obedience. But 'the divine commands does not make it wrong; it was already wrong.'[50]

At bottom, the clash between the two versions of justice touch on the worth of every human being. Here is Wolterstorff's reasoning:

> For the right order theorist, the violation of someone's natural rights is never, in itself and as such, the treating of a human being with less than due respect. It is always instead an indicator of the fact that some natural law of objective obligation has been disobeyed. A partisan of right order may point to the plight of the poor, he may say that their rights are being violated. But pointing to the victims is for him a roundabout way of calling attention to the more fundamental fact that that the powerful and the well-to-do are not living up to their obligations. It is not a way of calling attention to the fact that the worth of those human beings who are poor is not being respected. The worth of human beings does not enter into his way of thinking about rights.

The reason for this reflex, argues Wolterstorff, comes from two ways of reading the past history of Western intellectual thought – hence, the clash of two narratives.

The Clash of Two Narratives

Proponents of justice as right order hold to a 'declinist' view of the Latin term *ius* ('right'), i.e., that from a view of the right as a just society it declined toward the view that prevails in our day, that of justice as inherent rights. Some see the precipitating crisis in the philosophical nominalism of William of Ockham (d. 1347). In defending the Franciscans' right to use their properties and simple possessions, as they had made a vow of poverty, Ockham made extensive reference to natural subjective rights. The details need not detain us here,[51] but according to this narrative it was Ockham's nominalism that led him to defend 'natural' subjective rights and thereby promote an atomistic view of human society. Naturally, in this line of thinking, the great Western crisis came when Hobbes, Locke and their Enlightenment colleagues put to use this rights discourse to create political liberalism. Citizens were now seen as bearers of natural rights and the state's mission was to make sure those rights were respected without infringing upon their fellow citizens. More specifically, 'The "freedom rights" of individuals set limits to state action and to the actions of one's fellows; the "benefit" rights of individuals constitute entitlements to state action and to the actions of one's fellows.' In this wording, of course, it is easy to see a direct trajectory leading to the 1966 ratification of the ICCR and the ICESC.

That narrative is seen as a great decline in the understanding of justice only because in the minds of philosophers and historians like MacIntyre and O'Donovan justice as inherent rights is a child of modern liberalism which glorifies selfish individualism – people claiming all manner of rights for themselves and thereby creating a society torn apart by frivolous lawsuits, among other ills. Many people of faith, as well as many secularists, would agree that such a situation is a travesty of justice, but I would concur with Wolterstorff that its causes are not to be found in the concept of human rights.[52] There is another story, however.

The alternative narrative has grown out of a new body of scholarship that emerged in the 1980s and 1990s. Wolterstorff informs us that its main authors are medievalists who specialize in canon law, which largely grew out of Gratian's *Decretum* around 1140. Two seminal works are Brian Tierney's *God's Joust and God's Justice*[53] and his student Charles J. Reid, Jr.'s article, 'The Canonistic Contribution to the Western Rights Tradition: An Historical Inquiry.'[54] As Reid puts it, 'The chief difficulty with these two schools of thought [Ockham's nominalism and/or the Enlightenment], from the standpoint of the working medievalist, is that rights are readily identifiable in the legal systems of thirteenth century Europe.' Actually, rights were ubiquitous in the legal literature of the time. He explains:

> In fact, a close scrutiny of juristic materials reveals a sophisticated understanding of rights already operative in the legal systems of twelfth and thirteenth century Europe. This understanding of rights would become part of the medieval *jus commune*, the common law of Europe, that would in turn inform the polemical works of William of Ockham and the writings of early modern philosophers and theologians – figures as diverse and seminal in their own right as John Locke and John Calvin.[55]

Tierney and Reid agree with the partisans of the first narrative that in fact *ius* (or *jus*) for the ancient Roman jurists referred 'either to *the right*, in the sense of *the objectively right thing*, or to the benefits and burdens attached to some corporeal thing, such as a piece of property.'[56] But by the twelfth century it has become a close synonym of *lex* ('law') and it refers to subjective rights. Additionally, recent research has demonstrated that consistently in Justinian's *Digest* people 'have' *ius* and *ius* is used with a possessive pronoun, indicating that it 'belongs' to someone. So something happened in the early Common Era, argues Wolterstorff, to change the jurists' conception of *ius* from 'the right' to subjective rights. And, he adds, the evidence clearly points to the Church Fathers.

Already in Gratian's *Decretum* (the classic twelfth century work of canon law) we read about the poor, 'No one may call his own what is common, of which if he takes more than he needs, it is obtained by violence... The bread you hold back belongs to the needy, the clothes that you store away belong to the naked.'[57] Eventually canon law comes to assume that human beings all have a natural right to the necessities of life. But almost a millennium before this time the Church Fathers wrote about these concepts. In late fourth century Antioch, for example, the great preacher later revered by the Orthodox Church, John Chrysostom, was of this view. In several sermons commenting on Jesus' parable of Lazarus and the rich man he declared that to withhold one's possessions from the poor was to rob them. Here is a passage from one of his sermons on this parable:

> Need alone is this poor man's worthiness; if anyone at all ever comes to us with this recommendation, let us not meddle any further. We do not provide

for the manners but for the man. We show mercy on him not because of his virtue but because of his misfortune... I beg you remember this without fail, that not to share our own wealth with the poor is theft from the poor and deprivation of their means to life; we do not possess our own wealth but theirs.[58]

John's appeal here is to those who have means and he is 'begging' them to consider the needy person's worth as a human being, with no further qualification than his or her need. The poor, in other words, have a *natural right* to sustenance: 'the poor are *wronged* because they do not have what is theirs by natural right, what they have a natural right to.'[59] In the longer version of this sermon, John is appealing to other passages of the Bible, including the Old Testament. So I close this chapter with a few examples from that text.

Justice in the Hebrew Bible

From the outset let me say with Wolterstorff 'that my interpretation of justice in the Christian Scripture is one among others; there is no consensus interpretation.' Alasdair MacIntyre is a Catholic philosopher and Stanley Hauerwas is a Protestant theologian leaning toward the Anabaptist tradition (and a committed pacifist),[60] yet both would disagree with those of us who see the notion of human rights as taught by both Old and New Testaments. I will also be drawing from leading evangelical ethicists Glen H. Stassen (d. 2014) and David P. Gushee in their major work, *Kingdom Ethics*.[61]

In my own daily reading of the Bible, I am regularly amazed at God's passion for justice, whether in the courts, or in the conduct of kings, or in the way the poor and needy are treated by the wealthy. Here is a typical sentiment expressed by King David in one of his many psalms:

Justice do you rulers know the meaning of the word? Do you judge people fairly? ...

The godly will rejoice when they see injustice avenged ...

Then at last everyone will say, 'There is truly a reward for those who live for God; surely there is a God who judges justly here on earth' (Ps. 58:1, 10, 11).[62]

In the first of the four 'Servant Songs' (or poems) in the Isaiah tradition (Isaiah 42:1-4), we read about the messianic figure God will send to establish his kingdom, both humble and yet ultimately victorious in extending justice 'throughout the earth':

> 'Look at my servant, whom I strengthen.
>   He is my chosen one, who pleases me.
> I have put my Spirit upon him.
>   He will bring justice to the nations.
> [2] He will not shout
>   or raise his voice in public.
> [3] He will not crush the weakest reed
>   or put out a flickering candle.
>   He will bring justice to all who have been wronged.
> [4] He will not falter or lose heart
>   until justice prevails throughout the earth.

Like many other passages in the Hebrew Bible, God is concerned with all the nations. His servant will bring justice to all, and will start by ensuring that the weakest and most vulnerable will be cared for and protected. Justice will be served to all who have been wronged.

Stassen and Gushee point out that in the gospels Jesus quotes mostly from Isaiah, followed by the Psalms, in his preaching that centers on the kingdom of God now come in the person of Jesus of Nazareth.[63] They point to 17 passages in Isaiah, which emphasize God's dynamic reign among his people. Among the five main characteristics of this reign, notice the prominent role given to justice, which can also be translated as 'righteousness' in some instances:[64]

> *Deliverance* or *salvation* occurs in all the seventeen deliverance passages in Isaiah; *righteousness/justice* occurs in sixteen of the passages; *peace* in fourteen; *joy* in twelve; *God's presence as Spirit or Light* in nine (and God's dynamic presence is implied in all seventeen). These five characteristics of the reign of God are remarkably consistent in the deliverance passages. We may conclude that these are the characteristics of God's delivering action as described in Isaiah.[65]

Here is one of those passages often read in churches for Christmas celebrations:

> For a child is born to us,
>   a son is given to us.
> The government will rest on his shoulders.
>   And he will be called:

Wonderful Counselor,[a] Mighty God,
　　Everlasting Father, Prince of Peace.
[7] His government and its peace
　　will never end.
He will rule with fairness and justice from the throne of his ancestor David
　　for all eternity.
The passionate commitment of the LORD OF HEAVEN'S ARMIES
　　will make this happen! (Isaiah 9:6-7)

Launching into this topic, Wolterstorff seeks to refute Oliver O'Donovan's thesis that *mishpat* in the Old Testament is only about 'judicial performance,' or what he calls 'rectifying justice,' and not 'primary justice.'[66] Granted, retorts Wolterstorff, many passages do in fact refer to the way justice is served in the courts and law is applied in the land. But you cannot have rectifying justice without recognizing the existence of primary justice and injustice. Or in his own words, 'one cannot hold that the aim of the judicial system is to render justice to victims and offenders while at the same time holding that the offenses on which judgment is rendered are not offenses against justice.'[67]

O'Donovan claims 'that *mishpat* is primarily juridical judging, and secondarily juridical pleading,' and that 'it is not a state of affairs that obtains but an activity that is duly carried out.'[68] In doing this, he writes, the judge scrutinizes the case at hand in order to discern 'between the just and the unjust.' This, answers Wolterstorff, is precisely what primary justice is all about:

> With the eye on the demands of primary justice, the judge brings to light whether or not the accused has violated those demands. He brings to light *the state of affairs* on the matter: is the state of affairs that of the accused having *violated* the demands of primary justice, or is the state of affairs that of the accused *not* having violated those demands? The performance of juridical judgment, as an exercise of rectifying justice, presupposes the existence of a state of affairs of primary justice or injustice.[69]

Hence, it is possible that the laws on the books are themselves oppressive and unjust and that, as a result, the poor and needy are treated unfairly. What counts more than anything is not how laws are applied in the courts but the justice of those laws. Wolterstorff calls this passage to mind (Isaiah 10:1-2 NRSV)[70]:

> Ah, you who make iniquitous decrees,
> 　　who write oppressive statutes,

to turn aside the needy from justice
  and to rob the poor of my people of their right,
that widows may be your spoil,
  and that you may make the orphans your prey!

Even this famous passage from the prophet Amos, often quoted by Martin Luther King, Jr., shows that justice is much more than juridical procedure: 'But let justice roll down like waters, and rectitude like an ever-flowing stream' (Amos 5:24 NRSV).[71] The first line could likely refer to justice in the courts of law. But Hebrew poetry is built on parallel phrases, meaning that the second phrase emphasizes the meaning of the first. Yet the 'rectitude' of the second phrase, meant to be 'an ever-flowing stream,' 'is surely the rectitude of each and every Israelite, not only the judges. That makes it likely that the same is true for the justice of which he is speaking.'[72] So *mishpat* in the Old Testament, argues Wolterstorff, must cover both primary and rectifying justice.

Another important feature of justice in these texts is that it is frequently connected to the way widows, orphans, the poor and resident foreigners are treated. For instance, Moses transmits the following divine command in Deuteronomy, 'You shall not deprive a resident alien or an orphan of justice; you shall not take a widow's garment in pledge' (24:17 NRSV; cf. Exodus 22:21-22). In another passage this comes as a curse, 'Cursed be anyone who deprives the alien, the orphan, and the widow of justice' (Deuteronomy 27:19 NRSV). In Isaiah 1:17, we read, 'Learn to do good. Seek justice. Help the oppressed. Defend the cause of orphans. Fight the right of widows.'

This quartet of society's weakest members represents also those most vulnerable to being exploited and oppressed. The wealthy and powerful often knock them down and trample on them. Apparently, God's sense of justice is thereby offended. As Psalm 147:6 puts it, 'The Lord lifts up the downtrodden, he casts the wicked to the ground.'[73] In today's language of human rights, might we conclude that justice in these texts is more about social and economic rights than political rights? Walter Brueggemann, a preeminent Old Testament scholar, strongly implies this: 'the intention of Mosaic justice is to redistribute social goods and social power; thus it is distributive justice.'[74] Wolterstorff sees this as excessive. He believes one should find a middle path between Brueggemann and O'Donovan – an emphasis on primary justice, which also shines a light on rectifying justice in the judicial system. The focus on the most vulnerable was a sign that Israel's religion was focused on salvation in a practical way. It was about rescuing the downtrodden from the injustice they experienced every day.

I do not have the space to continue in detail my exposition of Wolterstorff's argument. He turns from the concerns of justice and injustice relative to Israel to the same concerns relative to the nations surrounding Israel.[75] And then he returns to the topic of justice as rights as opposed to justice as right order. He suggests that these texts often highlight 'the pervasive presence of social victims' over against the breaches of juridical procedures. This in itself, he contends, is a sign that the victims are not just the consequences of an order gone awry, but point to the deep structure of justice itself. For Wolterstorff two main themes emerge from these writings: 'God holds human beings accountable for doing justice; and God is himself committed to justice, both in the sense that God does justice and in the sense that God works to bring it about that human beings treat each other justly.'[76] To sum up, God loves justice. Therefore not just Israel is expected to uphold justice – though, because they have received his Torah, they are held to a higher standard. In fact, all human beings are accountable to their Creator to treat one another justly.

What is more, if Yahweh holds humanity accountable for doing justice, then 'Israel's writers were assuming that there already is a normative structure of rights and obligations.' This means that bribing judges was not a perversion of justice simply because the God of Israel said so. Rather, it is because bribes are a perversion of justice and that is the reason God proscribes it in the first place. In other words, 'Bribing judges is not unjust because God forbids it; God forbids it because it is unjust.'[77] That is part of God holding humanity to standards of justice.

With regard to God's love and commitment to justice, on the other hand, it makes no sense to say that whatever God commands is what justice is.[78] Since God holds us accountable to seek justice, and he himself is committed to justice, justice itself must be a standard outside both God and ourselves. So we are back to justice – and all ethical values – as an objective entity, or the philosophical position of ethical objectivism. This also implies that 'when we fail to do justice, we wrong God. We not only fail in our obligations to God. We wrong God, deprive God of that to which God has a right.'[79] That is why the theme of God's forgiveness is so pervasive in the Old Testament. When we disobey God, when we ignore his calls to act justly toward our fellow human beings, we incur God's righteous anger.[80] And so we humbly call on his compassion and mercy and plead for forgiveness, as in the words of the prophet Micah:

Who is a God like you, pardoning iniquity and passing over the transgression of the remnant of your possession?

He does not retain his anger forever, because he delights in showing clemency.

He will again have compassion on us; he will tread our iniquities under foot (7:18-19).

The Old Testament writers assume, then, that God, by virtue of his excellence and incomparable majesty and power, has the inherent right to be worshiped and obeyed; and thus, he also has the right to hold us accountable to act justly. His right flows out of his intrinsic worth. But contra to the right order theorists, Wolterstorff contends, there are also clear indications in these texts that human beings ('created in God's image') have rights flowing out of their own intrinsic worth. Psalm 8, for instance, gushes with pride at the thought of human worth – God has placed humans just under the angels and has 'crowned them with glory and honor.' He has also entrusted them with dominion over the rest of his creation.

No doubt, there remain important connections between the two traditions of Islam and Christianity on the theme of justice, and in particular how justice relates to love. It turns out that both face significant challenges in dealing with this issue as well, and perhaps more so today than ever. We started out in this chapter with a look at injustices committed by the Israeli state against Palestinians, especially in the Occupied Territories. Muslims have generally been more vocal about this issue than many Christians, and especially American evangelicals. Thankfully, this is slowly changing.[81] Here is an area where people from both traditions can work together in the United States, since up to now this is the nation with the will and power to veto all past UN resolutions calling for Israel to withdraw from the Occupied Territories. The occupation since 1967 has daily violated the individual and collective rights of Palestinians living there.

The next two chapters explore the theme of justice as it relates to Shari'a, which for Muslims is God's revealed path to a righteous and just society. In the next chapter we examine a spectrum of reformist views, whereas in Chapter 4 we focus on a more traditional jurist who has exerted a global influence for more than four decades.

Endnotes

1   Ateek 1989, 123.
2   'Uprising' in English, or the 'shaking off of the yoke.' It started as a spontaneous outburst of popular anger in the streets of one of Gaza's refugee camps

in December 1987; it then spread within days to the whole of Gaza and the West Bank. Our family was in the Jerusalem area starting in the autumn of 1992. Shops were only open in the mornings, as a means of non-violent protest against Israeli occupation. Palestinian youth routinely threw rocks at Israeli soldiers and were often shot as a result.

3   Ateek and his organization, Sabeel, are one of the founders of the bi-yearly conferences at the Bethlehem Bible College (where I taught for three years) called 'Christ at the Checkpoint'. See online, https://christatthecheckpoint.bethbc.edu/

4   His latest book is even more explicit about this issue: Ateek, 2008. See also books by Palestinian Lutheran pastor Mitri Raheb, and in particular his latest book, Raheb, 2014.

5   Quoted in Raheb, 122–123. In a separate resolution on the same day, the General Assembly said: that it

'1. *Reaffirms* that the Geneva Convention relative to the Protection of Civilian Persons in Time of War, of 12 August 1949, is applicable to Palestinian and other Arab territories occupied by Israel since 1967, including Jerusalem.

2. *Strongly deplores* the failure of Israel to acknowledge the applicability of that Convention to the territories it has occupied since 1967.

3. *Calls again* upon Israel to comply with the provisions of that Convention in Palestinian and other territories it has occupied since 1967, including Jerusalem.'

In the previous resolution, specifically in reference to the Geneva Conventions, it 'condemned' 'the Israeli annexation of parts of the occupied territories; establishment of new Israeli settlements and the expansion of the existing settlements on private and public Arab lands, and transfer of an alien population thereto; evacuation, deportation, expulsion, displacement and transfer of Arab inhabitants of the occupied territories and denial of their right to return ... destruction and demolition of Arab houses; mass arrests and administrative detention and ill-treatment of the Arab population; ill-treatment and torture of persons under detention; pillaging of archeological and cultural property; interference with religious freedoms and practices as well as family rights and customs; illegal exploitation of the natural wealth, resources and population of the occupied territories.' UN General Assembly Session 34/90B (Dec. 12, 1979); available at: http://www.un.org/en/ga/search/view_doc.asp?symbol=A/RES/34/90, accessed July 3, 2018. Those violations of Palestinian human rights have only multiplied over the years.

6   See online, https://www.btselem.org/

7   'Fake Justice: The Responsibility Israel's High Court Justice Bear for the Demolition of Palestinian Homes and the Dispossession of Palestinians,' B'Tselem 2019. Available at: https://www.btselem.org/publications/summaries/201902_fake_justice

8   B'Tselem 2019. Available at: https://www.btselem.org/publications/summaries/201902_fake_justice

9   On Christian Zionism see Sizer 2005; Chapman 2015; and Burge 2010.

10   Ateek expresses well what I have heard many Palestinians tell me: 'In fact, the great enigma is how can the Jewish people who experienced such suffering and dehumanization at the hands of the Nazis, turn around and inflict so much suffering and dehumanization on others? Why should the price of Jewish empowerment

after the Holocaust in the creation of the State of Israel be the oppression and misery of the Palestinians?' (Ateek 1989, 116).

11 On the Israeli side, 66 soldiers were killed, and six civilians, including a Thai worker.

12 Culzac 2014, available at: http://www.independent.co.uk/news/world/middle-east/israelgaza-crisis-reconstruction-of-flattened-gaza-will-cost-5billion-palestinian-officials-say-9713905.html.

13 Ateek 1989, 119.

14 Wacks 2014.

15 Wacks 2014, 3, without original reference.

16 Wacks 2014, 4, without original reference.

17 Especially in 'Maqasid al-Shari'a'; see also, Johnston 2015a, 113–48.

18 Wacks 2014, 25.

19 Hart 1961.

20 Austin in particular defined law as the clear command of a ruler who had the means to enforce it. Thus for him, international law, customary or even most of constitutional law, did not qualify as 'law.'

21 Wacks 2014, 47, emphasis his.

22 Wacks adds, 'The dominance of legal positivism, especially in Britain, was over the next four decades subjected to a comprehensive onslaught in the form of a subtle theory of law that is both controversial and powerful. His ideas continue to exert considerable authority, especially in the United States, whenever contentious moral and political issues are debated,' Wacks 2014, 49. Wacks devotes the third chapter to him, 'Dworkin: the moral integrity of law.'

23 Wacks 2014, 52.

24 Wacks 2014, 53.

25 To the contrary, a good judge according to Dworkin will consider what other judges have decided on similar cases and 'must think of their decisions as part of a long story he must interpret and then continue, according to his own judgment of how to make the developing story as good as it can be' (Wacks 2014, 54).

26 Wacks 2014, 61, emphasis his.

27 Dworkin 2011. The idea of hedgehogs comes from Isaiah Berlin's aphorism that 'The fox knows many things but the hedgehog knows one big thing.' For Dworkin that 'one big thing' was the 'unity of value.' He then turns David Hume's (d. 1776) famous principle that you cannot get an 'ought' from an 'is' (facts cannot tell you about value) on its head. Traditionally, this was understood as saying that morality cannot be derived from observing nature – a very skeptical view of morality and universal principles in general. Dworkin retorts that 'the proposition that it is not true that genocide is morally wrong is itself a moral proposition, and if Hume's principle is sound, that proposition cannot be established by any discoveries of logic or facts about the basic structure of the universe. Hume's principle, properly understood, supports not scepticism about moral truth but rather supports the importance of morality as a separate department of knowledge with its own standards of inquiry and justification' (Dworkin 2011, 63).

28 Johnston 2014, 899–920, at 905–912. Available at http://www.humantrustees.org/resources/item/134-indiana-law-review-hrs.

29 Johnston 2014, 899–920, at 905–912.

30 Johnston 2014, 107.

31 Wacks is certainly right about its antipathy as a movement for 'the methods, assumptions, and ideas of the analytical Anglo-American philosophical tradition' (Wacks 2014, 118).

32 See Benhabib Seyla's classic book, Seyla 1992.

33 Wolterstorff 2008, 15.

34 Wolterstorff 2008, 15.

35 Wolterstorff mentions an article written by Ronald Dworkin in the 1980s (though without referencing it) in which 'he argued that when one looks beneath the surface, one finds inherent natural rights at the basis of the theory' (Wolterstorff 2008, 16). That is not surprising, considering the wording in Rawls' first proposition.

36 Interestingly, this is the concept that University of Toronto legal scholar Mohammad Fadel puts forth in finding common ground between human rights and Islamic law. See Fadel 2007, 1–20.

37 Justinian I was an Eastern Roman Emperor who ruled in the first half of the sixth century. Under his sponsorship jurists collected laws and legal interpretations, which together represented the best of the Roman legal tradition. This 'Body of Civil Law' became the basis for the laws of most modern European countries.

38 Watson 1985, no pagination; quoted by Wolterstorff 2008, 22.

39 Wolterstorff 2008, 23.

40 Wolterstorff 2008, 25, emphasis his. He also adds that groups and organizations can also enjoy rights, including an indigenous group, an ethnic minority, or a business corporation. In another sense, he adds, animals and ecosystems enjoy rights as well, as I myself argued in Johnston 2010.

41 For example, the Qur'an says, 'Let harm be requited by an equal harm, though anyone who forgives and puts things right will have his reward from God Himself – He does not like those who do wrong' (Q. 42: 40).

42 *Justice*, 2008, 31.

43 O'Donovan 1996, 262, quoted in Wolterstorff 2008, 31.

44 MacIntyre, 1981.

45 This was from an article published by Bowdoin College, Brunswick, Maine, as the Charles F. Adams Lecture of February 28, 1983, at 12. But Wolterstorff does not provide the reference for that article (Wolterstorff 2008, 32).

46 Wolterstorff 2008, 33. Emphasis his.

47 Wolterstorff 2008.

48 Wolterstorff 2008, 34.

49 Wolterstorff 2008, 36.

50 Wolterstorff 2008, 37. We'll come back to that statement of ethical objectivism.

51 The discussion seems quite arcane today – Pope Nicholas III saying they had no rights by distinguishing 'right of use and simple factual use,' and William of Ockham arguing that though they have no positive right they do have a 'natural right.' Wolterstorff shows that this argument had nothing to do with Ockham's philosophical nominalism (the denial of all universals and, in the critics' view, a tendency toward social atomism). It has everything to do with a long history

of the use of natural subjective rights that goes back to the Church Fathers, and ultimately to the Bible itself, whence they had taken the idea in the first place.

52   This is not truly Wolterstorff's concern in this project, but I mention it, as I know it is a concern many people share and often in conservative circles (at least in the US) people blame it for an overemphasis on human rights. Moreover, it is surely related to the way capitalism preys on human greed, to the scourge of consumerism, to the individualism that contributes to the breakup of the nuclear family, and so on.

53   Tierney 2006.

54   Reid 1991, 37–92.

55   Reid 1991, 39–40. Cited in Wolterstorff 2008, 54.

56   Wolterstorff 2008, 54, emphasis his.

57   Wolterstorff 2008, 59–60.

58   Chrysostom 1984, 55 quoted in Wolterstorff 2008, 61.

59   Wolterstorff 2008, 62, emphasis his.

60   Hauerwas is a prolific author whose career spans four decades at the University of Notre Dame and more recently at Duke University. He was the first American in 2000 and 2001 to be invited to deliver the prestigious Gifford Lectures in Scotland. One of his recent books continues his relentless critique of the American civil religion and liberal democracy in general: Hauerwas 2011. Besides his attack on capitalism and its consumerist ethos, he lambasts the entrenched American industrial-military complex. We as a nation are addicted to war, he laments. But human rights discourse for him, as for his friend MacIntyre, only feeds on the destructive power of Western individualism and erodes any sense of community.

61   Glen Stassen, who spent the last 18 years of his academic career at Fuller Theological Seminary, is known internationally as the initiator of the 'just peacemaking' concept (cf. Stassen 1992; and as author and editor of Stassen 2008. Stassen died in April 2014.

62   As mentioned in the Introduction, unless indicated otherwise, my biblical quotes are from the New Living Translation, 2nd ed.

63   The gospel of Mark, the earliest one written, quotes more from Isaiah than all of the other canonical books combined.

64   Wolterstorff offers a similar explanation to that of Stassen and Gushee on the meaning of justice in the Old Testament. The word *mishpat* ('justice') is often paired with *tsedeqa*, usually translated as 'righteousness.' A better translation, he feels, would be doing 'the right thing,' or 'rectitude.' He refers to David Novak in his book *Natural Law in Judaism* (Novak 1998, 41) in saying that the pairing up of *mishpat* and *tsedeqa* 'can be understood as *correct justice*. Even better might be *true justice*' (Wolterstorff 2008, 69, emphasis his).

65   Stassen and Gushee 2017, 25.

66   He quotes from O'Donovan 1998.

67   Wolterstorff 2008, 72.

68   O'Donovan 1996, 38; quoted in Wolterstorff 2008, 72.

69   Wolterstorff 2008, 72.

70   New Revised Standard Version.

71   Wolterstorff changed 'righteousness' in the NRSV translation to 'rectitude.'

72 Wolterstorff changed 'righteousness' in the NRSV translation to 'rectitude,' 74.

73 This theme of the great reversal easily found its way into the song of the simple Galilean peasant, Mary: 'He has brought down princes from their thrones and exalted the humble. He has filled the hungry with good things and sent the rich away with empty hands' (Luke 1:52-53).

74 Brueggemann 1997, 736. Quoted in Wolterstorff 2008, 77. This was also my argument in Johnston 2014a which I end, for that reason, with Pope Francis' pastoral letter (cf. note 28).

75 It becomes clear that Israel in its calling to be 'a light for the nations' must in this mission demonstrate God's justice in its internal dealings. In short, it is 'an essential component of what it was to be a holy people' (Wolterstorff 2008, 83). The Torah, meant for all nations, was actually entrusted to Israel in the first place; but, as the prophets make clear, God meant it as a gift for all nations. In the meantime, God through his creation had in fact established a covenant with all nations. The prophets plainly believe that all nations are accountable to God for the way they deal with their own people and with other nations. Psalm 82, for example, imagines in very ancient Near-Eastern fashion a council in which all the gods come together to deliberate. From the beginning, Jahweh issues his complaint against these gods, 'How long will you hand down unjust decisions by favoring the wicked? Give justice to the poor and the orphan; uphold the rights of the oppressed and the destitute. Rescue the poor and helpless; deliver them from the grasp of evil people' (2-4). The psalm ends with a picture of God judging the whole earth: 'Rise up, O God, and judge the earth, for all the nations belong to you' (8).

76 Wolterstorff 2008, 89.

77 Wolterstorff 2008, 90.

78 Further on, he writes that if God's commands are praised as just, that justice cannot be linked to the fact that God issued those commands. It's a question of logic. He adds, 'God's statutes cannot be just because they conform to God's statutes' (Wolterstorff 2008, 94).

79 Wolterstorff 2008, 91.

80 Wolterstorff notes, 'The liberal tradition of Christianity finds it either offensive or embarrassing to think of God as angry; God is love. But as Jeffrey Murphy and Jean Hampton argue with great cogency in their book, *Forgiveness and Mercy* [Cambridge: Cambridge University Press, 1988], anger is the emotion one rightly feels when one recognizes that one has been wronged. It follows that full forgiveness requires forgoing claiming that right; it requires the abating of one's anger. And that is how Israel's writers describe God; God's anger will not last forever' (Wolterstorff 2008, 93).

81 One indication comes from the circulation of documentary films directed by young evangelical to justice and nonviolence in Israel-Palestine: *Little Town of Bethlehem* (Jim Hanon, EGM Productions); *With God on Our Side* (Porter Speakman, Jr., Rooftop Productions).

4

Justice as Shari'a's Central Purpose

In the last chapter I contended with Wolterstorff and others that justice requires that people's inherent rights be respected. In contemporary democratic polities, this means that each citizen has equal rights before the law. Religion, however, might be the most difficult identity marker to address when it comes to treating minorities fairly. The violent political fallout from the Protestant Reformation, including the bloodbath of the Thirty Years' War (1618–48), took about two centuries to resolve in Europe. The eighteenth century produced the Enlightenment, which then gave us the American Declaration of Independence, the Bill of Rights, and the French Revolution. But there was nothing linear about that progressive road to equality and justice. As mentioned before, it took two world wars for humanity to sit down and hammer out the Universal Declaration of Human Rights, and now we wonder if that liberal international order might not be unraveling.

That struggle to disentangle religion from civil and political rights is still a challenge in many Muslim-majority states. In a post- 'Arab Spring' book on democracy from Tunisia to Pakistan, Jocelyne Cesari uses the phrase 'hegemonic Islam.' By this she means that even so-called 'secular' states like Turkey use state power to enforce specific interpretations of Islam, which then impose restrictions on both Muslim and non-Muslim citizens. Thereby they display a 'lack of institutional separation, exclusive social role of one religion, and limited recognition of religious pluralism at the individual level.'[1] A similar dynamic is at play with the Buddhists in Sri Lanka, the Orthodox Church in Greece and Russia, or the Orthodox Jews in Israel.

At the heart of this issue is the right to religious freedom, as articulated in Article 18 of the Universal Declaration of Human Rights.[2] Pakistan is the nation I would like to use as a brief case study for this chapter, and the two related issues that are most often associated with it are apostasy and blasphemy.[3] The Blasphemy Law was first enacted under colonial rule in 1860; it was then reinforced under General Zia's regime in 1986, and then further given the death penalty in 1991. The definition includes insulting the Prophet Muhammad, speaking against the Holy Qur'an, and the like, but its interpretation in practice remains problematic.[4] Sara Singha shows that when one takes into account government corruption, a very dysfunctional judicial system, and the social status of Christians who are disproportionately poor and from the lowest caste, it is not surprising that most Christians in Pakistan have little to no chance of receiving due process.[5]

Three cases stand out. In 2009 a rural Christian woman, Asia Bibi, was accused and then charged with 'defiling the Holy Prophet.'[6] After being on death row for eight years, she was acquitted, mostly due to international pressure, then kept in one room with her husband in a secure location for close to a year and then finally allowed to join her children in Canada.[7] Second, a 12-year-old girl, Rimsha Massih, was arrested and imprisoned in 2012 for 'desecrating the Qur'an.' She was released eventually when evidence came to light that the cleric who accused her had an ongoing feud with her family. Yet he was never charged. Finally, this 2014 case is the most tragic of the three: 'A Christian couple working in an industrial brick kiln, Sajjid Maseeh and his wife Shama Bibi, were accused of burning pages of the Qur'an. Without any valid proof, they were attacked by a mob of 1,200 people and burned alive. Shama Bibi was pregnant.'[8]

As it turns out, such cases of blasphemy pale in comparison to other crimes committed with impunity against the majority of Christians whose forefathers were Christian converts from the Dalit, or 'untouchables' caste in colonial India. Still today these *chuhra* make up most of the workers in the 'dirty' profession of sanitation. In Punjab Province, for instance, 80 percent of the street sweepers are Christian.[9] About the same holds for sewage workers. These people, and especially their women, are much more vulnerable to attacks. The Catholic Church of Pakistan estimates that every year around 700 Christian girls are kidnapped and converted by force to Islam, because they are made to marry their kidnappers. At that stage they no longer have recourse to the civil courts but stand directly under the jurisdiction of the Shari'a courts. According to the Asian Human Rights Commission, the number of such kidnappings is closer to 1,800 every year.[10]

As mentioned in the last chapter, factors leading to injustice come from many directions and in many forms. Perhaps one of the most astute observers of this part of the world, James M. Dorsey, argues that the rise of extremism in Pakistan since the 1970s and the corresponding political violence is related to several factors. Near the top of that list are the following: a) General Zia's manipulation of Islam to tighten his grip on power; b) a reliance on Saudi money and the resulting spread the extremist Wahhabi ideology; c) the spread of Salafi ideology in turn helps to tighten the blasphemy laws, in effect giving impunity to the Sunni majority to persecute Pakistan's minorities. We mentioned Christians, but the Ahmadis have arguably suffered the most. Under Saudi pressure, the Ahmadis were officially declared non-Muslims in 1974 through a constitutional amendment enshrining the principle of Khatm-e-Nubuwwat (The Prophet Muhammad as 'Seal of the Prophets').[11] General Zia 'criminalized Ahmadi practices a decade later by barring Ahmadis from "posing as Muslims" or using Islamic titles, greetings, scriptures or calls to prayer.'[12] But then in March 2018 Islamabad's High Court judge Shaukat Aziz Siddiqi issued a ruling asking for the parliament to 'take measures which can completely terminate those who scar (the belief in Khatm-e-Nabuwwat).'[13]

Naturally, people wondered what Siddiqi, who is known to have labeled blasphemers 'terrorists,' meant by 'terminate.' In fact, this was a legal response to a request made by a subgroup from among the thousands of protesters who had blocked one of the capital's main arteries for almost a month. Their chief complaint was that the government was softening its position on blasphemy. In the end, they succeeded in obtaining the resignation of the justice minister who failed to refer to the Prophet in the constitutional bill in question. This ruling, which was clearly aimed at the Ahmadis, would have at the very least barred them from public service. But by 'terminate' was he also referring to the death penalty or possibly inciting violence against them?

These are not theoretical questions in Pakistan, where two top-level politicians were assassinated in 2011 for speaking out against the blasphemy laws. One was a Christian, Shahbaz Bhatti, the first Federal Minister for Minority Affairs, the second was Punjab's governor, Salman Taseer.[14] Fortunately, that is not the whole story. Lawyers and human rights activists condemned this ruling and called for its review by the Supreme Court on the grounds that it was hate speech. Election results indicate that there is a large segment of Pakistanis, including among the ruling elite, who disagree with the Salafi-inspired extremists. But these forces remain strong. The protesters were mostly from the Tehreek Labbaik Pakistan party (TPL), which in turn is connected to Tehreek Labbaik Ya Rasool Allah (TLR), a movement behind massive protests all over Pakistan after Salman Taseer's assassin, Mumtaz Qadri, was executed in 2016.

The issue of blasphemy laws and religious freedom is good to keep in mind in this chapter, which examines a popular strategy in Muslim jurisprudential circles, the so-called *maqasid al-shari'a*, or 'objectives of Shari'a' approach to Islamic law. How promising it might be for crafting democratic laws in a religiously pluralistic state with a Muslim majority remains to be seen. But I agree with Ebrahim Moosa when he argues that historically classical Islamic political theology was forged in the context of empire and molded by a civilization grown accustomed to hegemony and political dominance. Policing the borders of 'orthodoxy' in order to systematically stamp out manifestations of heresy seemed quite natural in that context. Reconsidering the twin issues of apostasy, says Moosa, and especially of blasphemy 'would require some serious re-thinking about how the Shari'a is imagined and how it is formulated.'[15]

Justice and the Shari'a's Objectives

At least in my experience, Muslims are more naturally poised to talk about justice than are Christians. It is a common theme in the Qur'an and it has often taken center stage in a religious tradition that prides itself in providing a legal blueprint for a just society on earth. The Arabic words expressing the idea of justice, *'adl* and *qist*, can be found about 50 times in the Qur'an; references to 'injustice' (*zulm*) number in the hundreds. This may well be the most cited Qur'anic verse on justice, here in the popular Yusuf Ali translation:

> O ye who believe! Stand out firmly for justice as witnesses to God, even as against yourselves, or your parents, or your kin, and whether it be (against) rich or poor; for God can best protect both. Follow not the lusts (of your hearts), lest ye swerve, and if ye distort (justice) or decline to do justice, verily God is well acquainted with all that you do (Q. 4:135).

I stated in Chapter 1 how the Universal Declaration of Human Rights (UDHR) in 1948 opened a new era in the global discussion of religion and ethics. That representatives from Muslim nations took an active part in and truly helped to shape the global conversation on rights from 1946 to 1966 is a little known fact.[16] The UDHR and the two covenants ratified in 1966, forming the International Bill of Human Rights,[17] offered international legal standards that purported to define how human beings *ought* to be treated in all human societies everywhere. In particular, though the word 'justice' is absent, the UDHR assumes that people understand the concept of equality before the law and fair legal procedure, both through negative definitions,[18] and the positive use of the adjectives 'fair' (once: 'Everyone is entitled to a fair and public hearing by an independent and impartial tribunal,' Article 10) and 'just' (twice: 'just and favorable conditions of work,' Article 23.1; and 'just and favorable remuneration,' Article 23.3).

The assumption that people in all cultures broadly understand what it is to tip the scales of justice fairly or unfairly is a common sense intuition. True, justice in human society may not be perfectly obtainable, the thinking goes, but the ideal is somehow ingrained in the human psyche. Within a religious framework, however, the relationship between justice (or 'the good' in general) and the divine will is often problematic.

I have already cited Plato's famous Euthyphro Dialogue, in which Socrates demonstrates to Euthyphro that an action is not good or just simply because it is commanded by the gods; rather, the gods command this action because it is good or just in itself. It is this conviction of an objective good that human beings can come to know as they exert their capacity of reason that drives Platonic and Aristotelian philosophy.

In the third Islamic century (ninth century CE) this was also the assumption of the 'Rationalists' whose theological clout was rising fast at the time in Abbasid Baghdad, until that trend was decisively reversed in the next century by the 'Traditionalists' – at least in circles that were to become Sunni Islam.[19] In schematic form, the ethical objectivism of these Mu'tazilites (justice exists independently of both God and our own opinions about it) was replaced by the ethical voluntarism (an act is good because God commands it) of the partisans of al-Ash'ari (d. 935), or Ash'arites, the trend that inspired the 'great rationalist-traditionalist synthesis' until the modern period.[20]

In a study highlighting the debate between and within juridical schools on the issue of human acts before the revelation of the Qur'an, Kevin Reinhart has demonstrated that although all Islamic jurisprudence is concerned with the categorization of people's acts, there developed two distinctive views of human reason ('aql, or 'the ability to know') and two corresponding views of revelation. Mu'tazilites all assumed the existence of an objective standard of the good and the just applicable to all humans, Muslims or not.[21] The early Mu'tazilites, particularly in Baghdad, tended to couple the ontology of an act's assessment with its being per se, while the later Basran school removed the assessment of an act from the act in itself and saw it as a more transitory quality in light of particular circumstances.[22] Thus a lie could in fact be a good act if, for instance, it saved a human life. In both cases, however, the ontological statement had epistemological consequences. On this view, the human person is endowed with the capacity to know the good and thus make moral judgments independently of revelation.

This perceived devaluation of the divine Shari'a was anathema to the Ash'ari majority, who then retorted that according to the Mu'tazilites God's law was shriveled down to a few bare indications of when to pray and how many genuflections and prostrations to perform.[23] Revelation is then only one source of moral knowledge among others. For Sunni Ash'arites, revelation *is* 'the foundation of the Islamic legal-moral edifice.'[24]

Having said this, the Sunni consensus over time was a compromise between the extreme traditionalism of, for instance, the founder of the Hanbali school of law, Ahmad b. Hanbal (d. 855), and the rationalism of the Mu'tazilites.[25] The official persecution of the traditionalists in Baghdad (the Miḥna of 833–848) was not just about whether the Qur'an was created or not. It was mostly about the role of human reason in the interpretation of the sacred scriptures.[26] All positions in the end allowed for human reason to make moral judgments in areas where the sacred texts were silent. On the question of human agency as well, a middle way was developed between the determinism of Ash'arism and the freewill of Mu'tazilism by al-Maturidi (d. 944) and his followers, yet their position on justice and the good was virtually identical to that of the Ash'arites.[27] While Shi'i thinking always retained some of the rationalistic bent of Mu'tazilism, ethical voluntarism continued, by and large, to dominate Sunni ethical discourse until the modern period.[28]

Interestingly, parallel to the ongoing ontological debate about the good, justice was at the heart of early Muslim ethical discussions, according to Majid Khaddury in his classic work, *The Islamic Conception of Justice*. These debates emerged as a by-product of the political struggles surrounding the Prophet's succession. While the Sunnis and Shia argued about the legitimacy of the caliph from two 'elitist' vantage points (either elected by Quraysh tribal leaders or a direct descendant of the Prophet), the Kharijites insisted that all believers are equal and the only valid scales of justice are to be found in the Qur'an and Sunna. Hence, they called themselves *ahl al-ʿadl* (the people of justice).

Then as opposition grew to the autocratic rule of the Ummayad caliphs in Damascus,[29] the political debate about legitimacy turned unmistakably theological, with the Mu'tazilites picking up from the early Qadarites, who emphasized free will in order to bolster the idea of divine justice (how could God justly condemn the acts of people who were not free to choose them?) and were determined to apply that standard of justice to Umayyad governance. However, the Mu'tazilites, or the 'partisans of justice and oneness' (*ahl al-ʿadl wa-l-tawḥīd*), were only one party in a multifarious and centuries-long debate by jurists, philosophers and other thinkers on the question of justice. Khaddury's chapters reflect the widening societal debate within the Muslim world: from political and theological justice, to philosophical, ethical, legal, international and social justice. But let it be said here, and this will be reiterated at several points in this book, Khaddury's survey cogently underscores that these ethical debates about justice were always much broader than the 'Islam' many islamists[30] today claim should be reduced to Shari'a – and Shari'a itself to *fiqh* (applied jurisprudence). In a sense, the definition of what 'Islam' is, beyond its ritual and textual givens, has always been contested terrain. As I will continue to reiterate, the debate can always be pinpointed somewhere along the continuum between reason and revelation.

The modern period also, despite its imposition of cataclysmic changes on Muslim lands, reveals much of the same past tensions between sacred text and reason, accommodation to change (including assimilation of outside norms) and revivalist reflexes of return to revealed norms, and particularly as believers take up afresh the question of God's justice and how it might be applied to human affairs. On the one hand, central to the contemporary Muslim discourse on human rights and democracy is the notion that the Qur'an enjoins social justice both as the foundation and goal of Muslim society. The Arabic root *ʿadl* is used at least 22 times in the Qur'an to exemplify the relationships of equity and fairness God intends for people to actively seek and exemplify in their action (e.g., 'God commands justice, good deeds...' Q. 16:90).[31]

On the other hand, although the affirmation of the centrality of justice can be found along the full spectrum of Islamic views on human rights, the more conservative writers find it difficult to circumvent the traditional Ash'arite voluntarist reflex. This is especially so, because from an Islamic perspective, ethics and law are intertwined. Yet, in the midst of a predominantly voluntarist and strongly textualist climate (particularly among the Sunni majority), a potentially subversive method of interpretation developed in the late medieval period, which became prominent in the last century. It focuses on the ethical purposes of the Divine Law (*maqāṣid al-sharīʿa*) with justice and human welfare (*maṣlaḥa*) at the top of the list.[32]

This rethinking of traditional theology in a new context of Enlightenment ideals and colonial realities led to a fresh emphasis in legal theory on the spirit of the law, that is, on the overall objectives of Shari'a, and less on past crystallizations of *fiqh* (Islamic jurisprudence, including the body of past rulings and their evolution within the five main schools of Islamic law).[33] Ebrahim Moosa, however, has argued that this 'purposive strategy' adopted by contemporary Islamic legal experts, while it has provided some needed flexibility in a maelstrom of changing sociopolitical conditions, has not fully dealt with the traditional rulings in the texts that contravene current norms of human rights, and particularly with regard to gender issues.[34]

In the end, the classical literature on scholastic theology (*kalām*) and legal theory (*uṣūl al-fiqh*) never resolved the philosophical status of the moral good. In the twentieth century Muslim legal scholars followed Muhammad Abduh's (d. 1905) lead in paying lip service to traditional Ash'arism, while at the same time proclaiming that Islamic law, when properly understood, is the best and most comprehensive legal system, because it fulfills humankind's deepest aspirations and harmonizes with people's innate sense of justice. This nod to ethical objectivism is easily legitimized by following the purposive strategy in legal methodology, which the three Muslim thinkers examined in this chapter develop in different ways.

Jamal al-Banna: Social Justice First

Jamal al-Banna is the younger brother of Hasan al-Banna (d. 1949), founder of the first Muslim mass movement of the modern era, the *al-ikhwān al-muslimūn* (The Muslim Brothers) in 1928. In the next chapter we will look at the most popular scholar to have come out of the Muslim Brotherhood orbit, Yusuf al-Qaradawi. But Jamal al-Banna, a tireless union activist, has not adopted his brother's ideology. Ironically, he died during the only year the Muslim Brotherhood ruled Egypt (January 30, 2013). As the titles of nearly 80 books he authored will show, he was keenly interested in Islam, but mostly as a faith which defends the rights of workers, women and other weaker members of society. When he was invited to conferences, he attended in his capacity of eminent 'Islamic thinker': his books regularly deal with issues of law,[35] theology,[36] and hermeneutics.[37] But he was also a favorite target of the powerful Egyptian islamist movement, as his views on women, secularism and especially his critique of their ideology consistently draw their ire.[38]

One may glean some clues to al-Banna's ideas and influence by noting his participation in two conferences aiming at the 'reformation' of Islamic thought today. The first took place in Paris between August 12–13, 2003 at the invitation of the Cairo Institute for Human Right Studies (CIHRS).

Al-Banna was one of six thinkers and human rights activists who made presentations. The papers then sparked in-depth discussions by the participants (29 altogether) from eight different Arab nations. The final declaration of the meeting entitled 'On Practical Means Of Renewing Religious Discourse' lays out the overarching goals of the renewal movement, mostly focused on creating more space within Muslim circles for the wealth and fullness of the Islamic heritage (including the contributions of the Mu'tazilites, the philosophers, the Sufis and others).[39]

Al-Banna's particular role is more clearly defined in the second gathering, the Islamic Reform Conference in Cairo, October 5–6, 2004.[40] As convener of the conference and founder of the Ibn Khaldun Center for Developmental Studies, sociologist Saad al-Din Ibrahim gave the opening address to what he called 'the first gathering of the Islamic Religious Reform Program in Cairo.'[41] Muslims today are facing a 'grave crisis,' he declared, which came to a head in the horrific events of September 11, 2001, with 'its disastrous after effects that continue to shake us and the entire world, from Afghanistan to Iraq to Chechnya.' Here Ibrahim's words are worth quoting in full – particularly in light of his own imprisonment by the Mubarak regime from 1999 to 2002:[42]

> Among the first to recognize the Muslims' crisis among modern Muslims was our great brother Jamal al-Banna. Ever since he joined the board of the Ibn Khaldun Center, he has been insisting that we take the initiative in the challenging battle of reforming Islamic thought to renew it, and to reach a living, ever-changing jurisprudence that fits the spirit of this age and adapts to its speedy changes.

> Brother Jamal al-Banna's insistence transformed into a deafening shout as I sat in my prison cell in Turra, after the horrifying events of September, as I read about what he wrote on those events. He did not bow to the misguided mainstream that had somehow engulfed the Arabs and Muslims, who either were in denial that the attacks had taken place or that some Muslims were responsible. He did not deny nor doubt either fact. He repeated his mantra: reform, reform, reform.[43]

So what does this reform of Islamic thought look like close-up? In his book, *The Theory of Justice in European and Islamic Thought*, al-Banna attempts to trace the concept of justice in the West as it was portrayed in Plato's Republic, then in Roman law, then in the lead-up to the modern period in the work of Hobbes and Machiavelli.[44] His conclusion is that in the European civilization justice was never a central concept. When it was sought after, however, it was assumed to come as a result of a powerful state that resorted to violence, if necessary, to enforce it. Conversely, the controlling concept of the modern period, starting with the ideals of the Enlightenment and the resulting French Revolution, has been freedom. This emphasis, coupled with a declaration of the innate dignity of the human person, opened the way for the oppressed classes to literally fight for their freedom, overthrow the dictatorship of monarchies and eventually create trade unions; enact laws to protect the weak; secure women's right to vote and initiate other practical steps to bring greater justice to society as a whole.

Turning to Islamic thought, al-Banna notes that if oneness characterizes Islam's belief in God, it is plurality that sums up its view of creation: from the male-female pairs mentioned in the Qur'an and the infinite variety of species, stars and substances, to the diversity of tribes and nations, God, the heavenly Maestro, designed the rhythm and role of each part so that the whole produces a marvelous symphony. This is possible, he writes, because God has made justice 'the virtue of all virtues,'[45] and particularly in human society. Despite what many Muslims may think, 'legitimate power in Islam is exercised through law, not politics' (*wa-l-ḥukm fī-l-Islām qaḍā' wa-laysa siyāsa*). To make sure his readers understand, he adds, 'the rule of law,' *ḥukm al-qānūn* (no mention of Shari'a here). This is so, because justice is 'giving each one his due' (*i'ṭā' kulli dhi ḥaqqin ḥaqqahu*) and 'putting things in their rightful places' (*waḍ'u al-umūr fī mawāḍi'ihā al-ḥaqqa*).[46]

To justify this viewpoint, Jamal al-Banna explains that we find over 300 references to justice in the Qur'an – mostly actions we are to initiate that give others their proper due and ensure harmony in societal relationships. Besides these, there are 300 other verses that warn about the disastrous consequences of unjust behavior (*al-ẓulm*), either in this life or in the next. The crucial point to make in the end, he argues, is that justice is something that emanates from God and by which God, therefore, abides. Sura 3, verse 18, states clearly that 'God, his angels and those endued with knowledge stand firmly on justice (*qā'iman bi-l-qisṭ*).[47] Particularly when one considers the Qur'an's testimony to God's coming judgment, His justice is portrayed through the analogy of the scale (*al-mizān*).

This picture, reasons al-Banna, might lead some to ask the question, 'Did Islam bring forth justice, or was it justice that brought forth Islam?' We are back to Socrates' query here. 'The question itself is skewed,' he answers, 'for Islam and justice are separate entities, but it is God – may He be exalted – who brought them both into being.'[48] Here, then, is an unambiguous claim – an ontological one – that, according to scripture, justice has objective existence.[49] Al-Banna, then, deliberately opts for ethical objectivism. On the other hand, he refuses to be trapped by old controversies debated by the practitioners of *kalām* (scholastics) about whether justice is an attribute of God or not, or trapped by the philosophers, about whether justice is a Platonic Form or not.

Not surprisingly perhaps, at one point in the book, he discusses Mu'tazilite doctrine. The Mu'tazilites are closer to the truth than the Ash'arites, he opines, particularly when they argue that God would be unjust if He rewarded the sinner and punished the righteous. The Qur'an itself assures us that His judgment on the Last Day will be strictly fair – 'even an atom of good will be counted' (Q. 99:7-8). For al-Banna, the Ash'arites are plainly in error when they allege that God would still be just if he sent all of humanity to hell.[50]

A strong critic of Western-led globalization, the oppressive power of transnational corporations, and the moral decay eating away at Western societies, al-Banna ends up a stronger critic of the moral complacency, political corruption and rampant injustice within Muslim countries themselves. Ironically, he writes, more justice finds its way in the mechanics and dynamics of Western democratic societies. Yet Muslims should know better, he moans. And then this memorable phrase – a jarring phrase, indeed – calculated to impel Muslims to action: 'It may well be that Islam is alive in a land that ignores its name, a land in which the banner of the cross is unfurled, more than in a land that raises the banner of the crescent.'[51]

How, might one ask, can he move so quickly from ethical issues debated by Mu'tazilites and Ash'arites to contemporary issues of governance and economic disparities? This is not only because he was one of Egypt's greatest twentieth-century trade union activists, but also because of his Qur'anic hermeneutic. As versed as he is in traditional *fiqh*, he does not take past legal formulations at face value. Much like Farid Esack[52] and other political activists, he brings to the sacred text the questions raised by his daily struggles for social justice. Like Esack too, who fought the evil structures of apartheid in South Africa along with Christian liberation theologians, he adopts a hermeneutic that assumes that the Qur'an's meaning unfolds in history, in each situation and in the changing conditions of humankind.[53]

Jamal al-Banna expands on the theme of reformism in his paper delivered to the Cairo conference ('The Islamic Reformation Required').[54] There he begins by dispelling the common notion among reform-minded Muslims, that Muslim society will be renewed by reforming either its economic or its political structures. The urgent reformation required, he contends, begins upstream from that; it starts when people's way of thinking changes. Al-Banna sees two inner dimensions of thought that need to be acquired: (1) a rational or critical thinking, that is, refusing to believe in fables or preoccupying oneself with secondary matters of law and ritual; (2) a renewal of one's conscience – a human faculty prized in all the religions, but that can easily be dulled and sidelined when the legalistic details of religion overshadow the weightier matters of human oppression and injustice.[55] What is needed is not a renewal of rituals or even of legal theory (*uṣūl al-fiqh*) but rather 'the moralization of the human self.'[56] In essence, the Protestant Reformation represented for Europe 'a religious movement that invited people to think freely and liberate the captive conscience.'[57] Clearly for al-Banna, attempts at imposing reform through Western secular methods and concepts will never work. Reform starts within the minds and hearts of individuals, as authentic Islamic ideals and values are reinterpreted and applied by people willing to honestly grapple with the realities of their age.

Al-Banna made no claim to be a legal scholar (*faqīh*), at least in the traditional sense. Over the years, however, his writings on theology and law culminated in his three-volume work, *Toward a New Jurisprudence*.[58] After the last volume appeared in 1999, a conference was convened by leading Cairo jurists to discuss it, amidst vociferous cries for its banning in some circles. It is imperative that this summary edition of al-Banna's three volumes be published, writes the publisher, for since it was destined for the educated classes from all occupations, it had to be made available to them in a more readable and affordable format. For him (or them), al-Banna's thought represents the best chance for the reformation of Islamic law today.[59]

In the end, however, al-Banna is difficult to pin down. He is unmistakably bold in his redefinition of Shari'a, particularly in the traditional category of sociopolitical and economic rulings (*mu'āmalāt*, or 'human interactions').[60] Under this rubric, he proposes, a literalist approach must be discarded in favor of rulings derived from the general ethical imperatives of the Qur'an.[61] In this realm, reason prevails over text, thus opening the possibility for a serious discussion of the Shari'a's objectives.[62] Further, his view of justice is plainly aligned with Wolterstorff's view of justice as rights and he believes in justice as the main purpose of God's law. Yet the pull of traditional Islamic *fiqh* is still noticeable in his views.

Although al-Banna comes across as 'progressive' on issues such as apostasy (no penalty, since the Qur'an teaches each person is free in their own conscience) and women's rights (total equality with men, and the veil is a culturally-conditioned ruling of the past), he nevertheless calls for a conditional application of the traditional penalties for theft, adultery and armed robbery (ḥudūd, the 'limits').[63] Yet because he has made prison reform one of his life-long projects, al-Banna also stresses the need for rehabilitation, the shortening of prison sentences and, in general, for the application of the cardinal Qur'anic virtue of mercy.[64]

Mohammed Hashim Kamali: Benefit may Trump the Text?

Mohammed Hashim Kamali, an Afghan legal scholar who has been teaching in Malaysia for over three decades, comes to similar conclusions, but through more traditional methods of Islamic jurisprudence.[65] In his book, *Freedom, Justice and Equality in Islam*, Kamali defines justice as 'placing something in its rightful place ...according equal treatment to others or reaching a state of equilibrium in transactions with them.'[66] It overlaps with equality, yet goes beyond in the sense that justice in certain situations calls for inequality in order to compensate for past injustice done to one party. For Kamali also, justice is 'a universal concept in that its basic meaning does not seems [sic] to vary a great deal between the major traditions of the world.'[67] Following a brief excursion into the concept of justice in Plato, Cicero, and the idea of natural law among medieval Christian thinkers,[68] Kamali briefly summarizes John Rawls's theory of justice, showing how the classical Greek connection between justice and personal virtue has now become in modern terms a contested issue between individuals and the state and how social, economic and political goods can be evenly distributed among citizens – or, distributive justice. Broadly speaking, this is the agenda of social justice: not just the distribution of economic goods, but the fairness of a legal system and the health of all social and political institutions. How much voice do minorities have? Or, to what extent are various classes and sub-groupings of society empowered to participate in the political process?

This vision is not in the least foreign to the Qur'an, explains Kamali, since 'justice is a supreme virtue ... and one of the overriding objectives of Islam to the extent that it stands next in order of priority to belief in the Oneness of God (*tawḥīd*) and the Prophethood (*risāla*) of Muhammad.'[69] After quoting several prophetic sayings and Qur'anic verses, he cites Shaykh Yusuf al-Qaradawi, who states that in the sociopolitical realm, '[a]ll means, procedures and methods that facilitate, refine and advance the cause of justice, and do not violate the Shari'ah are therefore valid.'[70] Thus throughout, Kamali underscores the 'objectivity' of justice (ethical objectivism) – in part referring to the necessity of witnessing to justice, even if that means to stand against one's kin (Q. 4:135; 6:152), and more importantly, as an ethical value that God observes and which He holds his human creatures accountable to pursue.[71]

The Qur'an holds human leaders accountable to rule with equity and fairness in mind: 'God commands you to render trusts to whom they are due, and when you judge between people, judge with justice' (Q. 4:58). The word 'trusts' (*amānāt*) here is a broad concept that includes all means of reaching the objective of justice, whether in the content of laws enacted, or in their application to the citizens. 'Justice in the Qur'an is intertwined with the parallel concept of *khilāfah*, that is, the right to rule, or the vice-gerency of man on earth.'[72] Hence, justice is meant to be the hallmark of a nation's politics, its judicial system, its economic policies, and the chief virtue of its individual citizens, as a prime manifestation of their moral excellence (or 'God-consciousness,' *taqwā*). Notice that this is the first place in which Kamali ties together ethical theory and theology. In a step away from the letter of the text, Kamali (along with most modern Muslim thinkers) links the human trusteeship to the Qur'anic virtue of *taqwā,* and the two in turn to the good functioning of a modern nation-state.

Kamali then focuses more specifically on the modern judicial system in a section that retraces in broad lines the historical development of the Islamic judiciary, including the concept of appellate review. The traditional literature consistently held out the possibility that judges might emit faulty pronouncements and that if it were the case that a judge had erred by straying from the principles of Shari'a or had engaged in the miscarriage of justice, that case must be reviewed. This leads Kamali to examine the attention paid to procedural matters – that is, how the courts actually function, both the strictly Shari'a courts and the more secular courts set up by the rulers (*maẓālim*) – or, procedural justice. Even more to the point, however, is his next section on a branch of law that developed on the subject of political rule (*siyāsa shar'iyya*). Interestingly, neither Qur'an nor Sunna offers any exposition of this concept of political statecraft (*siyāsa*), but the blanks were progressively filled in by the 'objectives of Shari'a' literature (*maqāṣid al-sharī'a*). Here we move into what Moosa called 'the purposive strategy': in Kamali's words, '*Siyāsah* in its widest sense has five purposes: the protection of faith, life, intellect, lineage, and property.'[73] He continues, 'The *'ulamā'* are unanimous on the point that the protection of these values constitutes the ultimate objective of the *Shari'ah* itself.'

No less than the towering intellectual and mystic Abu Hamid Muhammad al-Ghazali (d. 1111) brought together some of the disparate strands on this issue, declaring that these five values represented the highest level of human benefit toward which the Shari'a reached – that of 'necessity.'[74] Others followed him, developing still further the thesis that these five values should guide the enactment of rulings in evolving social and political contexts. Kamali had dealt with this purposive reasoning in a previous article, arguing that *ijtihād* in the absence of a clear text, should rest on the overall purposes of the Shari'a. What are these purposes? More broadly, and now quoting Ibn Qayyim al-Jawziyya (d. 1350), they are 'justice, mercy and wisdom.'[75]

Kamali insists that with changed conditions fresh rulings should be produced, which seek to promote justice and the common good.[76] Traditional legal scholars should work hand in hand with social scientists and lawmakers in elected assemblies in order to creatively embody these principles in a democratic society. In particular, he adds, they should be guided by four Qur'anic directives, each of which presupposes a sociopolitical order in which the moral autonomy of the individual is required: a) the basic monotheistic conviction of *tawḥīd* 'has a liberating effect on the personality and outlook of the individual';[77] b) the principle of *ḥisba*, or call for individual initiative in promoting good morals in society, 'takes for granted his basic liberty of action';[78] c) and d) are almost synonyms: *naṣīḥa* (good counsel, sincere advice) and *shūrā* (consultation) both point to 'an inherently participatory process,' exploiting 'individual liberty and initiative in the pursuit of socially constructive goals.'[79]

Traditionalists easily proffer similar ideals. The difference comes when one raises the issue of classical rulings of *fiqh,* which contravene current ethical convictions regarding human dignity, signed into international law. In a more recent article dealing with this topic, Kamali faces this issue head-on. The implication in his previous writing was that *ijtihād* only takes place when the texts are silent. Now Kamali writes,

> Social reality was not prone to rapid change and a *mujtahid* familiar with it could attempt to engage in *ijtihād* with a degree of predictability that is no longer the case. The much accelerated pace of social change and the complexities it generates has meant that *ijtihād* ought now to be multi-disciplinary and should not be inhibited by fear of departing from earlier formulations of Islamic law.[80]

This means, among other things, that the old rule 'no *ijtihād* in the presence of a text' will have to be changed. In his words, 'in the event where *ijtihād* can advance the spirit and purpose of the Shari'ah beyond the confines of a given text, should this not be seen as a valid form of *ijtihād*?'[81] He then cites areas that need to be rethought: 'the disability of non-Muslims in the matter of evidence in the courts of justice';[82] the issue of polygamy and divorce; the death penalty for apostasy; and finally, women's rights. In essence, the spirit of the law can on occasion override its letter.

That is what I wrote on the basis of that 2002 article. In an essay forming the first chapter of a 2018 edited book examining 'the Promises and Challenges of the Maqasid al-Shari'a,' Kamali's tone is a bit more cautious.[83] The scope of his presentation is wider, including useful theological notes on human intellect (*'aql*) and sound human nature (*al-fiṭra*), and a section listing 32 legal maxims used by classical jurists, which as a whole point to the use of a purposive *fiqh* in service of flexibility and the favoring of human benefit. Yet he offers no indication that any 'clear' text could be set aside for that reason. I will come back to this collection of essays, which originally came out of a conference organized in 2014 at the University of Paderborn (Germany), mainly because the volume as a whole puts a damper on this legal movement.[84]

Tariq Ramadan: Justice and Pluralism

In this chapter we examined the writings and activism of Jamal al-Banna, whose work remains completely overshadowed by the monumental reputation of his elder brother Hasan.[85] Here we look at Hasan's grandson (through his daughter), Tariq Ramadan, who grew up in Switzerland and obtained a PhD in philosophy at the University of Geneva. Unlike his great uncle Jamal, however, he is one of the most influential Muslim reformists today.

Until recently Professor of Islamic Studies and Theology at Oxford University, Ramadan is no stranger to controversy. Indeed, he shocked the American Muslim establishment by boycotting the 2014 conferences of the Islamic Society of North America (ISNA) and Reviving the Islamic Spirit (RIS). The reasons he gave were ISNA's silence in light of the Israeli 'war crimes' committed in the last war in Gaza and continued US heavy-handed interference in the Middle East and RIS's support of dictators in the region.[86] Ramadan, whose flawless French has seen him through in many spirited debates on French television, is both sought after by European politicians as a leader of European Muslims and reviled as an islamist in sheep's clothing.

His 2012 book, *Islam and the Arab Awakening*, offers useful analysis.[87] Noting the uneven results and sometimes dire developments in the wake of what some have called the 'Arab Spring,' Ramadan issues a challenge not only to Western nations in their dealings with these states but also to their Muslim inhabitants. Notice the objectives of Shari'a discourse, as well as his emphasis on ethical values over literal readings of the texts:

> If the shari'a is to be pervaded by and founded upon the vision of the *higher goals* of dignity, justice, freedom, and religious, political, and cultural pluralism; if *ijtihad* is seen as the effort of resisting racism, corruption, and dictatorship, allied with a commitment to the reform of the individual's being and of society in the light of these finalities, then and only then will Muslim majority societies be able to throw off their shackles and cast out their demons.[88]

Likely Ramadan's most controversial move among his fellow Muslims was to publish in May 2005 'An International Call for a Moratorium on Corporal Punishment, Stoning and the Death Penalty in the Islamic World.'[89] Although Ramadan had preceded this public act with innumerable conversations on this topic with Muslim scholars ('*ulamā*') over seven years, and though many of them had agreed with him, the reaction of Muslim leaders after his 'Call' was either deafening silence or defensive posturing. He subsequently contributed a chapter to a book on the 'new reformist thinkers' in Islam on this issue.[90]

At stake here are the penal laws in the Islamic sacred texts, both Qur'an and Sunna, referred to above as the *ḥudūd*, or 'limits.' These include 'the punishments of flogging for fornication, false accusation of illicit sex and consumption of alcohol, stoning to death for adultery and amputation of the hand for theft.'[91] Yet the Call went beyond that. It sought to preclude all corporal punishment and to ban the death penalty at least for a time. Even traditional '*ulamā*' in general agree that such prescriptions are indeed Islamic but that the conditions under which they can be applied today are quasi-impossible to meet. So, in essence, they were rarely applied in Islamic history, just as they are rarely implemented today. Yet that is precisely the problem, retorts Ramadan:

> Yet behind this "almost never," the somber reality is that women and men are punished, beaten, stoned and executed in the name of *ḥudūd*. Worse, these penalties are applied almost exclusively to women and the poor, not to the wealthy and powerful. More unjust still, the accused often have no access to defense counsel or other fundamental legal safeguards.[92]

International action against these blatant human rights abuses is just as selective and unjust, remarks Ramadan. In his words,

The international community's denunciations of these penalties have been selective and calculated for the protection of geostrategic and economic interests. A poor African or Asian country trying to apply the ḥudūd will face the mobilization of international campaigns, while their ongoing and well-known application in oil-rich monarchies and allies of the West is condemned only reluctantly, if at all.[93]

What is particularly tragic in Ramadan's view is that the Islamic resurgence in piety starting in the 1970s has produced a superficial understanding of the faith, which links 'true Islam' with the literal application of these penal laws, while in reality it is a betrayal of Islam's central value of justice. Part of the problem, he adds, is that 'the literal application of the ḥudūd is taken to be authentically Islamic for the simplistic reason that it is denounced by the West.' Unfortunately, the 'ulamā', who are supposed to be 'the guardians of fidelity to the objectives of justice and equality and proponents of a deep reading of the texts and of the analysis of conditions and social contexts,'[94] are loath to confront these popular sentiments, fearing for their credibility and professional standing. Hence the Call was aimed at the conscience of every Muslim, woman and man, with the hope that Muslim civil society would mobilize in order to pressure its leaders in this direction.[95]

The expression 'guardians of fidelity to the objectives of justice and equality and proponents of a deep reading of the texts and of the analysis of conditions and social contexts' is the centerpiece of Ramadan's 'radical reform.'[96] It is an energetic critique of the Islamic legal establishment and its leaders who at best have conceived of reform in terms of adaptation to the contemporary world. This 'adaptation reform,' as he calls it, has clearly reached its limits. He has kind words for Kamali whose work tries to open interesting prospects.[97] Yet in the end, for Ramadan, he too represents the limits of a methodology that despite its reliance on the objectives of the Shari'a and the privileging of values over legal rules does not do justice to the realities of our day.

That is why the traditional 'geography of the sources of uṣūl al-fiqh must be radically revisited.'[98] Islamic law is traditionally based on the sacred texts. That is fine, says Ramadan. No one here is questioning the divine modality of inspiration of the Qur'an or the authority of the Prophet Muhammad as prime interpreter of that revelation. But there are in fact two 'Books,' or two 'Revelations,' argues Ramadan. Those sources of 'applied Islamic ethics' (significantly, law takes a back seat in Ramadan's book) are the texts, Qur'an and Sunna, 'and the Universe on an equal footing.'[99] The second

Book includes the ongoing progression of science, from the exact sciences to the social sciences, which also touch on the study of human history, cultural production and the arts, political science and law, both national and international. From the two Books Islamic law can be inferred in new and fresh ways, yet always focusing primarily on 'the higher principles and objectives' of God's 'Way' (Ramadan's usual reference to Shari'a).[100]

Ramadan summarizes his intended reform in a figure, the top level of which is composed of the two Books – 'Revealed Book' and 'Book of the Universe.'[101] Each Book then leads to two groupings of 'sciences': text sciences (the traditional Islamic sciences) and context sciences ('exact, experimental, human sciences, etc.'). Only as these two constellations of disciplines come together in mutual consultation does one have the 'sources of law and jurisprudence,' which in turn yield the theoretical underpinning of ethical reasoning, 'higher principles and objectives.' Those principles are then reformulated and elaborated in more practical ways by the scholars in each of those fields – the text scholars (*'ulamā' al-nuṣūṣ*) and the context scholars (*'ulamā' al-wāqi'*).

What all this means, of course, is that Ramadan is proposing a division of labor among the specialists that significantly displaces the traditional Islamic sciences and their scholars and jurists, the *'ulamā'*. Only in tandem can the text specialists and the context (or 'reality') scholars produce a meaningful 'applied Islamic ethics' that will contribute to the benefit of humanity. At this level, through the use of 'induction, identification categorization of the objectives of the Way' these two groups as they collaborate are able to give direction both to the Muslim community and the wider society in the fields of, for instance, 'sciences, ecology, cultures, economics, politics, gender studies, education, etc.'[102]

That is why Ramadan's fourth part of *Radical Reform* includes five chapters as case studies of possible (and he adds, badly needed,) areas of application: 'Islamic Ethics and Medical Sciences,' 'Culture and the Arts,' 'Women: Traditions and Liberation,' 'Ecology and Economy,' and finally, 'Society, Education and Power.' Perhaps the best summary of what this 'radical reform' aims to accomplish is this passage taken from his Conclusion:

> The meaning and function of the Quran's message – in keeping with all divine, spiritual and philosophical messages – lies in its capacity to educate our hearts and minds to resist the aberrations of humankind and societies and seek to transform and fashion the world into what is best for human beings: *dignity, justice, love, forgiveness, welfare,* and *peace* ...

The alliance of faith and intelligence, of confidence and resistance, must liberate intellectual energies and give life to true freedom, which refuses alienation and mobilizes knowledge, human creativity, and ethical sense to transform the world and make it a better place.[103]

Ramadan's message aims to accomplish two main tasks, it seems to me. First, he intends to shake Muslims from their sense of inferiority and defensiveness and give them the confidence and the tools that will enable them to contribute solutions to humanity's urgent problems today. And second, in a spirit of dialogue with people of other faiths and other 'spiritual and philosophical' reference points, he wants to nurture an attitude of pluralism, as Muslims go about this crucial calling. Notice too that justice and love stand side by side, framed by human dignity and forgiveness. Human rights naturally come up here and there in his case studies. But a perfect way to end this chapter is found in a section in his chapter on 'Society, Education and Power', entitled 'Public Sphere, Private Sphere, and Rights.'[104]

Recalibrating the sources of authority in Muslim-majority nations will also impact how civil society is regarded, notes Ramadan. By that he means that the *'ulamā'* (or specifically jurists, or *fuqahā'*) must team up with 'thinkers ... and agents of civil society ... to produce new, dynamic thought able to meet today's challenges.'[105] This also means participating in some of the ongoing debates taking place within Western societies about pluralism, multiculturalism and the application of democratic principles in light of Europe's mass influx of immigrants. Rawls, who according to Ramadan advocated for a neutral public sphere, was wrong.[106] Others like Charles Taylor and Tariq Modood have shown that no such neutrality can exist. Every group in France is affected to some degree by the nation's former Catholic heritage, just as Middle Eastern Christians 'are influenced by what the Islamic reference has infused into the common culture.'[107] What is important, whether in Western or Muslim nations, is the issue of power. Do all citizens enjoy, in fact, *equal* rights? So the issue of justice and equality ought to loom large in such discussions.

It is in this context that Ramadan raises the issue of racism – one that figures prominently for Muslims in France, for instance, mostly because the majority of them come from North Africa. But it also touches on other forms of discrimination targeting the poor and marginalized and thus on realities of structural injustice, all of which figured in the discussion on Pakistan that opened this chapter. Justice as rights, as we saw in the previous chapter, has a direct bearing on the complex, multi-layered forces in Pakistani society. Keep that discussion in mind when listening to this challenge issued by Ramadan. Racism or blatant Islamophobia in Europe is the mirror image of entrenched prejudice against the Shia, Christians and Ahmadis in Pakistan, and the unjust blasphemy laws. Here he has just stated that policing a public space for the sake of neutrality can seem oppressive to some minorities. He goes on:

> But this is only one of the dimensions of the reflection: it is also important to undertake a critical analysis of all that, in social logistics, collective symbolisms, and institutional management, can hinder access to *justice* and *equality*. Fundamental reflection – far more sophisticated than the formulas of the Islamic ideal and of good human intentions – should be developed about racism and its structural dimension (which sometimes deliberately targets religious affiliations): institutionalized or tacit discrimination against the poor, immigrants, or foreigners.[108]

Conclusion

In this chapter we examined the views of Muhammad Hashim Kamali, a leading Muslim reformist legal scholar, and saw how his attention to public benefit as the overall purpose of God's law could enable Muslim jurists to renew Islamic jurisprudence expressly in the service of justice and human rights. We also took stock of an Egyptian union activist and self-taught scholar in the Islamic sciences, Jamal al-Banna, who saw justice as one of the main objectives of God's revealed law. In fact, it was more important that the five traditional objectives laid out by the proponents of the purposive jurisprudence. And for al-Banna it had more to do with ethics than law. Consciously reviving the ancient Muslim debates between Ash'arites and Mu'tazilites, he called for Muslims to develop critical thinking based on the objective values of what is right and just for both individuals and society at large.

Like his younger relative Tariq Ramadan, al-Banna urged Muslims to renew their conscience, 'a human faculty prized in all the religions, but that can easily be dulled and sidelined when the legalistic details of religion overshadow the weightier matters of human oppression and injustice.' Though blood relatives, al-Banna and Ramadan essentially came from different worlds. That said, there must have been a keen affinity between them, as both were calling for a deep-seated reform in the Islamic mind. In the next chapter we weigh the teaching and activism of someone who has consistently sought to advance the message and example of al-

Banna's older brother, Hasan al-Banna. Here we examined three examples of reformist thinking, but now, using the categories we mentioned above relative to the period of classical Islam, we move from the rationalists to the traditionalists, though with an activist strain. In Yusuf al-Qaradawi's life we find embodied in dramatic relief the priorities and values of moderate twentieth-century islamism.

Endnotes

1   Cesari 2014, 119.

2   'Everyone has the right to freedom of thought, conscience and religion; this right includes freedom to change his religion or belief, and freedom, either alone or in community with others and in public or private, to manifest his religion or belief in teaching, practice, worship and observance.'

3   For a survey of countries that outlaw blasphemy, see the following Pew Research article, Theodorou 2016, online, http://www.pewresearch.org/fact-tank/2016/07/29/which-countries-still-outlaw-apostasy-and-blasphemy/?utm_content=buffer1e801&utm_medium=social&utm_source=twitter.com&utm_campaign=buffer (accessed July 14, 2018).

4   Moataz El Feglery shows that in Islamic literature over the centuries both blasphemy (*sab*) and heresy (*zandaqa*) were subsumed under the wider category of apostasy and as a result the definition kept widening to cover more and more aspects far beyond the initial charge of insulting God and the Prophet. See El Feglery 2017 in a report, 'Islam and Human Rights: Key Issues for Our Time', published by the Atlantic Council. He also points to a rise in cases of arrest of bloggers and other human rights activists using religious pretexts when the crackdown has everything to do with the politically repressive nature of these regimes.

5   Singha 2018, 229–258, at 242.

6   The source Singha cites records the actual words that convicted her: 'Our Christ sacrificed his life on the Cross for our sins. Our Christ is alive.' This was from an article, 'Pakistani Court Overturns Asia Bibi's Death Sentence', CBN News 2015, online, www.cbn.com/cbnnews/world/2015/July/Pakistan-Court-Overturns-Asia-Bibis-Death-Sentence/ accessed July 13, 2018; cited in Singha 2018, 243.

7   'Aasia Bibi leaves Pakistan for Canada after years on death row over blasphemy case', Associated Press for NBC News, May 8, 2019, online https://www.nbcnews.com/news/world/aasia-bibi-leaves-pakistan-canada-after-years-death-row-over-n1003186, accessed May 22, 2019.

8   'Pakistani Christians Burned Alive Were Attacked by 1,200 People', NBC News, November 7, 2014, online, https://www.nbcnews.com/news/world/pakistani-christians-burned-alive-were-attacked-1-200-people-kin-n243386, accessed July 13, 2018.

9   Singha 2018, 238. This fact of caste creates puts the Christians in the urban slums and in rural areas as lowest of the low. Muslims often will avoid utensils touched by Christians as 'impure', and will not use them.

10   Singha 2018, 241.

11   Ahmadis especially run afoul of the Khatm-e-Nubuwwat doctrine since they believe their 19th-century founder, Mirza Ghulam Ahmad, was a prophet.

12   Dorsey 2018, https://mideastsoccer.blogspot.sg/2018/03/will-real-pakistan-stand-up-please.html accessed July 14, 2018.

13   This is the doctrine that Muhammad was the Seal of the Prophets, meaning the last and greatest of all the prophets because he mediated the Qur'an, God's final revelation. He is therefore deserving of the utmost respect.

14   The Introduction to *Under Ceasar's Sword* begins with the story of Shahbaz Bhatti. A Roman Catholic, he intentionally refrained from marrying, knowing how perilous his calling was. Bhatti had founded the influential NGO, All Pakistan Minorities Alliance, with the goal of uniting Christians, Ahmadis, Shia Muslims and others, in order to secure greater religious freedom for all. He had recorded a video shortly before he was gunned down, saying: 'I believe in Jesus Christ who has given his life for us, and I am ready to die for a cause. I'm living for my community ... and I will die to defend their rights' (Philpott and Shah 2018, 1).

15   Moosa 2012, 1–10, at 5.

16   I am grateful to Ann Elizabeth Mayer who led me to Susan Waltz's groundbreaking essay, 'Universal Human Rights: The Contribution of Muslim States,' see Waltz 2004, 799–844. Further, it was in large part due to the quasi-natural law formulation of the Universal Declaration of Human Rights, which studiously avoids any reference to the divine, that it won the approval of all nations present in 1948, which included the Muslim states of Afghanistan, Egypt, Iran, Iraq, Pakistan, Syria and Turkey. Only Saudi Arabia abstained.

17   As mentioned in the Introduction Introduction (see Chapter 1) they are the International Covenant on Civil and Political Rights (ICCPR) and the International Covenant on Economic, Social, and Cultural Rights (ICESCR). They came into force in 1976.

18   For instance, torture and all forms of discrimination are banned, as well as 'arbitrary arrest, detention or exile' (Article 9). Also, the Universal Declaration of Human Rights states that one may not 'be held guilty of any penal offense on account of any act or omission which did not constitute a penal offense (Article 11.2) and '[n]o one shall be subjected to arbitrary interference with his privacy, family, home or correspondence' (Article 12).

19   Hallaq 2005.

20   Hallaq 2005, 122–126. Ethical voluntarism was the dominant position in medieval Judaism, yet a minority position among Christian theologians. For Thomas Aquinas, voluntarism was heresy, and no doubt he remains the greatest medieval contributor to modern theology. Catholic philosopher Jacques Maritain rightly connects the voluntarism of Duns Scotus (d. 1308) and William of Ockham (d. 1350) to Islamic moral theology, but seems to be ignorant of the Mu'tazilite tradition of rationalism (Maritain 1964: 91; quoted in Makdisi 1983, 50–61).

21   Reinhart 1995, 40.

22   Reinhart 1995, 138–45. Basra, along with Kufa near Baghdad, was a garrison town built to house many of the Arabian warriors who had conquered these territories

in the first generation of Islam. It is today the most populous (and oil-rich) Iraqi city and the centre of its Shi'i population.

23 Reinhart 1995, 174.

24 Reinhart 1995, 174–175.

25 The Hanbali school of law is one of four Sunni schools still functioning today; it is also the most literal and uncompromising, and as such, Saudi Arabia is the only Muslim country to have adopted it officially. Add to that its ideology that sprung from the writings of eighteen-century Islamic reformer and Hanbali scholar Muhammad bin Abd al-Wahhab (d. 1792) and you have the recipe for a very restrictive view of Islamic law. It is commonly known that Saudi Arabia since the 1970s used its vast petro-dollar wealth to spread far and wide its Wahhabi ideology. See for instance, Crooke 2014, available at http://www.huffingtonpost.com/alastair-crooke/isis-wahhabism-saudi-arabia_b_5717157.html last accessed July 15, 2018.

26 Hallaq 2005, 124–125.

27 Fakhry 1991, 47; Khaddury 1984, 60–64.

28 Brown 1999, 181–192.

29 The Umayyads dynasty ruled in Damascus from 41/661 to 132/750, until the second dynasty, the Abbasids, took over from them, moving their capital to Baghdad.

30 I write 'islamist' with a lower-case 'i' since it refers to an ideological position combining religious belief and political orientations – much like the adjectives 'fundamentalist', 'socialist', or 'reformist'.

31 For an evaluation of the Qur'anic data on this issue, see Hourani's chapter 'Ethical Presuppositions of the Qur'an' in Hourani 1985, 23–48. In the first footnote of another chapter (from an article he had published later than this one), he writes, 'Support for an objectivist theory of value in the Qur'an is far more definite than I had realized before writing "Ethical presuppositions of the Qur'an." On the other hand the Qur'an emphasizes itself and the Prophet as the principal sources of ethical knowledge, without altogether ruling out the possibility of rational knowledge' ('Two Theories of Value in Early Islam' in Hourani 1985, 57–66, at 57).

32 See Adis Duderija 2014 for an edited volume on this topic and as a reminder, Johnston 2004 and Johnston 2007a.

33 While there have been dozens of schools at different times, four major Sunni schools survive today, and one Shi'i school. If the reader is confused about the connection between *shari'a* and *fiqh*, he or she is not alone. This is one of the most debated topics among Muslim scholars today.

34 Moosa 2001–2002, 1–46.

35 al-Banna 1986; al-Banna 1995a.

36 al-Banna 1994a; al-Banna 2005a.

37 al-Banna 2003a.

38 al-Banna 1994b; al-Banna 2003b; al-Banna 2003c.

39 This approach is consistent with that of much contemporary Islamic reformist thinking: the distinction between 'Islam' and the political history of Muslims; sweeping political reform in order to secure the necessary freedom of thought and conscience that will in turn help spark the needed 'renewal of religious discourse'; the belief in 'the relativity of human knowledge' as also essential to create

a climate which encourages innovation (Cairo Institute for Human Rights Studies; Paris Declaration 'On Means of Renewing Religious Discourse,' August 2003).

40   This was sponsored by The Saban Center for Middle East Policy at the Brookings Institution and the Ibn Khaldun Center for Developmental Studies, in association with the Center for the Study of Islam and Democracy (Washington) and the Islamic Dialogue Forum (London). The 'Concluding Statement' is available online, http://www.brookings.edu/~/media/Events/2004/10/05%20islamic%20world/ cairoclosing.pdf last accessed November 10, 2014.

41   'Opening Statement' Ibrahim 2004, 2.

42   No doubt due to his leadership in human rights advocacy, Saad al-Din Ibrahim (also spelled 'Saad Eddin') was arrested and imprisoned for several months without charge; then in November 2000 he was sentenced to seven years in jail for 'illegally accepting foreign funds, sullying Egypt's image abroad, and embezzlement.' His release in February 2002 was the result of a sustained international campaign on his behalf.

43   Ibrahim 2004, at 2.

44   al-Banna 1995.

45   al-Banna 1995, 77.

46   al-Banna 1995, 83.

47   al-Banna 1995, 88. Al-Banna scrutinizes a sampling of the numerous Qur'anic verses (about 300, he says) using the word 'truth' and argues that *'adl* and *ḥaqq* are used for the most part as synonyms in the Qur'an. Here is his conclusion: 'According to the noble Qur'an, justice (*'adl*) is truth (*ḥaqq*) applied, and truth is justice in the abstract. ...Both are among God's beautiful names,' al-Banna 1995, 98.

48   al-Banna 1995, 79.

49   Still, the formulation reveals his lack of training in theology and philosophy. If God 'brought into being' justice, did he also create all other ethical values? It would be better to say from a theological standpoint that justice along with all other ethical values somehow inhere in God's own character as attributes or qualities of his person. Then philosophically we could point to them as standing on their own, objectively, so that non-theists could refer to them without any connection to God. This is the way human rights discourse is seen today – an ethical theory intuitively grasped by people worldwide, and therefore not in need of any particular metaphysical justification.

50   al-Banna 1995, 103–104. I am not saying that al-Banna proclaims himself as a follower of the Mu'tazilites. He criticizes them for other reasons in several passages elsewhere. He is attempting to widen the scope of traditional debates, however, and to argue that, at least on the issue of justice, their position was more reasonable than that of the Ash'arites.

51   al-Banna 1995, 137.

52   Esack 1997.

53   This is one of the central themes of Omid Safi's edited volume, see Safi 2003.

54   Available online, http://www.yabiladi.com/forum/read-44-719276-719276.html last accessed, November 10, 2014.

55   http://www.yabiladi.com/forum/read-44-719276-719276.html. 1–4.

56 In his own words, 'The problem is essentially that of misconception in the minds and souls of many Muslims, something that the government can do very little to change. It means that one is free to hoard one's wealth or spend it irresponsibly, largely ignoring other, impoverished, members of society. Instead of being aware of the needs of others, one's conscience is too preoccupied with ritual worship and the routine practices of one's religion', al-Banna 2005b, 3.

57 al-Banna 2005b, 3.

58 The three volumes were published successively in 1995, 1997 and 1999 by his usual publisher (Dār al-Fiqh al-Islāmī, 'Home of Islamic Thought').

59 al-Banna 2001, Publisher's Preface.

60 His 'thee levels of authority for *fiqh*' (which is now subsumed under *'aqīda*, or personal belief – that is, law relating to individuals) represents an equally dramatic break from tradition: (1) the Qur'an; (2) the Sunna; (3) legal rulings and writings of the past ('laws of the *fuqahā*', pl. of *faqīh*). It is as if to say that what most traditionalists consider 'Shari'a' is of little consequence. Everything with the evolution of human societies needs to be considered afresh in each new generation.

61 Also, he dramatically scales down the number of reliable *ḥadīth*, the reports of Muhammad's sayings and deeds, and states that the Sunna must be judged by the Qur'an – against the traditional view, which elevates the Sunna on par with the Qur'an and sometimes even giving it the power to abrogate specific Qur'anic injunctions.

62 al-Banna 2001, 137–152. Following others, but especially the fourteenth-century Hanbali scholar, Najm al-Din Tufi, he declares that the first objective of Shari'a is human benefit (*maṣlaḥa*), closely followed by a second, justice. Significantly, Tufi was rediscovered by Rashid Rida (a fact also pointed out by the publisher, whom al-Banna knew personally before he died in 1935. Just the same, Tufi has remained a controversial figure, especially in his claim that even commands in the sacred texts could be set aside for the sake of human benefit.

63 See, in my discussion of Tariq Ramadan.

64 al-Banna 2001, 133–141.

65 Kamali studied and taught law at Kabul University and then obtained a PhD at London University. He also taught at McGill University, before taking his present position as Professor of Law and Dean of the International Institute of Islamic Thought and Civilization at the International Islamic University, Malaysia. His first book was published by E. J. Brill (Leiden) in 1985: *Law in Afghanistan: A Study of the Constitutions, Matrimonial Law and the Judiciary*. Recently he has published *Shari'ah Law: An Introduction* (London: Oneworld, 2008).

66 Kamali 2001, 103.

67 Kamali 2001.

68 Kamali 2001, 104.

69 Kamali 2001, 107.

70 Kamali 2001, 110. This is somewhat ironic coming from Qaradawi, considering the material we will cover in the next chapter.

71 Kamali assumes that justice, along with other ethical values, is common to all the religions: 'All religious traditions have taken a close interest in the basic humanitarian values that have been the subject of this presentation. Islam has often been

characterized as a social uprising against injustice, a fact borne out by the degree of attention justice has received in the Qur'an' (Kamali 2001, 156).

72 Kamali 2001, 113. Recall that 'vicegerency' is the archaic word many Muslim scholars use to translate the Qur'anic concept of humanity's *khilāfa*, or trusteeship, or deputyship (literally, caliphate). That was the theme I developed at length in Johnston 2010a.

73 Kamali 2001, 146.

74 The two lower levels are, in order: needs (*hājiyyāt*) and improvements of human conditions (*tahsīniyyāt*).

75 Kamali 1989: 215–235, at 225.

76 I use 'common good' here for *maslaha*, generally translated as human benefit.

77 Kamali 2001, 227.

78 A concept broad enough to encompass the positive efforts of government, '[*h*] isbah thus encourages the participation and involvement of the individual in society and sees him as a morally autonomous agent who is alert to the problems and concerns of the community' (Kamali 2001, 157).

79 Kamali 2001, 157.

80 Kamali 2002, 617–634, at 627.

81 Kamali 2002, 631.

82 Kamali 2002, 630.

83 Kamali 2018, 7–33.

84 It does so by its very structure: Part I contains essays affirming the use of this purposive method in some way, while Part II offers essays by scholars who doubt its usefulness and even call it a tool of the elites often used by authoritarian governments to keep people in line. So it clearly ends with an emphasis on 'challenges,' one of the words used in the title.

85 The Muslim Brotherhood, after all, was the first and remains the most influential islamist movement. Islamism is a modern social movement and ideology. Although Hasan al-Banna was more of an activist, organizer and preacher than a writer, his influence endures as the father of the movement that is still one of the most potent forces in the Muslim world today.

86 See Azad 2014, available at http://www.aljazeera.com/indepth/opinion/2014/09/ tariq-ramadan-reconfiguration-is-20149214173222672.html accessed June 19, 2019.

87 Ramadan 2012.

88 Ramadan 2012, 118.

89 This text can be downloaded as a pdf document on his website, available at http:// tariqramadan.com/blog/2005/04/05/an-international-call-for-moratorium-on-corporal-punishment-stoning-and-the-death-penalty-in-the-islamic-world/ (accessed November 17, 2014).

90 Ramadan 2009a, 163–174. This project for the promotion of religious freedom was sponsored by the Norwegian government through the University of Oslo and became the Oslo Coalition. This included three international workshops in Yogyakarta, Indonesia (2004); Sarajevo, Bosnia-Hezegovina (2005); and Istanbul, Turkey (2007). Finally, this led to the publishing of the above book.

91 Ramadan 2009a, 164.

92 Ramadan 2009a.

93 Ramadan 2009a. Think of the murder, dismembering and secret disposal of the body of the Washington Post columnist Jamal Khashoggi, inside the Saudi consulate in Istanbul. Khashoggi, a Saudi citizen who wrote critical articles about the policies of Crown Prince Muhammed bin Salman had been tricked into going to the consulate to collect his divorce papers in preparation for his marriage. Despite all the evidence which the CIA reportedly passed on to the White House, suggesting Khashoggi's murder was ordered by the Saudi State and likely the Crown Prince himself, as of today, President Trump has mostly remained silent. The same could be said about the war waged by the Saudis and Emeratis in Yemen, a conflict in which the UN says that both sides have likely committed war crimes. See Dunning 2018.

94 Dunning 2018, 164–165.

95 For a spirited debate on this issue, see Al Jazeera English's Head to Head programme at the Oxford Union, available at https://www.youtube.com/watch?v=cpmsqABAmCo (accessed November19, 2014).

96 Ramadan 2009b.

97 Ramadan 2009b, 135.

98 Ramadan 2009b, 126.

99 Ramadan 2009b, 127.

100 Ramadan goes further than the usual distinction made by legal scholars today between Shari'a and *fiqh*, God's divine will for humanity as expressed in the texts and human understanding of those general principles. By focusing on the two Books he is referring to two orders: 'The two orders, mirroring each other as to the study of definitive and changing laws and principles, unite and harmonize at the level of essence and meaning of creation and of life. Here, the believing conscience finds a Way (*ash-shari'ah*), a direction (*hudā*), the meaning of a free and therefore responsible destiny ... The two orders are not opposed, each of them complements the other, gives it meaning and perfects the path of knowledge be reconciling the "why" and the "how," thus enlightening the mind and appeasing the heart' (Ramadan 2009b, 99). This construct is only possible by positing wide powers to human 'critical reason,' as he calls it. Further, the human mind is skillfully linked to the human heart as the receptor of divine guidance. This is a theological reasoning to which, as a Christian, I can connect as well. The main difference, though, would be the choice of divine texts.

101 Ramadan 2009b, 129.

102 Ramadan 2009b.

103 Ramadan 2009b, 316–317, emphasis his.

104 Ramadan 2009b, 266–271.

105 Ramadan 2009b, 266–267.

106 He fails to take into account the later Rawls, author of *Political Liberalism* (Rawls 2005 [1993]).

107 Ramadan 2009b, 267–268.

108 Ramadan 2009b, 269.

Yusuf al-Qaradawi: Shari'a's Objectives and Social Justice

Egypt has proportionally and numerically the highest number of Christians among Arab nations, about 10 percent of its total population of 98 million. Nine-tenths of those Christians are Coptic Orthodox believers who boast about their church's founding in the first century by the evangelist Mark. That so many Christians still exist in Egypt compared to the rest of North Africa and the Middle East certainly speaks of tolerance on the part of the majority Muslim population over the last 1,380 years since the Arabian army of Amr Ibn al-Aas invaded it.

Still, the number of attacks on Christians in Egypt has risen sharply since the 2011 'January 25 Revolution.' First, the army killed 27 Christians and jailed another 31 others for peacefully protesting in October of that year (the 'Maspero Massacre'). Second, dozens of churches were destroyed, burned, or badly damaged in the aftermath of the July coup against President Mohammed Morsi. Third, a number of church bombings have occurred, including one in Cairo in December 2016 (Botroseya, 29 killed, 47 injured), and a two-pronged attack on Palm Sunday April 9, 2017 (Tanta, 30 killed; Alexandria, 17 killed).

What is worse is that there has been a longstanding discrepancy between the *de jure* rights of the Christian minority in Egypt and its *de facto* rights, noted Sarah Yerkes, a Brookings researcher. Although the status of Christians has been well established by successive constitutions since Anwar Sadat's coming to power in 1970, she writes, 'there is little Christian representation in government, and sectarian violence is all but commonplace.'[1] While the 2014 constitution guarantees 'absolute' freedom of religion, it also proclaims Islam as the religion of the state and Muslims may not leave Islam. Moreover, several public figures, mostly secular, have been jailed for blasphemy.[2] President Sisi vowed from the start of his first term in office (2013) that he would protect Christians. In fact, his public words emphasize the unity of all Egyptians, Christian or Muslim. But as Yerkes argues, this is to ignore the actual discrimination Christians face on a daily basis. She adds, 'This is most evident in the disproportionately low level of Christian representation in government, particularly within the influential security establishment.'[3]

In this chapter we scrutinize the writings of an influential Egyptian Muslim scholar who spent most of his life in Qatar. Yet so popular was he that at age 85 he was flown in to lead Friday prayers in Tahrir Square barely three weeks after President Mubarak had been toppled by the throngs of protesters in that central Cairo plaza. Here's how he began:

> The usage of preachers, for their sermons, is to say 'O Muslims!' but me, I say in this Square, 'O Muslims and Copts! O children of Egypt!' This is the day of the children of Egypt all together. It is not the day of the Muslims alone. I am addressing them from this tribune (*minbar*), and from this Square, Tahrir Square – or, rather, from this day onwards, it ought to be called the 'Square of the Martyrs of the January 25 Revolution.' O Brothers, I am addressing you from above this tribune and from the Square of the Martyrs of the January 25 Revolution, this revolution which has taught the world how revolutions should be.

> It was not a usual revolution but it was a revolution meant to teach a lesson. The youth who have triumphed in this revolution did not triumph over Mubarak only. They triumphed over Mubarak, *they triumphed over injustice*, they triumphed over falsehood. They triumphed over robbery and they triumphed over plundering. They triumphed over egoism and they initiated a new life by this revolution .... 'And say: Truth has come and falsehood has vanished away. Surely, falsehood is ever bound to vanish' (Q. 17:81) .... It was inevitable that this revolution should triumph, and that its believing children should triumph over this tyrant (*ṭāghūt*), over this Pharaoh who threatened and menaced. But the believers – Egypt once it believes – made answer to Pharaoh.[4]

Thus spoke Yusuf al-Qaradawi (b. 1926) in Tahrir Square on February 18, 2011. New York Times correspondent David D. Kirkpatrick emphasized the homecoming nature of this unprecedented *khuṭba* (Friday prayer sermon) in a public square: 'After Long Exile, Sunni Cleric Takes Role in Egypt.'[5] The government's official figure of two million attendees was surely overblown; yet Kirkpatrick and others believed the crowd to be over a million. Only this al-Azhar-educated mufti, self-exiled for 50 years and arguably the world's most popular Sunni cleric, could command such a crowd in this revolutionary setting.

Notice too how the very beginning of his speech addresses all Egyptians, both Muslims and Copts (referring to Christians): 'This is the day of the children of Egypt all together. It is not the day of the Muslims alone.' In light of the deteriorating situation of Christians in Egypt since the January 25 Revolution, was Qaradawi speaking sincerely? We cannot know, of course, but I would assume he was. Considering that he spent most of his life in the Gulf, he would not be aware of the decades-long, state-sponsored discrimination of Christians. Nor could he have imagined that in two years the Muslim Brotherhood-affiliated president would be removed from office by the army and that the personal prejudices of many Egyptians against Christians – and especially those who sympathized with the Brotherhood – would only be exacerbated after the coup. In those circumstances, some of them likely took out their rage and bitterness on the Christian community that overwhelmingly favored the coup.

Before launching into Qaradawi's contribution to the current of 'the objectives of Shari'a' in Islamic law, allow me to state from the outset that any assessment of his popularity in the Muslim world must go hand in hand with some of the controversy he has also stirred up over time. Consider for instance, that Qaradawi has been banned from entering the US since 1999, the UK since 2008, and France since 2012.[6] In part this is likely due to his high-profile fatwa declaring the permissibility of Palestinians using suicide bombing to fight the Israeli occupation of Palestinian territories.[7] The Wikipedia article on Qaradawi cites many other sources that provide translated remarks he has made over the years on al Jazeera and other Arab outlets that are are virulently anti-Semitic.[8] There is no escaping the controversial aspect of Qaradawi's expressed views, particularly from a Western perspective.

That said, in the Muslim world Qaradawi's reputation derives in part from his immensely popular show on al Jazeera satellite TV ('Shari'a and Life') and in part from his double presidency of the International Association of Muslim Scholars and the European Council for Fatwa and Research. He has also been savvy when it comes to the media.[9] One of the most frequented Islamic websites, IslamOnline.net, runs under his authority, and his sermons, addresses, and fatwas are disseminated on his own website, Qaradawi.net, as well as on several TV outlets besides al-Jazeera, and on many print outlets. Author of over 120 books, it is his ability to exploit the new media, nevertheless, that sets him apart from other Muslim scholars or jurists.[10]

Besides his active participation in international Islamic organizations and conferences and his projected image as leader of the 'moderate' current (al-ṭayar al-waṣaṭiyya), Qaradawi has had a longstanding relationship with the Egyptian Muslim Brotherhood. Born in 1926 in the Nile Delta region of Egypt, he was 14 years old when he first heard its founder Hasan al-Banna speak. He knew then and there that he would join this organization. Six years later, while a student, he started the first Muslim Brotherhood chapter at the world-renowned al-Azhar University in Cairo. He even traveled to spread its message to various parts of Egypt, and in 1952 he visited Syria for that purpose. So when the great miḥna struck in 1954 (the so-called 'persecution' or in this case, 'purge' at the hands of the military junta), like others he was imprisoned, but he was fortunate to be released in 1956. Thereafter he established his reputation as a preacher in various mosques, taught in a private school and then at the Institute of Islamic Culture at al-Azhar. It was this position that enabled him to be officially delegated by al-Azhar to Qatar in 1961, where he has lived ever since.[11]

Thanks to his close relationship with the Emir of Qatar (1972–1995), 'he fundamentally shaped the religious educational system in Doha,' establishing in particular the Sharia faculty of the University of Qatar, which opened in 1977. Partly through his own charisma and partly through the open policy of his host country, Qaradawi found himself at the center of a vibrant community of Islamic scholars and activists, including many Muslim Brothers who had come from Egypt and elsewhere.[12]

Today many of these people see Qaradawi as their global mouthpiece, though he himself has been at pains since the 1990s to distance himself from them, at least officially.[13] Still, there is no doubt that Qaradawi's Egyptian Brotherhood credentials were dramatically on display when he led the Friday prayers in Tahrir Square in Cairo, exhorting his hearers not to squander the gains of the Revolution and to remain united, Muslims and Christians. A book came out the next year with 80 colored photographs and a collection of sermons, speeches and fatwas by Qaradawi to emphasize his crucial political role as an 'ālim (singular of 'ulamā', alim from now on) in the unfolding revolution. The title in English is 'The January 25 Revolution of the People: Sheikh Qaradawi and the Egyptian Revolution.'[14]

Unmistakably, Shaykh al-Qaradawi in that moment was reaching the pinacle of a long career devoted to leading Muslim youth to embrace their religion with passion, yet without falling prey to the fanaticism of the Salafis,[15] and especially to the militancy and violence of the jihadis. With the whole world watching, this was a golden opportunity to showcase his 'middle path,' or 'moderate' Islamic way (*al-manhaj al-wasaṭiyya*). In doing so, he supremely embodied the proverbial Islamic scholar/jurist who guides his people in the ways of justice at a grave political junction. Indeed, this is the dream of islamism, that ideology born in the yearning of Muslims living under colonial regimes and then fueled by their dashed hopes as new, and mostly bitter postcolonial realities emerged. Tentatively before, but firmly in the twenty-first century, Qaradawi has embraced multi-party democracy and a religously plural citizenship. Now he wants the Muslim Brotherhood to rise up to the occasion and lead his fatherland in the way of Shari'a and justice. And yes, there is more than just a touch of national pride here.

Qaradawi is convinced that the 'middle path,' his *wasaṭiyya* message, embodies God's justice. This has been a consistent theme of his teaching, writing and preaching for over a half century, as echoing the Qur'anic injunction, 'Thus We have appointed you a *middle nation*, that ye may be witnesses against mankind, and that the messenger may be a witness against you' (Q. 2:143, emphasis mine). So the question I ask in this chapter is whether Qaradawi's more recent adoption of the *maqāṣid al-sharīʿa* emphasis ('The Purposes of Shari'a') has changed his conservative views as self-appointed guardian of 'ulamā' values and social position.[16] And then, how does this relate to the views of the reformists we examined in the last chapter?

Intellectual Roots of Qaradawi's 'Purposive Fiqh'

In the previous chapter I pointed to the growing movement in Islamic jurisprudence (*fiqh*) built around the 'overall objectives,' or 'purposes of Shari'a.'[17] In fact, the Arabic literature has become so abundant that the expression '*al-fiqh al-maqāṣidī*' ('purposive jurisprudence') or '*al-fiqh al-maqāṣidī*' ('purposive thinking') has now come into common usage. Even the English literature on the subject has begun to use the adjective '*maqāṣidī*' to denote this 'purposive' methodolgy in jurisprudence. Wael Hallaq, a highly respected Canadian scholar in the field, in his early 1990s work had already alluded to the 'utilitarianist' trend with roots in the nineteenth century which placed an unprecendented emphasis on *maṣlaḥa*, 'benefit' or 'welfare' or even 'the common good' in the sociopolitical realm.[18]

Three of the most cited scholars in this field of 'purposive jurisprudence' are from the fourteenth century, Najm al-Din al-Tufi (d. 1316), Ibn

Qayyim al-Jawziyya (d. 1350), and Abu Ishaq al-Shatibi (d. 1388). Tufi is clearly the most controversial, since he taught that the purpose of revelation is human well-being (*maslaha*) and that it is the chief source (*dalil*, pl. *adilla*) for extending God's law into new areas of human experience.[19] Although not in the area of religious rituals and creed (*'ibadat*), in the area of *mu'amalat* (human interactions) considerations of *maslaha* for Tufi can trump the rulings of the sacred texts.

Ibn Qayyim (d. 1350) was the disciple of Ibn Taymiyya, the famous Hanbali scholar from Damascus who highlighted the use of *maslaha* in the sociopolitical realm, *siyasa shar'iyya*. Ibn Qayyim went beyond his teacher, however, by widening the use of *maslaha* as the *ratio legis* (the reason for the particular ruling) behind all of the Shari'a's injunctions. In fact, the following quote from Ibn Qayyim I found in Yusuf al-Qaradawi's recent book entirely devoted to the purposes of Shari'a is virtually ubiquitous in the contemporary literature. Referring to his own rather recent turn to this purposive legal reasoning, Qaradawi tells his readers how it started:

> The idea kept coming to me in greater clarity and depth and this word from Ibn Qayyim implanted itself in the depths of my heart: "The Shari'a is built and solidly anchored on the benefits (*masalih*, pl. of *maslaha*) it bestows on humankind. It is altogether justice, altogether mercy, altogether well-being (*maslaha*), altogether wisdom."[20]

Finally, by far the most quoted and studied today among these forerunners of the purposes of Shari'a movement is the Maliki jurist from Andalusia (Islamic Spain) al-Shatibi (d. 1388), the only one to establish a sophisticated legal hermeneutic based on considerations of *maslaha*. For him, the universal sources of the law could be known through an inductive methodology tied to the three levels of *maslaha* as mapped out by Ghazali. These universal sources (or 'comprehensive,' *kulli*) bring certainty to the jurist's task of discovering God's law in new contexts. Conversely, the specific texts yield only probability, as they are tied to particular historical moments or geographical contexts.[21]

This kind of hermeneutic resurfaced in the modern period in several guises. In 1928 Rashid Rida (d. 1935), Muhammad Abduh's disciple and co-founder of the *al-Manar* journal ('The Lighthouse'), published a booklet entitled *Yusr al-islam wa-usul al-tashri' al-'am*, 'The Ease of Islam and the Foundations of General Legislation.'[22] This book more than any other, it seems to me, is what has inspired Yusuf al-Qaradawi's long career. First, his primary audience was the youth, who, because the teaching of the *'ulama'* seemed both so complicated and so demanding, were sorely tempted to leave religion behind.[23] Second, Qaradawi modeled his concept of *wasaṭiyya* ('the middle path,' or 'the moderate path') on Rida who saw Muslims in the 1920s as divided in three camps:

a) the fierce advocates of *taqlīd* (following very literally the past rulings of one's legal school)
b) the secularists, who see the west as their guiding light
c) the 'moderate reformers who maintain that Islam can be revived and its true guidance renewed by following the Qur'an, the authentic Sunna, and the inspiration of the righteous forbears, with the help of the imams of all the schools of law, but without being attached to any particular rules in the books of jurisprudence and the theoretical peculiarities of each school, as is the case of the first group.'[24]

Much more could be noted about the intellectual roots of this purposive bent in Islamic jurisprudence, but the jurists I have mentioned give a sufficient indication of the possible directions this movement could take in the contemporary era. Yet before delving into Qaradawi's use of this approach, we must take a quick pulse of this movement in contemporary Muslim legal circles.

The Thriving Purposive Legal Theory Movement

I offer here only two manifestations of the popularity and influence of this *'maqāṣid al-sharīʿa'* movement today, one institutional and the other a high-level academic conference followed by a book. First was the establishment of the London-based Al-Maqasid Research Centre in the Philosophy of Islamic Law founded by Sheikh Ahmad Zaki Yamani in 2005 with Yusuf al-Qaradawi, Muhammad Salim al-Awa[25] and 14 other *'ulamāʾ*. Although Qaradawi is still on the board of directors, he did not write anything in the book that collected the papers for that maiden conference. This is because Qaradawi was the keynote speaker at a London conference the year before (2004) and his address became the first item in his own book entirely devoted to the objectives of Shari'a published in 2006.[26] The prime mover behind this initiative, Ahmad Zaki Yamani, is a fascinating combination of a Harvard-educated lawyer, the long-time Saudi Minister of Petroleum and first Secretary General of OPEC – and a self-taught *'alim*.

The second sign of this movement's prominence can be gleaned from the large two-volume collection of 'The 22ⁿᵈ General Conference of the Supreme Council of Islamic Affairs in Cairo, February 2010; the last of these annual conferences organized by the al-Azhar University and the Egyptian ministry of Awqaf before the January 25 Revolution. The theme that year was: 'The Purposes of the Islamic Shari'a and Contemporary Issues: Research and Realities.' Delegates from over 30 countries participated and their papers can be read in the two volumes.[27] Qaradawi does not appear in either volume, since he did not attend the conference. This is simply to point out that, as dozens of recent books on this subject also suggest, this movement is widespread. In fact, I am arguing here that Qaradawi jumped on the *maqāṣidī* bandwagon well after it had gained momentum.[28]

Qaradawi's Gradual Embrace of the *Maqāṣidī* Movement

So my next question is 'how new to this *maqāṣidī* thinking is Qaradawi?' I was surprised to read in his 2006 book, *A Study in the Jurisprudence of the Shari'a's Purposes* that he had written about these ideas in ten other books, ranging from the late 1980s through the early 2000s. His doctorate from al-Azhar in 1973 had been on *fiqh* – how *zakat* could be applied today;[29] but he did not write anything of substance on legal theory (*uṣūl al-fiqh*) until the 1980s.[30] For instance, much of his writing in the 1970s was in an activist mode – how to move the burgeoning islamist movement forward – like *al-Ḥall al-islāmī farīda wa-ḍarūra* [The Islamic Solution: Both a Duty and a Necessity].[31] Nothing in there deals with *maṣlaḥa*; nothing even touches on 'the ease' in the interpretation of rules. The concept of *wasaṭiyya* comes up a good deal in the 1970s, but it is about the middle road between socialism and capitalism.[32]

By the 1980s, though, *wasaṭiyya* for Qaradawi was about disassociating himself from the radicals who killed President Sadat (1981) and threatened other acts of terrorism. The 'middle path' now looked much more like what Rashid Rida was writing about in the 1920s. Then in the next decade, on the far side of the Cold War, a new challenge came to the fore: Islam in the eyes of Samuel Huntington and the western media in general was being tarred as a threat to democracy and a harbinger of violence. His second volume of fatwas published in 1993 locates his *wasaṭiyya* discourse as the happy medium between the exaggeration (*ghulūw*) of the zealots and the neglect (*tafrīṭ*) of the secularists.[33] The key text here is *Introduction to the*

Study of the Islamic Shari'a also in 1993, with a second edition (identical, as far as I can tell) in 2001.[34] Qaradawi has finally written on legal theory and concluded that the 'objectives of the Shari'a' is the path for today. Let me explain.

The first chapter after the introduction compares the Shari'a to the 'previous laws,' both religious jurisprudence and secular law; the second chapter presents the two 'sources,' Qur'an and Sunna, while mentioning that there are other sources besides the two everyone had agreed upon in the past – consensus (*ijmā'*) and analogy (*qiyās*). But he only lists them in one sentence: *istiṣlāḥ* (human welfare, synonym of *maṣlaha*), *istiḥsān* (legal equity, or preferrential choice), *istiṣḥāb* (presumption of continuity), '*urf* (local custom), previous legal systems, opinion of the Companions, etc. There is no space to go into the details in such an introductory work, he says. So the next chapter is entitled, '*al-Maqāṣid al-ʿāmma li-l-sharīʿa*' (The General Objectives of the Shari'a).

In a nutshell, he argues that all past scholars and jurists agreed that all the ordinances of the sacred texts 'safeguard the welfare (*maṣlaha*) of those responsible to obey the law, protect them from harm and fulfill the utmost good in their lives.'[35] He then launches into how Ghazali (d. 1111) classified the three levels of *maṣlaha* and how Shatibi interpreted his thought more systematically. The next section covers the old refrain from the pen of Rashid Rida: 'The ease of *maṣlaha* and its comprehensiveness with regard to God's law.' Building on that, his next chapter reads, 'Remarks about the Shari'a's Objectives.' There he explains the five areas God's law seeks to protect (life, religion, mind, progeny, and possessions), how this perspective builds a better society; and how it enhances the values that are necessary for it to thrive – and above all, justice.

Qaradawi notes some reservations as well. *Maṣlaha* can easily be abused and therefore considerations of human benefit can never trump a clear text (*naṣ qaṭʿī*). But this is a short section, which leads into 'the necessity of knowing the objectives for those who study the Shari'a.' Chapter six again brings Rida to mind: 'Factors of ease and flexibility in the Shari'a.'[36] The 'purposes of Shari'a' are certainly present in this introductory work to Islamic law, but they are not central. Thirteen years later, Qaradawi wrote his monograph dedicated to the issue, *A Study of the Shari'a's Purposes*. I now come back to this book and examine it in more detail, as I try to determine whether this new twist in Qaradawi's discourse actually adds anything new to his legal opinions.

Do the 'Purposes' Change Anything in Qaradawi's Jurisprudence?

To begin with, apart from some window dressing, this 2006 book, *A Study in the Jurisprudence of the Shari'a's Purposes* offers little that Qaradawi has not written before. It is organized around a familiar theme: promoting the *wasaṭiyya* school of Islamic jurisprudence, and thus positioning it smack in the middle of the other two extremes – the strict textualists and the loose liberals, who out of love for the West find no problem in leaving the sacred text behind. This sets the stage for the 'Middle School,' which avoids the weaknesses of the other two, while building on their respective strengths.

The whole book, then, is about showcasing the balance and wisdom of the middle school (*al-madrassa al-wasaṭiyya*) and, unsurprisingly, it is evenly divided into three parts. Qaradawi first visits the 'School of the New Zahiriyya.' The Zahiriyya[37] was a short-lived school of Islamic law founded by Ibn Hazm (d. 1064), who according to Qaradawi may have been a genius, but was led astray by his literalist approach. The literalists today are the Salafis (although his only explicit reference to them is in a footnote),[38] who, like the Zahiriyya of old, stick to the letter of the text while refusing to look 'behind it' to the wisdom of God connected to his wider purposes for humankind.

The second third of the book is devoted to the School of the *Mu'aṭṭila al-judud* ('the New Deniers') – those who in their zeal to copy and ingest everything Western use *maṣlaḥa* as a cover to cancel out the clear texts of the Qur'an and Sunna. Mohammed Arkoun and the 'American' Amina Wadud are the only ones mentioned by name.[39] These Muslims, he intones, literally worship everything coming from the West, and it is their secular-ist assumptions that cause them to pick and choose what suits them from the sacred texts.

So the third school is the one which at the same time takes the texts seriously and, following Shatibi's inductive method, discerns the divine wisdom behind the shari'a as a whole. Against the first school, then, he maintains that slavish attention to rules misses the spirit of the law, which can only be discerned through the ethical values brought to light by the Shari'a's purposes – and above all the notion of human benefit (*maṣlaḥa*). This means that the protection of the five domains act as a rational scale against which the jurist can evaluate possible courses of action.

By contrast, followers of the New Zahiriyya (the Salafis, from now on) are rigid and fanatical, and their literalism leads them to ridiculous posi-tions – like saying that since there was no paper money in the Prophet's era, today's paper money is worthless and unfit to fulfill one's *zakat* duties.[40] How can the poor and destitute be helped if this is the case, asks Qaradawi?[41] Or consider their claim that Christians cannot be full citizens because they have to pay the poll tax as members of the 'protected minorities' (*ahl al-dhimma*). This is silly, retorts Qaradawi. If we were to apply these medieval rules literally, we would have to force them to wear different clothes so as to distinguish them from Muslims, as was the case in medieval times.[42]

So one might be tempted to say, 'if a strong dose of common sense is needed, then Qaradawi is coming down on the reason side of the reason-revelation dilemma.' Yes and no. Here's what he says to the 'new deniers',[43] the liberals who declare, for example, that the prescribed punishments in the Qur'an and Sunna (the five or six so-called *ḥudūd* penalties we discussed in the last chapter) are no longer applicable today.[44] Qaradawi considers these 'new deniers' to have in essence denied the divine origin of the texts by canceling out some of its specific injunctions. As he writes about them, he takes the role of an inquisitor, though stopping short of calling them infidels (*kuffār*): 'They deify themselves, they hand over God's right to legislate to his creatures by permitting that which is forbidden and by forbidding that which is permitted on the basis of their own whims and by cajoling their own demons. They want people to take them as lords in the place of God.'[45]

These scholars – like those we examined in the last chapter – are a new phenomenon, opines Qaradawi, mostly coming out of France.[46] They claim to know the Qur'an, but ignore the Sunna of the Prophet and the pooled knowledge of Qur'anic commentary and jurisprudence of the classical scholars. They have their own way of dealing with 'the specific objectives and the shari'a in general.' Their leader is the famous Sorbonne scholar, Mohammed Arkoun (d. 2010), who considers the 'objectives of the shari'a' approach as a mere tactic to get beyond the impasse of rigid interpretations of medieval Islamic law, and which will never succeed. The 'insurmountable obstacle' they are trying to overcome by their recourse to this tactic, he believes, is 'the gaping distance between the Qur'an and the Shari'a.' For Arkoun (from Qaradawi's perspective), 'Shari'a' simply denotes the Qur'an and 'what their minds have invented in the way of *uṣūl* (legal theory) and *aḥkām* (the specific rulings in the sacred texts) at the same time, without discernment.'[47] He and others of his ilk have no place for the Prophet or his Sunna,[48] or the great commentators of the Qur'an, or for the classical jurisprudence of Islam as a whole. In other words,

This Muslim branch, cut off from its umma and from its heritage, is so proud of itself that its vision of reality is completely blurred. These people look with derision and contempt at our heritage and our imams, while at the same time reserving great respect – to the point of making it holy – the West and its culture.[49]

In his chapter on 'The Central Tenets of the School of the Deniers of the Texts,' Qaradawi explains that the great mistake these scholars make is to elevate reason over revelation. It is true, he admits, that God created humanity with the capacity to reason, and therefore to develop science and technology. But from there to come to God's text and say that this or that ruling goes against human welfare (*maṣlaḥa*) – that is to go down a dangerous path. For them, when the Qur'an states that God wants to remove hardship from the lives of the believers, that means they can pick and choose whatever seems best to them. But that's not what God meant, protests Qaradawi. His Word forbids many things people once took for granted, whether it was killing baby girls or depriving women of property in the Prophet's day, or sexual immorality, drugs and alcohol today. We have also seen how both capitalism and communism have led people into terrible predicaments. All said, concludes Qaradawi, the human mind needs the aid of revelation to enlighten and guide it.[50]

Now we are in a better position to answer the question of whether Qaradawi's turn to the purposive jurisprudence changed any of his views. I contend that it did not. There is here no modification of his basic stance as promoter of the middle path; it did, however, give him more ammunition against the literalists and more flexibility in the sociopolitical realm. Perhaps the main reason for the incremental changes came less from his legal methodology than from the fact that, as a result of his personal investment in European Islam from the 1980s on, he was feeling pressure to reconsider Islamic law from a very different perspective and hence, propose solutions that contravene traditional *fiqh*.[51] Let's follow his argument in the third chapter covering the third school, 'Central Tenets of the Moderate School' (*al-madrasa al-wasaṭiyya*).[52]

Qaradawi offers five main headings, which I will simply list here to give the reader an idea of the relative sophistication of his hermeneutical (methodology of interpretation) framework:

1. 'Finding out the purpose before issuing a ruling'
2. 'Understanding a text in the light of its reasons and its context'

3. 'Discerning between the permanent objective and the changing means – declaring a shari'a objective without setting a means for reaching it'
4. 'The rightful relationship between the fixed and the changeable'
5. 'Discernment of the differences of meaning between matters of worship and matters of human relationships'

Under the first heading, right from the start, Qaradawi addresses himself to all *mujtahids*. These are the '*ulamā*', the professional jurists who after many years of training in a wide spectrum of Islamic sciences have reached the desirable level of expertise allowing them to issue rulings on new issues that arise (*ijtihād*, from which the word *mujtahid* comes from). The clear subtext here is, 'move over lay people, let the '*ulamā*' take their rightful place!'

So practically speaking, what difference does knowing the purpose or objective of a textual injunction make in a jurist's issuing of a particular ruling? Above all, he must discern on which of the three levels of human benefit his judgment belongs. He must ask himself, 'is this case related to the top level of the five necessities, or that of general needs, or simply that of making life more comfortable and removing unnecessary hardships?' Take the example of wearing beards for men. Authentic hadiths clearly say it is not necessary. Shall we make it an obligation then? Qaradawi then produces three hadiths that plainly command Muslims to wear their hair and beards differently from the Zoroastrians, Christians and Jews – and to dress differently too. The *'illa* (*ratio legis*, or reason behind the injunction) is obvious: by copying others in your outward appearance you might be tempted to follow their customs and beliefs as well. This was a necessary teaching in the early years of the faith, he says, as Muslims now propelled into new territories through conquest suddenly found themselves living among people of other faiths. At what level do we place this command? The necessary, needful or embellishment of life? Clearly, he concludes, it's on the the latter level. It has to do with a complementary command (*takmīlī*), not a foundational one.[53]

The wider issue is how Muslims are supposed to live in a religiously pluralistic society – very much the situation today, and especially for Muslims in Europe. Qaradawi goes to the heart of the matter: 'We also don't see the classical jurists blaming Muslims for dropping markers of difference between them and non-Muslims when there was a need for them to mix with people, so as to influence them and by all means call them to Islam.'[54] This is the case among Muslim minorities living in the west. Why should they be forced to create more discomfort for themselves and even animosity between them and the general population, when in fact they want to have a positive impact on their neighbors?

In fact, Muslims in the West should do their utmost to mix in with the Europeans and not live in ghettos. Nor should they exaggerate differences of dress or appearance. Above all, they should emphasize any common ground and build on it. This early 'differentiation from non-Muslims' was never a pillar of faith (*rukn al-dīn*). In our day, it is a 'necessity' for Muslims to cultivate a friendly relationship with people of other faiths 'so as to communicate the message of Islam by word and deed ... and to bring them closer to those who oppose their faith and yet are fellow citizens. The emphasis on distinction more often than not creates an obstacle between them and their compatriots.'[55]

Still, Qaradawi cautions his readers, when it comes to mandatory issues like women wearing the hijab, women in France should still wear it, no matter what the pressures against them might be. But, according to his fatwa on this matter, the *niqāb* (full face veil) would be an unnecessary exaggeration, and even a provocation.[56]

The Purposive Fiqh, Qaradawi's Legacy, and Justice

In the end, Qaradawi remains a traditionalist, a conservative, and yes, mainstream Muslim jurist. All the clear indications of the texts (*nuṣūṣ qāṭiʿa*) must be followed to the letter, whether the five 'penalties' (*ḥudūd*), like amputating the hands of thieves, or the rules of inheritance or divorce in the Qur'an, or the ban on charging interest on loans.[57] These rulings are unchangeable, non-negotiable. They represent the 'closed circle,' which also includes all the creeds, the five pillars of the faith, all the required virtues and ethical values, and all the prohibitions, like 'false accusations against chaste women believers,' 'rebellion against one's parents', abortion, assault on people's privacy, and much more.[58] True, the circle of the unchangeables is very small; still, it plays an important role in the life of Muslims by pointing 'to the umma's identity, its self-consciousness, and its distinction.'

By contrast, Qaradawi hastens to add, when it comes to the socioeconomic and political realm, there is great latitude. This is the vast space, I would argue, in which we do see Qaradawi affected by modern rationalistic thought. This is quite different from the rituals of worship and all the fixed rules of the sacred texts (the close circle) where we posit by faith that behind each one stands God's wisdom and commitment to human well-being. When it comes to politics, however, we must work for the common good of all people because the values of justice and human dignity are ingrained in all humankind. In his own words:

> There is more to human benefit (*maṣlaḥa*) than the protection of religion, life, mind, family and property. You have to add freedom, equality, fraternity, solidarity, and human rights. These are the building blocks of society, the umma and the state. It seems to me that the classical usulis were focused on the individual welfare of the responsible person ... They did not have the same level of concern for society, the umma, the nation, and international relations.[59]

Yet on the issue of the relative balance between human reasoning and the injunctions of the sacred texts, Qaradawi cannot be consistent – nor could Rashid Rida a century ago.[60] On the one hand, he wants a divine law that is responsive to changing conditions; on the other, since it is 'divine,' he doesn't want it to be the product of human ingenuity and effort. And so there's a whole area that is roped off and declared impermeable to human reason and values. Still, Qaradawi believes that goodness, justice and compassion are objective values and that people can access these outside of the revealed texts. His immediate endorsement of the Arab Spring as a leading jurist only reinforces this point.

In the end, it may be that Qaradawi has opened a door that he as an alim cannot go through, purposive jurisprudence notwithstanding. But just maybe a new generation will say, for instance, that everything in the texts outside of the rituals of worship is historically conditioned, and therefore subject to change as sociopolitical conditions change. Maybe then the traditional jurists, the 'ulamā', will have worked themselves out of a job. At the very least, considering the proliferation of opinions on the Internet and the growing influence of Muslim intellectuals without classical legal training, his campaign to rehabilitate the traditionally central role of the 'ulamā' is not likely to succeed.

Nevertheless, in February 2011 in Tahrir Square, Qaradawi spoke with the conviction of an alim who was bringing the central value of the God's law – justice – to bear on the sociopolitical realm. What could be more exhilerating than to address a crowd of young compatriots, both Muslims and Christian, that had been instrumental in overthrowing a dictator? Qaradawi took his role seriously before boarding his plane back to Qatar. He knew that part of the injustice of Egypt's politics is the ruling elite and the army's unwillingness to invest in infrastructure, public education, a fairer tax code, and the like – all of which would address the poverty and helplessness of the overwhelming majority of Egypt's population. In his sermon he says, 'I know that the children of Egypt have suffered a lot of injustice. Various groups of workers, peasants and employees, how long they have suffered injustice!'

Qaradawi also knew that many factories had been on strike in the wake of the revolution. His fatherly advice to the workers is to be patient, to get back to work and trust the new leaders (and the army, in the meantime) to get the country back on track:

> Surely, it is the right of all these Egyptians that they get their rights, that they obtain that which they deserve and that they be treated equitably, but it is also our duty to be patient with our brothers in the army, so that all hopes be achieved, one after the other. "And say to them: 'Act!' God will see your action, and so will His Messenger and the believers, and you will be brought back to the Knower of the invisible and the visible, and He will inform you about what you used to do" (Q. 9:105). Pray to God Most High and He will hear your prayer.

It may be that Jamal al-Banna, Mohammed Hashim Kamali, and Tariq Ramadan, would have agreed with him that day. But they likely would be less comfortable with his 'middle path.' Certainly Ramadan has had little sympathy for the Muslim Brotherhood's Freedom and Justice Party that fielded its candidate, Mohamed Morsi, who won the presidential election the next year.[61] But from the beginning Ramadan was wary about the so-called 'revolution.' Hence, his book on the 'Arab Awakening.' As a result, he refused to visit Egypt. After the military coup of July 2013, he wrote:

> I never shared the widespread "revolutionary" fervor. Nor did I believe the events in Egypt, any more than in Tunisia, were the result of a sudden historical upheaval. The peoples of these two countries suffered from dictatorship, from economic and social crisis; they rose up in the name of dignity, social justice and freedom …

> The Egyptian army has not returned to politics for the simple reason that it has never left. The fall of Hosni Mubarak was a military coup d'État that allowed a new generation of officers to enter the political scene in a new way, from behind the curtain of a civilian government …. The American administration has monitored the entire process: its objective ally in Egypt over the past fifty years has been the army, not the Muslim Brotherhood.[62]

Understandably, he had no patience with the US government, after the forcible removal of the democratically elected Egyptian president, which refused to call it by its name – a coup d'État. But beyond all the historical details that may be interpreted in various ways lies the very different approaches of Qaradawi and Ramadan. Part of it is politics. Qaradawi's allegiance, at least in terms of sympathies, with the Muslim Brotherhood is also aligned with the politics of his adopted home, Qatar. Saudi Arabia, together with the United Arab Emirates (UAE), bristled in October 2012 when the emir of Qatar, Sheik Hamad bin Khalifa al-Thani, visited Hamas in Gaza and pledged $400 million for various development projects.[63] Ramadan has a more European perspective, if a critical one.

What is most notable here is the difference in understanding how Islamic law is to be interpreted and implemented in the sociopolitical sphere. Even though both hold to an objective value for justice and other ethical norms, Qaradawi is bound to a literal understanding of the texts, which becomes most obvious when he writes about the *ḥudūd* penalties as non-negotiables. Ramadan, you will recall, wanted a moratorium for their implementation, and, reading between the lines, it seems that the temporary suspension he spoke of was only a tactic calculated to provoke enough discussion susceptible in the long run to spur Muslim jurists to conclude that those rules in the text are context- and time-bound.[64]

What is more, Qaradawi still prefers an 'Islamic state' in which Shari'a as interpreted and negotiated by the ulama takes pride of place. Ramadan was never comfortable with that position. In fact for him, the *'ulamā'* should listen to 'context scholars' and learn to read the signs of the times and discern the ethical implications of new scientific discoveries and evolving cultural norms.

Perhaps not surprisingly, Qaradawi never signed the 'Common Word' document, while Tariq Ramadan did sign it.[65] At the risk of speculating, it may well be that his conservative mindset found the idea that love of God and love of neighbor are at the heart of Islam a dangerous innovation. Still, knowing the influence he's had on the Qatari royal family over the decades, I would like to think that he was partly responsible for the relative freedom the foreign Christian community in Qatar (9.6% of the total population, nearly all guest workers) has enjoyed. Six Christian denominations are officially recognized and an important number of churches have been built or have gained permission for construction.[66] Even just for the Coptic Church in Egypt that is a very sore topic. Despite the official promises in 2013, practically none of the churches destroyed or damaged that year have been rebuilt.

As mentioned earlier, Qaradawi served for years as the president of the European Council for Fatwa and Research. Mouez Khalfaoui, professor and chair of Islamic law at the Eberhard Karls University of Tübingen, Germany, tackles Qaradawi's use of the purposive fiqh to establish an Islamic jurisprudence for Muslim minorities (*fiqh al-aqalliyāt*) in his 2001 book on this topic.[67] Here is a useful summary of Qaradawi's thesis:

> Qaradawi's approach toward questions of Muslim minorities is based on the notion of common good (*maṣlaḥa*), which he uses as a synonym for *maqāṣid*. Within this framework, Qaradawi refers to several key concepts when formulating his stance on Muslim minority law, such as "the flexibility of fiqh," "fatwas change with time and circumstance," and "the priority of living context vis-à-vis the Islamic texts." These norms, Qaradawi argues, should constitute the theoretical and methodological framework for *fatāwa* in the field of Muslim minority law.[68]

Iraqi-American scholar Taha Jabir al-Alwani (d. 2016), founder of the Fiqh Council of North America, has also written on this topic.[69] Khalfaoui contends that both Qaradawi's and al-Alwani's discourse on these issues are still tangled up, perhaps even unconsciously, in the classical distinction between the Abode of Islam and the Abode of War (*dār al-islām, dār al-ḥarb*). This means that they are making a moral differentiation between Muslim and non-Muslim territories. Put otherwise, they oppose a Muslim 'self' to a non-Muslim 'other.' They and other scholars working in this field, though shunning that traditional dualism, still end up assuming this 'premodern doctrine,' mostly by portraying a 'Muslim world' as harmonious, where Islamic law is practiced. And despite many positive values found in non-Muslim polities, including democracy and religious freedom, these scholars assume 'that living in non-Muslim environments will automatically lead to violations of Islamic norms' and that the best option for any Muslim is to move out and settle in a Muslim nation.

At least two objections can be made here, retorts Khalfaoui. First, because of globalization the problems faced by people everywhere are more similar than different. For example, 'factory workers in Muslim states and the West are equally debating the issues of praying during working hours; likewise, Muslim women in both non-Muslim and Muslim contexts are challenged by combining their role as housewives and working mums.'[70] Second, as societies are changing everywhere due to both local and global pressures, Muslim jurists, whether in Muslim or non-Muslim nations, will have to make more of an effort to study these changes and adapt their rulings accordingly.

Finally, in a day when Muslims are constantly in contact with other communities, 'it seems that the justification of a minority law has lost its validity, if it ever had any ... Accordingly, the Islamic minorities law would change into a general minorities law, applicable to minorities of different religious affiliations across the globe.'[71] But it is precisely the *maqāṣidi fiqh* that put these scholars in this dilemma – calling for 'an Islamic solution' and the drating of a 'sectarian law' to address human problems common to all. It is a dilemma also because demanding an application of Islamic law in Western contexts is more likely to accentuate differences between Islamic and secular law, which only increases the Islamophobia already present. How is this serving justice, we might ask? Khalfaoui suggests that Muslims cooperate with other minorities like the Jews, for instance, as they have in Europe and achieved remarkable results in the area of male circumcision 'and the private slaughter of animals during religious festivities.'[72]

There is perhaps a darker side to the *maqāṣidi* approach to Islamic law, notes Anver Emon in his Epilogue to the volume *The Objectives of Islamic Law*.[73] As evidenced in Kamali's opening chapter and others in the first half of the book dedicated to the proponents of this purposive jurisprudence, hope is the catchword and neatly captures the ethos of those who see the *maqāṣid al-sharīʿa* as the key to escaping from some of the confines of the classical *uṣūl al-fiqh* method. But if one looks at who is using this method and in what political circumstances, one might see it differently, and particularly from the perspective of 'the disenfranchized, the marginal, and the vulnerable of society.'[74] This is about a definition of justice, claims Emon. With their focus on 'technique and method,' the authors promoting it 'both avoid the history of *maqāṣid's* failures and police Muslims into a state of orthodox compliance by reference to a method that those with access to education claim to know and represent.' He then adds, 'Policing, in this fashion, is very much an enterprise of defining Islam or Islamic law from the top-down.'[75] This elite discourse more often than not ignores the voices of a wide variety of people and social groups on the margins, as highlighted by anthropologists of Islam Charles Hirshkind and Noah Solomon.[76]

Justice, after all, is about the rights of the most vulnerable. If the law does not protect those most at risk and the state does not enforce those laws properly – justly, then injustice prevails. Our case studies in this book amply demonstrate that this kind of injustice is found everywhere. Certainly it is minimized where civil society is allowed to protest and participate in the political process. That is why one has to point out the irony of Qaradawi praising a people's revolution that has toppled a dictator and exhorting leaders to allow trade unions to defend their workers when at home in Qatar (and the Gulf generally), the vast majority of the population is composed of foreign laborers not allowed to become citizens and often no better off than indentured servants.[77] True, in Europe Muslim migrants often live precarious lives economically and socially, with a lot of prejudice directed at them. But as Emon remarks, 'In the Gulf, these laborers come from India, Pakistan, Bangladesh, and the Philippines, and work in conditions where they have few rights (political, civil and otherwise) and limited mobility.'[78]

We began this chapter with the daily struggles experienced by Egyptian Christians and we heard Qaradawi strongly affirm their rights as citizens alongside the Muslim majority. Yet justice is so easily stymied, whether by discriminatory laws, or by the state's unwillingness to enforce laws protecting minorities, or by investigating and prosecuting acts of violence against them. But justice also makes a moral claim on individuals and civil society groups to work for the harmony and common good of all citizens. This is where the love equation comes into sharper focus.

In the next two chapters I turn more specifically to the theological perspective on God's love and mercy, and on how he enjoins that love in our lives as creatures. In Chapter 6, I examine the work of Prince Ghazi of Jordan, the author of that 'Common Word' letter, who thereby opened some fresh avenues for Muslim-Christian dialogue. I then return to Wolterstorff in the last chapter and in the conclusion I attempt to better unite the two strands, justice and love.

Endnotes

1   'Yerkes 2016.

2   El-Sayed Gamal El-Din, 'Egyptian writer Fatima Naoot sentenced to 3 years in jail for "contempt of religion,"' *Ahramonline*, http://english.ahram.org.eg/NewsContent/1/64/185963/Egypt/Politics-/Egyptian-writer-Fatima-Naoot-sentenced-to--years-i.aspx, accessed December 19, 2019.

3   Yerkes 2016, She mentions two other downsides to this unity rhetoric. First, 'he does not see Copts as a minority in need of protection and is therefore not willing to extend the necessary measures to proactively protect against or respond to attacks.' And second, Egypt bans the right of surveyors to ask a participant's religion during their research. This prevents policy makers from truly dealing with minority problems.

4   Qaradawi 2011.

5   Kirkpatrick 2011.

6   BBC 2004a. This article simply states the US ban on Qaradawi, though without giving reasons for it.

7   BBC 2004b.

8   https://en.wikipedia.org/wiki/Yusuf_al-Qaradawi#Controversy accessed July 21, 2018. That article mentions several other areas in which Qaradawi has made controversial remarks. A November 2018 article on the Jerusalem Center for Public Affairs website tells of Qaradawi's retirement from the leadership of the International Union of Muslim Scholars, which he founded in 2004: Yoni Ben Menachem, 'Muslim Brotherhood Religious Authority Resigns' (http://jcpa.org/muslim-brotherhood-religious-authority-resigns/). What is interesting in this substantial article is the tone. He is called 'extreme and supportive of Islamic terror,' and he is said to have called Osama bin Laden his disciple and a member of the Muslim Brotherhood.' What is not said, however, is that Qaradawi issued a fatwa condemning the 9/11 attacks and permitting Muslims to fight along with the Americans to root out al-Qaeda from Afghanistan.

9   See Feldman 2007, 104–119.

10   The first book on Qaradawi in English is recent: *Global Mufti: The Phenomenon of Yusuf al-Qaradawi*, see Gräf and Skovgaard-Petersen 2009. Qaradawi's output is not as vast as it seems, however. Having read or scanned a couple dozen of his books so far, I have noticed how often he repeats himself. Nor is his thinking particularly original, as I will argue here.

11   Gräf and Skovgaard-Petersen 2009, 2–3, see 'Introduction.'

12   Gräf and Skovgaard-Petersen 2009, 2–3, see 'Introduction,' 3.

13   See Tammam's 2009.

14   Qaradawi 2012.

15   An excellent study of the Salafi movements worldwide is *Global Salafism: Islam's New Religious Movement*, see Meijer 2009.

16   For more details on this, see Johnston 2014b.

17   By way of reminder, there is a heated debate today, both among scholars and Muslims more generally, about the exact meaning of the word Shari'a. To simplify, allow me to state that the majority view (and ascending one as well), is that Shari'a is God's ideal will for this world, partly revealed in the Qur'an and Sunna, and that *fiqh* is the human attempt to discover this divine will for particular places and particular times. Thus *fiqh* comes to represent the volumes of jurisprudence produced over the ages by the five extant schools of Islamic law, and because this body of knowledge's contextual nature by definition, it is a fallible human product that will need to be updated and improved upon with each succeeding generation of Muslims. So Shari'a and *fiqh* are not the same thing.

18   Hallaq 1999, 213–231. See also Opwis 2007 and Johnston 2007b.

19   In contemporary Islamic jurisprudence the traditional two-tiered characterization of *uṣūl* as 'sources' of the law (Qur'an, Sunna, *qiyās* and *ijmā'*) and its evidences, or proofs (*adilla*), like abrogation, *istiṣlāḥ*, *istiṣḥāb*, etc., no longer applies, as both terms are now used almost interchangeably (cf, Johnston 2004).

20   Qaradawi 2006, 12. The same quote from Ibn Qayyim appears again on p. 78.

21   Of late much attention has been paid to Shatibi. See Masud 1989; Hallaq 1997, Chapter 5, 162–206; I have located over 20 books in Arabic on Shatibi written in the

last two decades in our library of the University of Pennsylvania alone, including some new editions of books from the early twentieth century.

22 Rida 1984.

23 Recall Qaradawi's Friday Sermon at the start of this chapter: 'The youth who have triumphed in this revolution ... triumphed over Mubarak, they triumphed over injustice, they triumphed over falsehood.' Qaradawi's books were aimed at the youth whenever possible. In a sense, he has been a popularizer of Islamic law.

24 Rida 1984, 10.

25 A prolific author, he is another longstanding member of the Muslim Brotherhood movement, though certainly considered to be on the moderate side.

26 Qaradawi 2006. The same quote from Ibn Qayyim appears again on p. 78. The Maqasid Centre is a project of the Al-Furqan Islamic Heritage Foundation. Both are led by Sheikh Ahmad Zaki Yamani. For more information on this center, see 'The Chairman's Introduction' at http://www.al-furqan.com/en/al-furqan-foundation/al-maqasid/chairmans-introduction

27 Zaqzuq 2010. Vol. 1. Cairo: *Al-Majlis al-A'lā li-l-Shu'ūn al-Islāmiyya, Wizārat al-Awqāf, Jumhūriyyat Misr al-'Arabiyya* [The Supreme Council of Islamic Affairs, Ministry of al-Awqāf, The Arab Republic of Egypt]. Under the Supervion of the President Muhammad Hosni Mubarak.

28 Then, as I mentioned in the previous chapter, the movement has grown so much that it now has generated some pointed criticism, as seen in Rumee, Nassery and Tatari (2018).

29 Zakat is one of Islam's Five Pillars, that is, its ritual foundation. Zakat is the yearly obligation for Muslims to give 2.25 percent of their net worth to charitable causes.

30 *Uṣūl al-fiqh*, literally, 'the foundations of jurisprudence,' became a legal genre to which Muslim jurists contributed regularly from the fourth century onwards.

31 Qaradawi 1977.

32 For more details, see Betina Gräf, 'The Concept of *wasaṭiyya* in the Work of Yusuf al-Qaradawi,' in Gräf and Skovgaard-Petersen 2009, 213–238.

33 Qaradawi 1979, 1993, 2002. See below at footnote 36.

34 *Madkhal li-dirāsat al-sharī'a al-islāmiyya*, Qaradawi's 1993 edition was published in Beirut by MuŒassat al-Risāla, whereas Qaradawi came back to his usual publisher in Cairo for the 2002 edition, Maktabat Wahba.

35 Qaradawi 1993, 53.

36 The next edition of *Madkhal li-dirāsat al-sharī'a al-islāmiyya* which appeared eight years later, in 2001, is about 60 pages longer. No new chapters are added, and as far as I could tell, no new material was added. The difference in length is only due to a difference in typesetting.

37 It was known for its determination to root out any human reasoning in finding God's law, including the use of analogy (*qiyās*), accepted by the other schools as one of the four main 'sources' (*uṣūl*) of the law. Here, by branding the Salafis 'the new Zahiris,' Qaradawi achieves two objectives: 1) he sticks on them a pejorative label; 2) he also puts them on the defensive by saying that their theology rules out any consideration of God's wisdom or purposes behind his Shari'a being accessible to humankind.

38　'Like many of those preachers (*du'āt*) from the Salafi tendency, which now has many branches; their opponents include the 'Ahbash' (45). The Ahbash (lit. 'the Ethiopians') are an international movement of reformist Islam founded by an Ethiopian Shaykh Abdalla b. Muhammad b. Yusuf al-Harari from the town of Harar, who settled in Lebanon in the 1960s. For more information on the little known rivalry and polemics between the Salafi-Wahhabis and the Ahbash, see Kabha and Erlich 2006: 519–538.

39　Arkoun (d. 2010), originally from a Berber village in Algeria, taught as a professor of Islamic Studies for many years at the Sorbonne in Paris. Amina Wadud, an American academic, is best known for the controversy she stirred up by leading the Friday prayers in New York City in 2005. Her feminist books have been controversial for most Muslims as well.

40　This is the prescribed almsgiving in Islam and one of its five pillars.

41　Qaradawi 2006, 67.

42　Qaradawi 2006, 46. The most extreme example of Qaradawi's use of ridicule is when he brings up Ibn Hazm's commentary on the following hadith: 'Let no one urinate in stagnant water and then use it to wash himself.' A parallel version reads, 'and use it for his ablutions.' Ibn Hazm simply follows this literally, but without taking into consideration that it was the presence of urine in the water that was the issue. So he writes that one cannot perform the partial ablutions (*wuḍū'*) with it; still, it is fine to use it for the full ablution, for him or anyone else. It is also permissible for someone else to perform either *wuḍū'* with that water, or even drinking it, for that matter! Ibn Hazm, explains Qaradawi, refuses to weigh the differences between all these acts, but gets stuck with the letter of the hadith – no partial ablution with the water into which you have urinated. Let's say that someone urinated in water that subsequently flows into this body of stagnant water – for Ibn Hazm, that water is pure! How extraordinarily literalistic can one be! No wonder the majority of jurists distanced themselves from the Zahiriyya, exclaims Qaradawi!

43　From the mainstream Sunni perspective (which adopted Ash'arite theology around the tenth century), to deny (or 'suspend') God's attributes, a move made by the Mu'tazilites, is heresy. The Mu'tazilites emphasized God's unity to the extent that God's attributes (like seeing, hearing, knowing, etc.) seemed to be entities on their own and thereby threatening God's eternal unitary essence. Qaradawi uses this pejorative word in a different sense: whereas the early *Mu'aṭṭila* canceled out God's attributes, these people cancel out any part of the sacred texts that offends their sensibilities – something far worse! Naturally, the negative connotation of the word ('those heretics!') suits his purpose nicely.

44　They are usually listed as six, with their corresponding penalties: theft (amputation of the hand); highway robbery (death by sword, crucifixion, or stoning); illicit sexual intercourse (flogging for unmarried partners or non-Muslims; stoning for married partners); false accusation of sexual immorality (flogging); drinking alcohol (flogging); apostasy (death by sword). That said, classical jurisprudence in all five schools of law set up stringent standards of evidence in court for these to be implemented.

45 Qaradawi 2006, 87.

46 Significantly, he never mentions Tariq Ramadan. From what I have been able to gather, they remain on good terms – which, after his 2008 book, *Radical Reform*, seems amazing to me.

47 Qaradawi 2006, 87. He quotes Arkoun, who calls the *maqāṣidī* method 'the great deception which enables the spreading of the great illusion that makes every law they invent holy' (87). For them, 'renewal' simply means leaving behind the rulings of shari'a. He is quoting from an Arabic translation of the French original (Arkoun 1984).

48 They don't recognize the Sunna as a source of Islamic law, he adds, and for them 'Muhammad is not a prophet free from error (*maḥsūm*) in his reception of his Lord's message, as all Muslims believe. He is merely an Arab personality who did his best in his own time and place, in his own environment; he was right and he was wrong' (Qaradawi 2006, 89).

49 Qaradawi 2006, 88.

50 Qaradawi 2006, 101. He adds a footnote here, encouraging his readers to consult Muhammad Abduh's *Risālat al-tawḥīd* ('Discourse on Divine Unity'), his magnum opus which was first published in 1897.

51 Alexandre Caeiro and Mahmoud al-Saify contributed a chapter to *Global Mufti* on this very issue ('Qaradawi in Europe, Europe in Qaradawi? The Global Mufti's European Politics,' 2009, 109–48). There is no doubt that Qaradawi, whose stature as leader of the global Islamic Awakening (*al-ṣaḥwa al-islāmiyya*) was already established by then, also led the way in seeing the strategic importance of Muslims in the West. As Caeiro and al-Saify noted, 'It speaks of a shift in the political imagination of the umma whereby European Muslims, from the geographical periphery, seem to acquire a new religious centrality' (2009, 111).

52 This is by far the longest chapter (60 pages, 155–214) and the heart of Qaradawi's thesis. I can only delve into one small part of it in the space I have here.

53 Qaradawi 2006, 158. Qaradawi continues in this vein: several of the companions dyed their hair in old age. The obvious conclusion, Qaradawi opines, is that this was only a recommendation (*nadb*). Here's the corresponding maxim of the jurists: 'dislike (*karāha*) disappears with the slightest need (second category of *maslaḥa*)' – as it the case with a preference (*istiṣḥāb*). Even from the various hadiths narrated by Abu Amama we can see that sometimes the Prophet wore trousers and a shawl and at other times he did not (159). Muslims haven't been wearing those for centuries! 'But we don't see any of the umma's scholars blaming anyone for neglecting to wear the *izār* (shawl).

54 Qaradawi 2006, 159.

55 Qaradawi 2006, 160.

56 Qaradawi 2006, 161. Yet he does show a good deal of flexibility as well, pointing out two rulings made by the European Council for Fatwa and Research that go against traditional *fiqh*: 1) allowing Muslims in Europe to take out mortgages from banks that charge interest; 2) permitting a European wife to stay with her non-Muslim husband after she has embraced Islam. Classical Islamic law (*fiqh*) forbids a Muslim woman from marrying a non-Muslim man.

57 See for example on p. 123. Since these are unambiguous texts, they are meant to
    be obeyed for all times and places. Apparently, for him this applies to the Qur'an,
    though not quite so much to the Sunna, as was seen above.

58 Qaradawi 2006, 198.

59 Qaradawi 2006, 28.

60 As a Christian theologian, I would add that the 'proper' balance between reason
    and revelation bedevils all theologians of the monotheistic faiths. You can easily
    find evidence of Qaradawi's three schools among Jews and Christians too, and this
    in spite of Christian protests that there is no 'law' to be found in Christianity. In
    the end, it's still about how one is to read the sacred texts.

61 On the one hand, Ramadan argues, 'President Morsi cannot be fairly criticized
    for not doing all he could to establish relations with the opposition ... But his
    approaches were rejected out of hand, with the opposition bitterly opposing his
    every initiative.' Then on the other hand, 'The fact remains, however, that his
    management of the business of the state, his failure to listen to the voice of the
    people and even to some of his trusted advisors, his exclusivist relationship with
    the highest echelon of the MB leadership, his hasty and ill-considered decisions
    (some of which he later acknowledged as errors) must be unsparingly criticized.
    But on a more fundamental level, his greatest fault has been the utter absence of
    a political vision and the lack of clearly established political and economic pri-
    orities, his failure to struggle against corruption and poverty, and his egregious
    mismanagement of social and educational affairs' (Ramadan 2012).

62 Ramadan 2012.

63 Al Jazeera 2012. Five years later, Egypt joined Saudi Arabia and the UAE in block-
    ading and attempting to isolate Qatar, though at this writing there are signs that
    this is changing.

64 Qaradawi's views on apostasy are in line with the classical consensus (despite
    some exceptions) in Islamic jurisprudence on the death penalty for apostates.
    Furthermore, he distinguishes between hidden and open apostasy. A person keep-
    ing their own denial of the Muslim faith to themselves will only have God as their
    judge, but those who try to influence others in that direction should be given the
    chance to repent. But if they do not, then they should be killed. See Moosa 2012. A
    footnote in the Wikipedia article provides a short clip of an interview on Egyptian
    TV in 2013 in which he emphatically says that Islam's law of apostasy (*ridda*) is the
    death penalty, and that there would not be any Islam today were had that law not
    been applied in the past: https://www.youtube.com/watch?v=huMu8ihDlVA.

65 See the Introduction on this 2007 open letter to the pope and all Christian leaders.

66 See 'Christianity in Qatar,' Religious Literacy Project, Harvard Divinity School,
    online, https://rlp.hds.harvard.edu/faq/christianity-qatar.

67 *Fiqh al-aqalliyāt al-muslima* (Cairo: Dār al-Shurūq, 2001).

68 Khalfaoui 2018, 271–284, at 274–275.

69 See the translation of his original work in Arabic: *Towards a Fiqh for Minorities: Some
    Basic Refections*, trans. Ashur A. Shamis, 2nd ed., With an Introduction by Shaykh
    Zaki Badawi, Occasional Papers Series 18 (Herndon, VA and London: International
    Institute of Islamic Thought, 2010).

70 Khalfaoui 2018, 278.

71 Khalfaoui 2018, 281.

72 Khalfaoui 2018, 380.

73 Anver Emon and Rumee Ahmed are both Canadian scholars in their early 40s, already accomplished in their field. Emon is the Canada Research Chair in Religion, Pluralism, and the Rule of Law, and professor of Islamic law in the Faculty of Law at the University of Toronto. Ahmed is associate dean of arts and associate professor of Islamic law at the University of British Columbia.

74 Emon, Epilogue, Nassery and Tatari 2018, 285–96, at 290.

75 Emon, Epilogue, Nassery and Tatari 2018, 291.

76 Hirshkind 2009; Solomon 2016.

77 Qatar, to be fair, is the one Gulf nation that has made the most progress, but arguably because of outside pressure in light of its hosting the 2022 World Cup. See Amnesty International 2018.

78 Emon 2018, 293.

6

Justice and Love: Prince Ghazi and the Common Word

I begin this chapter with a case study about Christian-Muslim relations in Nigeria, which historian John N. Paden called 'a pivotal state in the Muslim World.'[1] Africa is dominated by three powers, he contends. Muslim Egypt in the north, the Christian south, and Nigeria, a major oil producer with by far the largest population (over 180 million as of 2016), and which also has the largest population of Christians and the largest population of Muslims on the continent simultaneously.

The case study concerns the decision made by 12 Northern states in 1999, the year the first democratic presidential election had taken place, to adopt Shari'a law. This development, at least in the beginning, caused no end of shrill condemnation by Nigerian Christians and the international media in general. Frieder Ludwig provides a useful summary of the issues and the violence that took place:

> Since most Nigerian Muslims tend to see the introduction of Shari'ah as the restitution of their rights which they had lost during the colonial period, while many Christians regard this measure as a step to Islamize Nigeria, there had been tensions and sometimes violent conflicts – as for instance in Kaduna (February 2000 and November 2002), in Bauchi (June 2001), in Jos (September 2001), and in Yelwa (February 2004).[2]

Although the issue of Shari'a was likely an important factor in this cycle of violence, there are many other layers to these tensions. One of the more violent incidents took place in Plateau State (Yelma, above), when in February 2004 78 Christians were killed and several churches were torched. Then in May, Christians took revenge, killing 660 Muslims (a number confirmed by Human Rights Watch). As a result of this massacre, somewhere between 40,000 and 60,000 people were internally displaced.[3] Note, however, that this was not one of the 'Shari'a states.'

Clearly this is not all about religion, at least in some of the more recent waves of killings. The original tribes of this so-called Middle Belt of Nigeria farm the land. Many Hausa-Fulanis from the north, traditional herders and nomads, have emigrated there in past decades and now complain about discrimination and the lack of many advantages enjoyed by the region's natives who are mostly Christian, along with numerous devotees of African traditional religions as well.[4] As Ludwig shows, these clashes 'expressed social tensions and ethnic conflicts.' In Kaduna, where some of the worst clashes related to the adoption of Shari'a law took place, 'there had been long-standing animosity between the ethnic groups of the Hausa and the largely Christianized Kajes and Katafs who had been integrated against their will into the Islamic region by the British.'[5] Further, in Jos, the capital of Plateau State, not one of the 12 states that implemented some form of Shari'a, Muslims originally from the south had to deal with threats both from recent Hausa settlers and from local Christians. Finally, when law and order breaks down, the vacuum draws in criminal elements. Then we see an older collegiality between Muslims and Christians coming to the fore:

> Christians and Muslims joined forces against troublemakers and plunderers. The Christian Association of Nigeria (CAN) called for investigations of the role of the police during the conflicts. At the same time talks also intensified between the representatives of religious communities. For example, the Catholic archbishop of Jos, Ignatius Ayan Kagama, invited all leaders of religious communities, Christians and Muslims, to joint consultations. Christian-Muslim talks were initiated in different parts of the city.[6]

Now that I have offered some general remarks about the tensions and at times violence between Muslim and Christian communities in Nigeria, I will focus on three aspects in order to tease out elements that will help us in our conclusion about justice and love as seen from both sides: the legacy of history, governance, and finally, reconciliation and ongoing cooperation between the two communities.[7]

In his book, *Religion and the Making of Nigeria*, Olufemi Vaughan contends that '[t]he critical foundation in the making of modern Nigeria was constructed on the convergence of two monumental world religious movements that transformed the Nigerian region, starting in the nineteenth century.'[8] Notice that for him colonialism is not the main force responsible for the shaping of modern Nigeria. It bears a large responsibility, as we shall see, but the two tectonic plates that began to rub against each other in the decades preceding the twentieth century are the most crucial element. The first was the expanding 'Islamic reformist movement' that gave birth to the Sokoto Caliphate among the Hausa tribes in Nigeria's North, and the second was 'a Christian evangelical missionary movement' that began transforming Nigeria's coastal Southwest region.[9] The British overpowered the Sokoto Caliphate only in 1903 and then proceded to give back to it a large measure of autonomy – 'indirect rule,' as it was called.

The friction between the two tectonic plates, which in their mutual interactions have underpinned the historical development of Nigeria since the early nineteenth century, also help to explain the relative underdevelopment of the Northern region. The British brought together North and South Nigeria as one entity in 1914, although in practice they managed the territory as two separate colonies. Under the Sultan of Sokoto, they allowed the Northern region to be ruled by the traditional mix of local customs and shari'a law, while grooming the military elite from their ranks.[10] The south, on the other hand was favored in terms of education and industrialization. The North, as a result, remained relatively impoverished. After World War II, with the advent of decolonization, the British and the Nigerians moved in the direction of a unified country, unlike Rhodesia, which split into Zimbabwe and Zambia, for instance.

To be fair, the British had also made an effort to reconcile the two regions, mostly by using the qur'anic paradigm of 'the people of the book.' With time, it seemed that the northern rulers had absorbed this paradigm, and Christians and Muslims came to feel that they had more in common as followers of an Abrahamic faith than they had with the devotees of traditional African religions. Paden puts it this way:

> During the early independence era, there was close cooperation in the north between Muslims (whether emirs, civil servants, or teachers) and their Christian counterparts (whether chiefs, civil servants, or teachers). During this period, the premier of the Northern Region, Ahmadu Bello, initiated the northernization policy in which Muslim and Christian northerners were promoted rapidly, both at the regional and the national levels.[11]

However, three events opened old wounds: first, a 1966 coup by Christian officers who killed several Northern leaders; second, the Muslim military leader, Ibrahim Bagangida, decided to integrate Nigeria into the Organization of the Islamic Conference (OIC) in 1986; third, the Shari'a movement, which gained national prominence in 1999.

One has to look at history to understand the complexity of issues that converge and, as in a kaleidoscope, that create new, unexpected combinations and landscapes. Throughout this historical presentation I hope the reader has noticed the important role of governance in bringing about justice in society – whether it was the reformist ideal of the Sokoto Jihad or the power sharing arrangements of the Nigerian political class as it emerged from the long period of military rule.[12] After Obasanjo finished his two terms, the Muslim governor of Katsina State was elected to the presidency of Nigeria. After Umaru Musa Yar'Adua was elected in 2007, many Katsina Christians complained that under his leadership Christians found it difficult to send their children to secondary public schools and thus had to send them to schools in other states. Furthermore, Christians were effectively barred from entering the army and rising to higher positions in the state bureaucracy; and the ban on preaching in public places seemed only to apply to them.[13] Still, Katsina leaders of the Christian Association of Nigeria (CAN) admitted that the situation for them had not worsened as a result of the imposition of Shari'a, that the state government was willing to make some compromises, and that finally, Christian advocacy in Katsina was severely hampered by the lack of church unity. Governance, especially in a democratic state, will always be a work in progress, with inevitable ups and downs, and very much dependent on the vitality of civil society.

But there has also been reconciliation and healing. Fortunately, those are also in great supply in the recent experience of Nigerians. The first step was for both sides to moderate their positions. Many Muslim leaders began to realize how the Shari'a discourse had been corroding Nigerian national unity. A government committee composed of Islamic scholars recommended that Sokoto State not expand its Shari'a policy until they had a chance to educate the local population as to what it entailed. Although the authorities went ahead anyway, their positions moderated considerably and Christians were largely spared any additional difficulties.[14] Thus Christians also toned down their discourse and began to openly accept that Muslims could implement moderate Shari'a laws for their own community.

Then there were more positive initiatives from both sides. In fact, they would be too numerous to mention. Vaughan mentions in particular influential intellectuals proposing 'an Academy of Peace' and in fact several regional dialogues did take place. One featured a Catholic priest, a Muslim cleric and a Pentecostal theologian. What is more, 'The federal government established the Nigerian Inter-Religious Council, and Yusuf Ameh Obaje was appointed as national coordinator.'[15]

In the end, the most inspiring story may well be the friendship of Imam Muhammad Ashafa and Pastor James Wue from the city of Kaduna. Both as religious zealots had taken up arms in the 1992 riots in their city but in 1995 a journalist brought them together saying, 'Gentlemen, you can keep Kaduna State together. I want you to talk.' Grudgingly at first, their conversations developed into a lasting friendship and the founding of the Interfaith Mediation Center, with seed money from the US Institute of Peace. Their first intervention was in Yelwa and Shendam, where they brought leaders from both sides together to discuss the way forward. As a result, that region has stayed calm over the last ten years. Their mediation efforts since then have successfully helped to bring peace to communities in Sri Lanka, Kenya, South Sudan, Iraq and elsewhere.[16]

It is particularly at the local level, where people meet face to face, that we see justice and love coming together in a beautiful way. Reconciliation involves forgiveness, the first step before friendship can be nurtured. Love expressed through forgiveness translates into a commitment to work for the good of the other, and in this case an enemy, with no strings attached. Jesus called his disciples to love their enemies. The Qur'an says, 'Good and evil cannot be equal. [Prophet], repel evil with what is better and your enemy will become as close as an old and valued friend' (41:34). And again, on forgiveness we read, 'Let harm be requited by an equal harm, though anyone who forgives and puts things right will have his reward from God Himself – He does not like those who do wrong' (42:40).

Such peacebuilding initiatives as we have seen have brought lasting changes to each of these Northern states. Years of riots and violence had taken their toll – flight of capital from many of the Shari'a states, the tarnishing of Nigeria's international reputation, the loss of life and destruction. Yet the Nigerian people resolutely showed their political will to remain united, especially through the years of Boko Haram terrorism. Now with a backdrop of 20 years since the 1999 Shari'a controversy, we have witnessed each state moderating its positions in its own way. Each one has been forced as well to deal with its own governance failures, and especially in actively working to eradicate poverty. It may be that no one said it better than the influential Nigerian Sanusi Lamido Sanusi, 14th Emir of Kano and former governor of the Central Bank of Nigeria:

> Over a period of four years, the euphoria seems to have fizzled out. After the initial sensational sentences of amputations and caning, and even stoning to death (which was not carried out) the people have come to realize that nothing in reality has changed and that the poor seem to be the only ones facing the wrath of the law. There is now a focus on the real problems facing the people, and questions are being asked about good governance, competence, and genuine commitment to the welfare of the people.[17]

Considering the tense and polarized history of Nigeria, such stories of growing political solidarity beyond the traditional religious dividers, and especially the stories of friendship between people on both sides, speak of expanding justice and even love in this young nation. Though on a much grander scale, this was the spirit that prompted Prince Ghazi of Jordan to launch this ground-breaking initiative we now simply refer to as the 'Common Word,' which, it bears mentioning here, five Nigerian leaders signed.[18] Examining that 2007 document will lead us to reflect on a thought dear to Wolterstorff, but which likely did not occur to him when he signed the full-page advertisement in *The New York Times* in November 2007, which was also the very first Christian response to that Muslim letter addressed to Pope Benedict VI and all Christian leaders.[19] The idea for this book came to me, at least in part, when I realized that there was a direct connection between Wolterstorff's project on justice (and especially his second book in 2011, *Justice in Love*) and the Common Word initiative. I will explain in what follows.

Pope Benedict's Regensburg Lecture

We already looked at the basic premise of the 2007 letter by Muslim leaders addressed to Christian leaders, 'A Common Word Between Us and You.' We saw that its primary objective was to foster peace and understanding between the two religious communities that accounted for more than half of the globe's population. We also stated that the 'basis for peace' was not only possible, but right at the heart of both traditions, namely love of God and love of neighbor. The Introduction then goes on to quote the Qur'anic verse that inspired the letter's title:

> Say: O People of the Scripture! Come to a common word between us and you: that we shall worship none but God, and that we shall ascribe no partner unto Him, and that none of us shall take others for lords beside God. And if they turn away, then say: Bear witness that we are they who have surrendered (unto Him) (Q. 3:64).

Yet, although I mentioned the controversy that sparked the Muslim reaction which a year later led to the signing of the Common Word letter, I gave no details about Pope Benedict's lecture at the University of Regensburg, Germany, on September 12, 2006. This I must do here, if only to clarify a context that is often misunderstood. As you will see, another subtext here is that no new initiative springs from a vacuum.

Pope Benedict XVI (b. 1927) had been an academic for 26 years when he was named Archbishop of Munich and Freising and Cardinal by Pope Paul VI in 1977. His last academic appointment was at the University of Regensburg in 1969, in his native Bavaria. As Pope (2005–2013), he was asked to deliver a lecture there on September 12, 2006, on religion and science entitled, 'Faith, Reason, and the University: Memories and Reflections.'[20] This was a topic dear to his heart and about which he had written much over the years. Truth is one, and as the two theological faculties on that campus indicate by their very presence, theologians use that same reason to probe the rational dimension of religious faith. And this, despite the accusation of many academics that these two faculties are 'devoted to something that does not exist: God.'[21]

Unfortunately, his point of departure in this lecture on faith and reason was a 1966 translation and commentary of a dialogue between one of the last Byzantine emperors, Manuel II Paleologos, and a Persian Muslim interlocutor, possibly in 1391, by Münster scholar Theodore Khoury. Keep in mind that the fall of Constantinople was less than 60 years away and that the Byzantine Empire was now a mere shadow of its former self, whittled away almost yearly by the armies of a much more powerful foe, the Ottoman Empire. The pope then admits that the topic of 'holy war' was only tangential to the dialogue, but that it fit well into the topic of his lecture. He then comments on the emperor's argument after citing Q. 2:256 ('There is no compulsion in religion'):

> He addresses his interlocutor with a startling brusqueness, a brusqueness that we find unacceptable, on the central question about the relationship between religion and violence in general, saying: "Show me just what Mohammed brought that was new, and there you will find things only evil and inhuman, such as his command to spread by the sword the faith he preached."

Note that the pope calls this harsh discourse 'unacceptable,' yet he does not stop to explain why he finds it unacceptable. Rather, he goes on to cite the emperor as he condemns the use of force to convert people: 'Whoever would lead someone to faith needs the ability to speak well and to reason properly, without violence and threats.'[22] Next Pope Benedict quotes the editor, Theodore Khoury: 'For the emperor, as a Byzantine shaped by Greek philosophy, this statement is self-evident. But for Muslim teaching, God is absolutely transcendent. His will is not bound up with any of our categories, even that of rationality.' Referring to Ibn Hazm, he says that God is not even bound by his own word. Put differently, an act is good if and only if God commands it. This is the classical statement of ethical voluntarism, the default position of Sunni Islam in its classical period in reaction to the rationalism of the Mu'tazilites. Yet anyone with some knowledge of Islamic law knows that Ibn Hazm of Cordoba (d. 1064) held extreme views according to Sunni standards. His rather short-lived school of Islamic jurisprudence even refused the use of analogy in discerning the teachings of the Qur'an and Sunna. For him that was to give reason too much leeway.

The reaction in the Muslim world was immediate. The next day people poured into the streets to protest in many Muslim-majority nations around the world.[23] Many statements by Muslim leaders were harsh in their criticism, and in particular Yusuf al-Qaradawi, who assumed like many that the pope agreed with the fourteenth-century emperor in his assessment of Muhammad. The pope never retracted this very disparaging remark about Islam, Qaradawi complained in his weekly Al Jazeera programme, although at his own request the International Council of Islamic Scholars had asked him to do so.[24] Tariq Ramadan, by contrast, used this as an example of a lost opportunity for the Muslim world to engage in an open discussion both internally and with those who disagree with them from the outside.[25]

In the end, it was Ramadan's view that prevailed. Thirty-eight influential leaders and scholars issued a letter to the pope, correcting what they thought was wrong in his lecture but also calling for open dialogue on the matter.[26] The pope subsequently expressed regret for what he called the misunderstanding of what he had said. Though he might have made his disagreement with the emperor more forthrightly, this row nevertheless led to a movement for greater dialogue with members of other faiths, and Christians in particular. Less than two weeks later, Pope Benedict received a visit from a number of ambassadors from Muslim countries at the Vatican, and among other things he said,

> Dear friends, I am profoundly convinced that in the current world situation it is imperative that Christians and Muslims engage with one another in order to address the numerous challenges that present themselves to humanity, especially those concerning the defence and promotion of the dignity of the human person and of the rights ensuing from that dignity.[27]

Although the pope's Regensburg lecture might have engaged the rich legacy of Islamic thought in a more constructive way, he certainly believed that followers of various faith traditions could come together on the basis of their common belief in human dignity and in the rights that this confers on all people.

Prince Ghazi's Common Word Letter

I will keep my own commentary on this letter brief, as it has been the subject of several books, numerous Master's theses and doctoral dissertations, and already dozens of Muslim-Christian conferences worldwide.[28] But perhaps the most useful lens from which to approach it here is through Prince Ghazi's answer to the letter's critics, both Christian and Muslim. Here are some of the things he asserts the Common Word is *not*:

1. *An attempt 'to trick Christians or to foist Muslim theology on them.'* Some Christians objected to the use of Q. 3:64 to seemingly press them into denying the Trinity ('we shall ascribe no partner to God'). Ghazi recognizes that Christians too 'insist on the Unity of God,' albeit in their own way.[29] But these words of Jesus about the two commandments, adds Ghazi, were uttered long before Christians come together to affirm the Trinity, which is not mentioned by name in the New Testament.

2. *An attempt 'to reduce both our religions to an artificial union based on the Two Commandments.'*[30] This theological common ground already existed in both traditions, he argues, and this is merely a way to leverage religion for positive and peaceful ends, far from the nefarious ways it has so often been put to use.

3. *A denial that God loved us first,* as some Christians have alleged. Allow me to explain the background here: more conservative Christians, likely Protestants, have accused the writers of the letter of forcing a view of salvation by works on Christian readers. 'God so loved the world that he gave his only Son,' they would quote from John 3:16. Prince Ghazi avoids the salvation issue by simply replying that of course God loved us first. He created us out of love as the apex of his entire creation .... end of quarrel. This is clear from Surat al-Rahman, 'Al-Rahman / Has Taught the Qur'an / He has created Man / He has taught him speech' (Q. 55:1-4). He explains, 'the very Divine Name *Al-Rahman* should be understood as containing the meaning 'The Creator-through-Love,' and the Divine Name *Al-Rahim* should be understood as containing the meaning 'The Savior through Mercy.'[31]

4. *A means to marginalize or exclude Judaism.* Jewish observers were in fact invited to the Common Word conferences at Yale and Cambridge. These are common truths to all three of the Abrahamic faiths. This initiative was simply addressed to the two religious communities

with the longest history of enmity and whose numbers of followers constitute the greatest potential for peacebuilding.

5. *A capitulation to Christian theology* (not 'one iota,' he adds). Nor does it expect Christians to desist from any of their convictions. It is about 'equal peace, not about capitulation.'[32]

6. *A Muslim aquiescence to expanded Christian evangelistic efforts among their ranks.* Definitely not! This is about bringing greater understanding betweeen the two communities, and the issue of evangelism has long been a thorn in the side of Muslims. Better to leave that bitter history behind, he urges.

7. *A concession to Christians by framing traditional Islamic discourse in the language of 'love.'* This common objection on the part of Muslims reveals the ignorance many have of their own religion, he says. Here Prince Ghazi should be quoted at greater length:

... this frequently underestimated aspect of our religion: the Grand Principle of Love. Indeed, the Holy Qur'an uses over fifty near-synonyms for love; English does not have the same linguistic riches and connotations, as was discussed in particular during the Yale workshop and conference in July 2008. If Muslims do not usually use the same language of love as English-speaking Christians, it is perhaps because the word "love" for Muslims frequently implies something different for Muslims than it does for Christians.

Our use of the language of love in "A Common Word" is simply, then, a recognition that human beings have the same souls everywhere, however pure or corrupted, and thus that the experience of love must have something in common everywhere, even if the objects of love are different, and even if the ultimate love of God is stronger than all other loves.[33]

Now as I glance at the copy of the Common Word letter in Volf et al., the following are the salient points I see about our love for God and the love God expects us to show to our fellow human beings.[34] With regard to God's love for his creation and humans in particular, the word 'love' is not used in the Qur'an or in this letter. This makes sense, as the common ground is about the two commandments – our call to love God and to love our neighbor. Had the letter been written by Christians, however, it would have started with God's love for us. So as it is, the first half of the letter is entitled 'Love of God,' and, as the text makes clear, it is only about our love for God and not vice versa. Yet in a footnote we do read about 'God's universal Mercy *which embraceth all things* (Al-A'raf 7:156); but God knows best.'[35] So in the sense of God's mercy, one could say that the Qur'an is full of God's love for all of his creatures, since the *besmillah* (the formula, 'In the name of God, the Merciful, the Compassionate') precedes all 114 suras but one.[36] But, as I said, love of God for humanity is not directly stated in the Common Word.

In Ghazi's exposition of the Islamic view of loving God, devotion is the central concept and it flows out of the two testimonies of faith (*shahadatan*), 'There is no God but God, and Muhammad is the messenger of God.' This is then expanded by the hadith (which comes in many forms, as he explains in his notes) that strings together various Qur'anic phrases: 'There is no God but God, He Alone, He hath no associate, His is the sovereignty and His is the praise and he hath power over all things.' Each of these phrases, he adds, 'describe a mode of love of God, and devotion to Him.'[37]

All of these sentiments resonate with Christians, and particularly 'He is the praise,' which 'remind Muslims that they must be grateful to God and trust Him with all their sentiments and emotions.'[38] He then quotes one of many Qur'anic verses that teach God's care of humanity through his creation, 'And if thou wert to ask them: Who causeth water to come down from the sky, and therewith reviveth the earth after its death ? they verily would say: God. Say: Praise be to God! But most of them have no sense' (29:61-63). Close to this sense of God's bounty in creation is the word 'grace,' which comes in the next two verses he quotes:

And He giveth you of all ye ask of Him, and if ye would count the graces of God ye cannot reckon them. Lo! man is verily a wrong-doer, an ingrate. (14:34)

Thee we worship, and Thee we ask for help. Guide us upon the straight path. The path of those on whom is Thy Grace, not those who deserve anger nor those who are astray. (1:4-7)

This means that our devotion to God flows not only out of God's absolute sovereignty and greatness but also out of gratitude for his grace and care for all his creatures. That is the first *shahada*, or 'testimony.' The second testimony, however, is unique to Islam, as it urges the believer to follow the example of God's messenger, Muhammad, to whom God says through the Qur'an, 'Say: Lo! my worship and my sacrifice and my living and my dying are for God, the Lord of the Worlds' (6:162). Ghazi offers the following commentary:

These verses epitomize the Prophet Muhammad's complete and utter devotion to God. Thus in the Holy Qur'an God enjoins Muslims who truly love God to follow this example, in order in turn to be loved by God: *Say, (O Muhammad, to mankind): If ye love God, follow me; God will love you and forgive you your sins. God is Forgiving, Merciful (Aal 'Imran, 3:31).*[39]

As mentioned above, Prince Ghazi admitted that 'the word "love" for Muslims frequently implies something different for Muslims than it does for Christians.'[40] This is certainly noticeable here in the conditionality of the above Qur'anic phrase, 'Say, (O Muhammad, to mankind): If ye love God, follow me; God will love you and forgive you your sins' (Q. 3:31). I will return to this issue of conditionality, but let me end Ghazi's exposition on the commandment to love God with his own conclusion, just after briefly commenting on the gospel account of that commandment. Stating that they are 'remarkably parallel,' he adds:

> In the light of what we have seen to be necessarily implied and evoked by the Prophet Muhammad's blessed saying ... [quoting again the above hadith], we can now perhaps understand the words: "The best that I have said – myself, and the prophets that came before me" as equating the blessed formula: *There is no god but God, He Alone, He hath no associate, His is the sovereignty and His is the praise and He hath power over all things*, precisely with the "First and Greatest Commandment" to love God, with all one's heart and soul, as found in various places in the Bible. That is to say, in other words, that the Prophet Muhammad was perhaps, through inspiration, restating and alluding to the Bible's First Commandment. God knows best, but certainly we have seen their effective similarity in meaning.[41]

Allow me to interject here an assumption that remains unstated in this letter. There is no hint anywhere, as Bible verses are quoted and analyzed, that the Jewish and Christian scriptures have been 'falsified,' as is commonly believed among Muslims. This is seldom brought up in scholarly Muslim-Christian dialogue settings, but it is inevitably mentioned in more casual conversations between Muslims and Christians relative to their respective sacred texts. I have no space, and actually no need to delve into the details here, particularly since University of Melbourne Islamicist Abdullah Saeed has written such a succinct and helpful article on the subject.[42] Although over a dozen Qur'anic verses imply some form of 'distortion,' particularly by Jews, only four verses have the word commonly used and understood, at least on a popular level, as actually changing the original text (*taḥrīf*). Saeed highlights the discussion of this word by Qur'anic commentators over time and shows how the issue of whether it was 'distortion of meaning' or 'distortion of the text' was never resolved. Part of the problem, Saeed avers, comes from two very different theories of revelation – 'dictation' by the Angel Gabriel reading from the heavenly book in the case of Muslims, and 'divine inspiration' of human speech, including narratives, poetry, law and more, in the case of the Bible.

That said, adds Saeed, many Muslim scholars realized how fragile such an allegation of textual corruption was, especially in light of 'the obvious lack, in the Qur'an, of any attack on either *Tawrat* (books of Moses, perhaps the entire Hebrew Bible) and the *Injīl* (the 'gospel,' and by extension, the New Testament).[43] As a result, less traditional Islamic scholars today take their cue from Qur'anic verses like these two:

> So if you [Prophet] are in doubt about what We have revealed to you, ask those who have been reading the scriptures before you. The Truth has come to you from your Lord, so be in no doubt and do not deny God's signs (10:94).

> We sent Jesus, son of Mary, in their footsteps, to confirm the Torah that had been sent before him: We gave him the Gospel with guidance, light and confirmation of the Torah already revealed – a guide and lesson for those who take heed of God. So let the followers of the Gospel judge according to what God has sent down in it. Those who do not judge according to what God has revealed are lawbreakers (5:46-47)

An interesting application of this clear affirmation of the trustworthiness of the Torah and Injil is found in the last footnote in the first section, 'Love of God.' As in several other places in the letter, the footnote does not seem to relate directly to the passage where it appears. Here, it comes at the end of the section and is given a title, 'In the Best Stature,' referring to Q. 95:4, 'Verily, we have created man in the best stature.'[44] Then the footnote quotes scriptures on a theology of humanity with two verses from the book of Genesis, one hadith, and six from the Qur'an. The introduction states, 'Christianity and Islam have comparable conceptions of man being created in the best stature and from God's own breath.' What is remarkable is Prince Ghazi's use of Gen. 1:27 ('So God created man in his image ...'). This is my first time hearing a Muslim quote this as a parallel to Q. 95:4. It certainly is a point I have made elsewhere in relation to the classical Qur'anic commentators who were loath to 'make any connection between humanity's capacities of reason and free will and God's attributes as their Creator.'[45] Still, one can find at least ten instances of this *hadith*, 'God created Adam in His image' (*'alā ṣūratihi*).[46] At the very least, this represents a conscious effort to build theological bridges where few had ventured before.

Now, what does the Common Word say about love for our neighbor? The key text here is the hadith that echoes Jesus' Golden Rule, 'None of you has faith until you love for your neighbour what you love for yourself.'[47] The resemblance between the two (the three, counting Judaism) traditions is indeed striking. Two verses from the Qur'an are also cited, with the word 'love' in both. In the first, aside the long list of practices that demonstate 'righteousness' in 2:177), there is this phrase: 'and giveth wealth, for love of Him, to kinsfolk and to orphans and the needy and the wayfarer and to those who ask...'[48] Charity here is tied to one's love for God, another common theme in the Bible, but it is also explicitly labelled as 'love' for the other, as in the following:

> He is the faithful God who keeps his covenant for a thousand generations and lavishes his unfailing love on those who love him and obey his commands (Deut. 7:9 NLT).

> Do not take advantage of foreigners who live among you in your land. Treat them like native-born Israelites, and love them as you love yourself. Remember that you were once foreigners living in the land of Egypt. I am the Lord your God (Lev. 19:33-34, NLT).

The other Qur'anic text cited is also related to almsgiving: 'Ye will not attain unto righteousness until ye expend of that which ye love. And whatsoever ye expend, God is Aware thereof' (3:92). The letter goes on to explain, 'Without giving the neighbour what we ourselves love, we do not truly love God or the neighbour.'

Now, we may wonder, *how is this interfaith letter focused on love connected to the central issue of justice from an Islamic perspective?* As one might expect, and counting titles, subtitles and scripture verses, the word love appears 77 times. Justice only appears six times, including twice in a Qur'anic verse. Still, the four instances are worth quoting for our purposes. Significantly, the first instance is in the opening words:

> Muslims and Christians together make up well over half of the world's population. Without peace and *justice* between these two religious communities, there can be no meaningful peace in the world. The future of the world depends on peace between Muslims and Christians.[49]

This is an uncontroversial statement – there can be no peace without justice. This letter aims to build peace in the world, and the two largest faith traditions which together make up over half of humanity can and should exercise a decisive influence in this direction. And this especially, because they have been at odds, to say the least, almost from the start. Yet such a cliché hardly gives us an idea of what he means by 'justice.'

The second reference to justice comes after a brief commentary on the verse that gives the letter its name, 'O people of the Scripture! Come to a common word between us and you ... that none of us shall take others for lords beside God...' (3:64). In a footnote after that phrase about not taking others as lords instead of God, Ghazi refers to 'one of the oldest and most authoritative commentaries' to explain its meaning as 'that none of us should obey the other in disobedience to what God has commanded.' Then he adds, 'This relates to the Second Commandment because justice and freedom of religion are a crucial part of love of the neighbour.'[50]

That last phrase seems quite a leap to me – from not allowing the religious other to pressure our community to disobey God to the human rights language of justice and freedom of religion. Perhaps his reasoning goes as follows. As Muslims invite Christians to highlight their commitment to monotheism in a way common to theirs (without thereby denying their distinctive view of God as Trinity), they are calling for a public alliance of sorts as two major religious communities, an alliance that builds on the central teaching in both traditions that each and every human being is worthy of God's care and mercy. And, what is more, they are called to be his trustees of the earth and of all its creatures. Thus humans, by virtue of this high calling, should seek to implement justice and freedom of religion in society. This alliance also empowers Muslims and Christians to model love of neighbor for others, whether they are Buddhists, Sikhs, Christians, Muslims, or atheists.

So I take the letter to be affirming that treating one's fellow humans with justice and an attitude of religious tolerance is one way to love them. Indeed, this is borne out by the last two instances of the word justice in the conclusion ('Part III: Come to a Common Word Between Us and You'). The letter underlines the fact that 'the Prophet Muhammad brought nothing fundamentally or essentially new.' It then quotes two Qur'anic verses to this effect, the second being this,

> Say (Muhammad): I am no new thing among the messengers (of God), nor know I what will be done with me or with you. I do but follow that which is Revealed to me and I am but a plain warner (46:9).

This then is the letter's comment on the verse. Notice the emphasis on commonality:

Thus also God in the Holy Qur'an confirms that the same eternal truths of the Unity of God, of the necessity for total love and devotion to God (and thus shunning false gods), and of the necessity for love of fellow human beings (and thus *justice*), underlie all true religion:

[First, it quotes Q. 16:36, then this verse:] 'We verily sent Our messengers with clear proofs, and revealed with them the Scripture and the Balance, that mankind may stand forth in *justice*....' (57:25).[51]

The last instance of the word 'justice' is at the very end. Having quoted Q. 16:90 ('Lo! God enjoineth justice and kindness, and giving to kinsfolk ...'), the letter mentions Mt. 5:9 ('Blessed are the peacemakers ...') and then comes the last sentence, 'Let us respect each other, be fair, just and kind to another and live in sincere peace, harmony and mutual good-will.'[52] To be sure, these references remain quite vague beyond the affirmation that part of loving our neighbor includes fair treatment and respect for religious difference. What might we learn from his magnum opus, *Love in the Qur'an*, about how he connects love and justice?

Ghazi's Perspective on Love and Justice

The Common Word letter was certainly the first place to look for Prince Ghazi bin Muhammad's view on love and justice, since he was the project's initiator.[53] To read his *Love in the Holy Qur'an* is to delve into a direct expansion of that thesis about love's central role in the Qur'anic worldview.[54] This interest in him seems to have developed over his whole academic career. What started as an interest in comparative literature (his Bachelor of Arts degree at Princeton University), developed more specifically around the theme of love, as in his Cambridge PhD dissertation, 'What Is Falling in Love? A Study of the Literary Archetype of Love.' When it comes to this book, the '7th Expanded Edition' of his original doctoral dissertation at al-Azhar University, three aspects stand out from the outset: the strictly literalist approach to the sacred text; his continued interest in love from a literary perspective; his apologetic aim throughout.

By 'literalist approach' I simply mean that one encounters the author's thoughts only in sparse comments interspersed between inumerable quotes from either the Qu'ran or Sunna. Everything is centered on the Qur'anic text, either by quoting verses that relate to the theme at hand, or by looking at instances of how one particular word is used in various places. His own opinions shine through more often than not through his

choice and ordering of the book's content and by quoting the classic commentators of the past. Thus even in two-and-a-half-page chapter 3 ('The
Definition of Love') Ghazi sticks to a combination of textual references and
the opinion of twelfth-century classical scholar Abu Hamid Muhammad
al-Ghazali. So based on several Qur'anic verses, including Q. 32:7 ('[God]
Who beautified everything that He created'), and Ghazali's definition of
human love ('the soul's inclination to something which suits it and pleases
it'), Ghazi offers the following definition of God's love: 'first of all the free
gift of existence and countless other favours (including beauty of various
kinds) to every created thing, and, second love of beauty as such.'[55] Then
he ends his short chapter with a lexical note. The main word used for love
in Arabic *ḥubb* comes from *ḥabb* ('seed'), 'thus implying a seed falls into the
ground, grows, then brings forth a new and beautiful plant.'[56] Then this
thought is further clarified, he notes, by the following verse:

> The likeness of those who expend their wealth in the way of God is as the
> likeness of a grain (*ḥabb*) that sprouts seven ears, in every ear a hundred
> grains; so God multiplies for whom He will; God is Embracing, Knowing
> (2:261).

Improbably, he concludes from this verse that 'love is like a seed from which
comes forth a plant which God multiplies as He wills for whom he wills.'[57]
I write 'improbably,' because this verse is about generosity toward the
poor, which God multiplies many times. Generosity should be motivated
by love, certainly, but that is still an indirect reference from this verse.
Ghazi's pointing to this verse, however, has more to do with the word *ḥabb*
(seed, or grain). It's a lexical hermeneutic. That said, perhaps one of the
advantages of such a strict textualist methodology is that these kinds of
word associations within the text can be made quite freely, it would seem,
and meanwhile the reader is comforted by the thought that everything is
actually derived from the text.

  This leads us to Ghazi's previous study of love in comparative literature,
which can also be intimated through the book's outline. Part One tackles 'Divine Love' in just over 40 pages; Part Two quotes the Prophet ('The
Messenger of God's Love') in barely eight pages. By contrast, Ghazi devotes
the bulk of his book to human love, with Part Four serving as a 100-page
philosophical treatise on 'Love,' and yet with each chapter pegged to specific verses in the Qur'an or Sunna. Finally, as one might have guessed,
Ghazi displays his admiration for Sufism, the dimension of Islam that
has always highlighted divine love and the spiritual path that leads the

devotee to loving union with God. Hence, Part Five wraps up the book with a 30-page mystical treatise on the beatitude of meeting with God in this world and the next ('The Beloved').

Still, Part Four, I would argue, represents the heart of the book, as it dissects human love by kinds, by stages, by hierarchies and opposites; and by exploring its end and nature, both on earth and in Paradise. There is even a chapter entitled 'Falling in Love,' which revolves around a tripartite division of the human person (body, soul and spirit) that is explored through the use of these terms in the Qur'an. But again, there is very little personal commentary and a good deal that is devoted to explaining how related words are used in the sacred text.[58] Still, the reader can easily guess the questions with which Ghazi came to the text – questions most certainly inspired by his research on love in various branches of world literature.

Finally, I mentioned 'his apologetic aim.' By this I mean that Ghazi has two audiences in mind, which he states in his goals.[59] I also gather this from the efforts he made to launch the Common Word project. The historical circumstance is that of the unprecedented attacks on American soil of September 11, 2001 and the series of al-Qaeda-inspired attacks in places like Madrid, London and Bali. That, at least, was behind the spectacular Jordanian effort to gather all major branches of contemporary Islam in order to issue a common declaration on what is 'true Islam' (the Amman Message).[60] Yet the backdrop of recent 'Islamic terrorism' is only the trigger perhaps. Veteran American Islamic scholar Seyyed Hossein Nasr, in his Foreword to the book, puts his finger on a longstanding wound inflicted by Christians on Muslims. 'Love is in fact one of the central themes of the Noble Qur'an,' he writes, 'whatever naysayers, whether non-Muslims or even some Muslims who see only the external dimension of things, may assert.' A good portion of the next paragraph is worth quoting in this regard, as it aptly captures the sting felt by Muslims over at least two centuries of debates with a dominant religious other:

> This unique work, therefore, is of great importance not only for Muslims, who at the present moment are so much in need of a deeper understanding of their religion and realization of the central importance of the Prophetic virtues of love, compassion, mercy and forgiveness, but also for non-Muslims and especially Westerners. *For too long Western critics of Islam have asserted that while Christians view God as Love, Muslims hold the view of God as a vengeful God who emphasizes His justice alone at the expense of his Love and Mercy.* This false and malicious view of the Islamic conception of God has been propagated over and over in orientalist writings and also asserted again and again by Christian missionaries who preach to those Muslims who would listen to

them that the Islamic emphasis upon the Divine Attributes of Justice eclipses and nullifies the reality of the Divine Attributes of Love, Compassion and Mercy. The present book is a powerful response to this erroneous but prevalent view that is such a major obstacle to better understanding between the two religions.[61]

I certainly hope that the present book represents a tangible, if humble, Christian response to that perceived collective injury.

After this brief introduction to Ghazi's *Love in the Holy Qur'an*, allow me to highlight three aspects of how love and justice are paired therein: the 'balance' of justice and love; the 'balance' of love and beauty: justice as 'inalienable rights.'

The 'Balance' of Justice and Love

Ghazi's Chapter 5 bears the title, 'Love Is the Root of Creation.' After five pages of Qur'anic quotes and commentary, he summarizes his thesis in these terms:

> Thus it is clear and beyond doubt that God created human beings and the world *out of mercy* and *for mercy*; and since Divine Mercy is inseparable from Divine love [sic] (as we have already discussed in Chapter 4: God and Love), this means that the world and human beings were created *out of love* and *for love* as well.[62]

Then, as he does in several chapters, he adds in bold in the margin, 'A Question.' Here, 'If the world and human beings were created *out of* mercy, and thus love, and for mercy and thus love, then how can it be that God does not love certain (evil) people?' Here we come back to the question of the conditionality of God's love, raised earlier. In his 'Executive Summary'[63] under 'Divine Love' he cites from the Qur'an the eight types of people God loves and then the 12 kinds of people he does not love.[64] So is this a contradiction? Anticipating another chapter in which he deals with this at greater length, Ghazi answers that nowhere is it said that God hates anyone. Clearly, does not love evil deeds nor evil doers. But since the Qur'an plainly states that humankind was created 'in a state of moral purity, and in the best stature and the best form,' they were equally created out of mercy and love. At the same time, they were created with the ability and freedom to choose between good and evil.

This of course touches on two philosophical dilemmas for all three monotheistic faiths. Where did evil come from if God is both all good and all powerful? And if God is all powerful and controls everything that happens, then how can human beings be said to have free will? Or, from another angle, how can he justly condemn sinners to hell if he himself is finally responsible for their actions? Ghazi is not concerned with such far-reaching questions here, however. His dilemma is more pedestrian. If God created all people out of mercy and love, how can he not love certain people? In essence, Ghazi answers, evil exists (and we won't try to explain it) and God by definition cannot love evil or those who decide to commit it. He has given them free will and that is how they decide to exercise it. This is similar to one verse in the biblical Proverbs, in which God hates both sin and evil doers:

> There are six things the Lord hates, seven that are detestable to him: haughty eyes, a lying tongue, hands that shed innocent blood, a heart that devises wicked schemes, feet that are quick to rush into evil, a false witness who pours out lies and a person who stirs up conflict in the community (Proverbs 6:16-19 NIV).

Besides the fact that I could not find any other example of God either 'not loving' or 'hating' people in the Bible, at a deeper level for Christians this idea is problematic, because:

1) all humankind practices sin since the fall of its first pair
2) 'God so loved the world that he gave his one and only Son that whosoever believes in him should not perish but have eternal life' (John 3:16 NIV).

Hence, the theme of redemption that is so central to Christianity.

Still, Ghazi's point is well made. Speaking in the context of the Islamic worldview, God is a *just* Judge on the Last Day. 'And God created the heavens and the earth with the truth and so that every soul may be requited for what it has earned, and they will not be wronged' (45:22). The theme of justice comes again in Surat al-Rahman:

> It is the Lord of Mercy who taught the Qur'an. He created man and taught him to communicate. The sun and the moon follow their calculated courses, the plants and trees submit to His designs. He has raised up the sky. He has set the balance so that you may not exceed in the balance: weigh with justice and do not fall short in the balance (55:1-9 Abdel Haleem).

Here the idea of justice is tied to the concept of 'balance,' seemingly tied to creation (it was set up with the creation of the heavens) and to an ethical standard (not to be contravened). Yet the third instance takes on a more down-to-earth meaning, that of just weights on a market scale. Commentators usually connect this to the scales of God's judgment on the Last Day.[65] But Ghazi offers no comment whatsoever, as is his custom. He simply goes on to the next verse, and so on. His introductory phrase reads, 'And "so human beings might keep the balance with justice," for God says ...' Though Ghazi offers no answer to this question here he does so in the chapter opening his Part Five ('Beauty and Its Components'). For Ghazi, love and justice would be incomplete without adding beauty.

Love, Beauty and Justice

To begin his discussion of beauty, he quotes from Raghib al-Isfahani as he does throughout the book,[66] in order to define 'beauty' as used in the Qur'an:

> Raghib says: '*Jamal* means great beauty (*ḥusn*), and there are two aspects to this: the first is the beauty with which a person is characterised in soul, body or actions; the second is that which connects to something else. In this regard, it is related that the Prophet said: "God is beautiful, and He loves beauty," which indicates that all goodness flows from Him, so He loves those who are characterised by this goodness.'[67]

Naturally this idea connects to God's 'beautiful names' (*al-asmā' al-ḥusnā*), and further research into the usage of these two words (*jamāl* and *ḥusn*) in the Qur'an reveals that they are 'basically synonyms.' This leads to the second and last section of this short chapter, 'The Components of Beauty.' Here he comes back to Surat al-Rahman (55:1-9), mentioning that 'the balance' (*al-mizān*) is mentioned three times. Now he offers his own analysis. After noting that God mentions the balance with regard to various elements of nature, he remarks,

> God does not speak of rewards and punishments, or other things that come to mind when justice is spoken of. Perhaps, then, the mention of "the balance" here is an allusion to a greater "balance," namely the natural harmony and equilibrium of God's Creation. Our evidence for this is the "measure" (*ḥusbān*) of which God speaks in connection with "the balance": "The sun and moon follow a measure,[68] / and the grass and the trees prostate."[69]

This is the context in which he now quotes Q. 32:7, 'Who beautified everything that He created. And He began the creation of man from clay.' This idea of beauty must also be connected to the Surat al-Rahman passage, he argues, because the Prophet spoke of the virtues (*faḍā'il*) of various

Qu'ranic suras; and in particular he said, 'Everything has a bride, and the bride of the Qur'an is [Surat] Al-Rahman.'[70] This, asserts Ghazi, can have no other meaning but that 'the balance' in that passage 'must contain an allusion to beauty.' Why is this significant? It is because many Muslim scholars have divided 'God's Most Beautiful Names ... into two categories: The Names of the Divine Essence (such as the 'One'), and the Names of the Divine Qualities,' which include 'the Names of Beauty (such as: 'The Compassionate' and the 'Beautiful'), the Names of Majesty (such as: 'The Almighty' and the 'The Irresistible'), and the Names of Perfection (such as: 'The King' and 'The Lord').'[71]

Ghazi on Justice and Rights

The last point to be made here is that justice and love relate to human rights for Ghazi. This is to be found in Chapter 17, 'Love of Others (All Humanity; The 'People of the Scripture'; Believers and Friends).' Since all human beings were 'created from a single soul' (e.g., Q. 6:98) and since they all descend from one pair, Adam and Eve; and finally, since the diversity of languages, ethnicities and cultures are among the Divine Signs (*ayāt*) (Q. 30:22; 49:13), 'God values every single soul as if it were all humanity, when it comes to saving its life or not causing its death' (Q. 5:32). After quoting several other verses, he notes, 'Thus God commands Muslims to be peaceful and to be just toward every single human being, except those who wage war upon them, destroy their places of worship and drive them out of their homes.'[72]

After three more pages of Qur'anic quotes, Ghazi offers this summary. Note here the connection between justice, forgiveness and rights:

> In summary: God has given each and every human being inalienable rights, and has obliged Muslims to have respect for all human beings; not to commit aggression against anyone; to be peaceful and to be just; to be merciful; to empathize with all human beings; to forgive them; to pardon them; to restrain themselves from anger; and even to repay evil deeds with kindness and "turn the other cheek" – and to do this with all people, whoever they may be and regardless of their faith (or lack of it) all the times, so long as they are not first waging war against Muslims.[73]

After the next two-page section on 'The people of Scripture' Ghazi offers this summary that, unsurprisingly, does not mention love (that word is not in any of the verses cited):

God enjoins upon Muslims – in addition to having respect, justice and mercy in general towards all humanity – to have affection and admiration for the People of the Scripture in general (notably Christian and Jews). God says in the Holy Qur'an that the Jews were His most favoured people and that Muslims have a special affinity with Christians in particular; and God knows best.[74]

There is no mention of 'rights' here, but 'affection' for this class of religious people is certainly paired up with 'justice and mercy.' As this quote ends our survey of Prince Ghazi's book on the topic of love and justice, I can only conclude that he leans in the direction of Wolterstorff's thesis (justice is about inherent human rights and love is closely connected to it), but since this book is an exegetical and literalistic commentary on Islam's sacred texts, there is little room here for any expansion on this theme. Yet as we saw in the above quote, Ghazi vigorously embodied his own words, 'God has given each and every human being inalienable rights,' and 'Muslims have a special affinity with Christians' through the Common Word document and his bold diplomatic initiatives on both sides of the divide. As the truism goes, actions speak louder than words.

We began this chapter with the tense, often violent context of Muslim-Christian relations in Nigeria in which people in both communities have forged friendships on both sides and called for national unity and peace. We then discovered how the text of the Common Word and the writings of Prince Ghazi can provide a needed space to discuss the theological implications of justice paired with love, and opportunities to implement and protect rights for battered minorities. Nigeria as a nation with such a large and roughly equal population of Muslims and Christians is exceptional. Practically everywhere else, either Christians or Muslims form a large majority. Attending to the rights of a Christian or Muslim minority is the challenge at hand.

In the next chapter I will attempt to sum up some of themes raised by several Christian writers on justice and love, beginning with Wolterstorff. I will also begin with the very real struggles Muslims in most western nations face in a climate of Islamophobia.

Endnotes

1   Paden 2008.
2   Ludwig 2008, 602–637, at 603.
3   Ludwig 2008, 618.

4   Ludwig notes that politicians who win in the polls, almost to the last one, engage in a public Christian thanksgiving service (Ludwig 2008, 617). Nigeria's 'Middle Belt' states were traditionally considered 'northern' by the Fulani-Hausa rulers and there has been considerable pushback against this notion, particularly in Plateau State. As of this writing I found this article today: Alexis Akwagyiram, 'Nigeria grazing violence kills many more than Boko Haram, poses serious threat-think-tank,' Reuters (July 26, 2018), online, https://af.reuters.com/article/topNews/idAFKBN1KG18X-OZATP, accessed December 20, 2019. Two hundred people were killed by Boko Haram between January and June of 2018, whereas violence between 'semi-nomadic cattle herders and and settled farmers has killed over six times more people.' This violence is in the Middle Belt.

5   Ludwig 2008, 619.

6   Ludwig 20018, 619. On May 18, 2004, the Christian president, Olusegun Obasanjo, declared a state of emergency in Plateau State. Most Muslims and Christians welcomed the decision.

7   A 4,000-word version of this case study is available online, http://www.human-trustees.org/resources/item/183-nigeria-case-study.

8   Vaughan 2016, 13. Vaughan is the Geoffrey Canada Professor of Africana Studies and History at Bowdoin College. From my several visits to Nigeria my guess is he is from the Yoruba tribe, which dominates the southwest of Nigeria, and which has both a large Christian and Muslim population, along with practitioners of its traditional religion.

9   Naturally, the missionary movement in the south would not have been so extensive without the protection of the colonial powers. Yet many other factors created by Western influence, mostly cultural, social, and economic, contributed to the rapid spread of Christianity. Some factors were local too, like the Yoruba wars, for instance, during most of the nineteenth century (Vaughan 2016, 25–29).

10   Ludwig explains that at Independence the Nigerian government introduced a new Penal Code for the Northern states, 'basically English in derivation, but also incorporated various principles of Islamic and customary law.' Islamic criminal law, which had operated under the British, was now abrogated and the Shari'a courts were limited to questions of personal and family law. In a centralizing move, the state established one Shari'a Court of Appeal for the whole Northern region, the decisions of which along with those of the Regional High Court, were irrevocable. The Shari'a movement of the late 1990s sought to decentralize much of this structure, and in the end, Shari'a is applied differently in every state. Throughout this process, the federal system in Nigeria was strengthened (Ludwig 2008, 608).

11   Paden 2008, 22.

12   In the longer version of this case-study I explained that reformist scholar Usman dan Fodio, his brother Abdullahi and his son Mohammed Bello, launched a military movement (the Sokoto Jihad) in the first half of the nineteenth century which eventually allowed them to rule the northern half of today's Nigeria (the Sokoto Caliphate). A central part of their reform had to do with uniting Hausa talakawa commoners and disaffected Fulani masses with the idea of bringing justice to all.

13   Ludwig 2008, 630.

14   Vaughan 2016, 195.

15 Vaughan 2016, 196.

16 See the US Institute of Peace article about them here: https://www.usip.org/publications/2017/09/nigerias-imam-and-pastor-faith-front-video. See also this three-minute YouTube video where they explain their story: 'Nigeria's Imam and Pastor: Faith at the Front,' https://www.youtube.com/watch?v=bL2qA6Gt6Ko.

17 Sanusi 2007, 177–188, at 185.

18 This was among the initial list of 138 signatories. The very first one was 'His Royal Eminence Sultan Muhammadu Sa'ad Ababakar, the 20th Sultan of Sokoto; Leader of the Muslims of Nigeria.' There were also several Shia leaders, although fewer Sufi ones.

19 See the full text republished in *A Common Word*, Volf et al., 2010, 51–75. This includes a commentary by Miroslav Volf, Joseph Cumming, and Melissa Yarrington.

20 The full text is available here under the title, 'Papal address at University of Regensburg,' https://zenit.org/articles/papal-address-at-university-of-regensburg/. It has eight pages and 4,000 words. Only three paragraphs mention Islam (#2, 3, 4).

21 Pope Benedict XVI 2006, 1–2.

22 Pope Benedict XVI 2006, 1–2.

23 This included some acts of vandalism against churches, notably in the West Bank and Gaza, but also a nun was shot and killed several days later in Somalia, presumably in response to this affair. See 'Gunmen slay Italian nun in Somali capital,' https://www.news.com.au/national/gunmen-slay-italian-nun-in-somali-capital/news-story/59282bf4be5b3ab86fb335d175143ee7 accessed July 23, 2018.

24 'Arab Reactions to the Pope's Visit: Signs of Hope,' Qantara.de [a website funded by the German Foreign Office to foster dialogue between the West and the Islamic world since 2003] (Oct. 10, 2009), http://en.qantara.de/content/arab-reactions-to-the-popes-visit-signs-of-hope accessed July 23, 2018.

25 Ramadan 2006, online, https://www.nytimes.com/2006/09/20/opinion/20iht-edramadan.2876272.html. In this article Ramadan also critiques the Pope's thesis that Europe and its universities should return to the Hellenistic use of reason while strongly implying that Islam, unlike Christianity, was incapable of functioning as a reasonable dialogue partner. In essence, he concluded, Islam is banned as the 'other' and therefore cannot be adopted as a European religion.

26 'Muslim clerics reach out to Pope,' BBC (October 14, 2006), online, http://news.bbc.co.uk/2/hi/europe/6050156.stm accessed July 23, 2018.

27 A copy of this short speech is available on the Vatican website, http://w2.vatican.va/content/benedict-xvi/en/speeches/2006/september/documents/hf_ben-xvi_spe_20060925_ambasciatori-paesi-arabi.html accessed March 19, 2019.

28 I am gleaning this from Prince Ghazi's introduction to the first official book on the Common Word, see Volf et al., 2010, 13–15.

29 Prince Ghazi, 'On "A Common Word Between Us and You,"' in Volf et al., 2010, 9.

30 Volf et al., 2010, 10.

31 Volf et al., 2010, 11.

32 Volf et al., 2010,

33 Volf et al., 2010, 11–12. He then quotes from Qu'ran 2:165: 'Yet of mankind are some who take unto themselves (objects of worship which they set as) rivals to

God, loving them with a love like (that which is the due) of God (only) – [but] those who believe are stauncher in their love for God.'

34 Ghazi, 'A Common Word Between Us and You,' in Volf et al., 2010, 30–50.

35 Volf et al., 2010, 37, note 12, emphasis his.

36 Still, there are verses that make clear that God's love for human beings is conditional.

37 Volf et al., 2010, 31.

38 Volf et al., 2010, 32.

39 Volf et al., 2010, 36. Qur'anic verses in his text are in italics without quotation marks.

40 Volf et al., 2010, 12.

41 Volf et al., 2010, 42..

42 Saeed 2002 and online as a pdf, http://quranandinjil.org/sites/default/files/pdfs/The-Charge-of-Distortion-of-Jewish-and-Christian-Scriptures_Abdullah%20Saeed.pdf last accessed, Jan. 15, 2015.

43 Saeed 2002, 434.

44 This is taken from *The Noble Qur'an: Interpretation of the Meanings of the Noble Qur'an in the English Language*, al-Hilali and Khan, 1999.

45 Johnston 2010, 300. That connection between God and humanity, however, is common in Sufi literature. Sayyid Hossein Nasr begins his Foreword to Prince Ghazi's *Love in the Qur'an* (after stating that 'one of God's Beautiful Names is Love or al-Wadud') by quoting the *hadith qudsi* central to Sufi literature and spirituality, 'I was a hidden treasure; I loved (*aḥbabtu*) to be known; therefore, I created creation so that I would be known' (xv). The implication drawn from this is that human beings, as God's trustees on earth, are called to know God by climbing the path that leads to unity with Him.

46 Johnston 2010, 300, note 100.

47 'A Common Word Between Us and You,' in Volf et al., 2010, 44. That comes from *Sahih Muslim* (*Kitab al-Iman*, 67–71, *Hadith* no. 45), whereas he also cites a similar hadith from *Sahih al-Bukhari*, 'None of you has faith until you love for your brother what you love for yourself.'

48 Volf et al., 2010, 44.

49 Volf et al., 2010, 28, emphasis added.

50 Volf et al., 2010, 29.

51 Volf et al., 2010, 46. In what follows, both in the Common Word letter and in Ghazi's book *Love in the Qur'an*, I will use his quotes from the Qur'an. He does not specify which translation he is using. More likely, the translation is his own.

52 Volf et al., 2010, 50.

53 He was the original author, although this statement is no longer to be found on the official Common Word website (I remember reading it before and so does the author of the Wikipedia article on the letter). That is easy to understand, for two reasons. First, for the 128 scholars and high-ranking Muslim leaders to have signed it, one imagines that the text underwent significant changes. Second, either because of the prince's humility or as a way to promote greater buy-in from a wider swath of Muslim scholars, this fact has been deemphasized.

54 Ghazi 2013. The 8th edition came out in 2019.

55   Ghazi 2013, 13.

56   Ghazi 2013, 14.

57   Ghazi 2013, 14.

58   For those familiar with the traditional Islamic sciences, this is not surprising. Some scholars were indeed specialists in grammar, others in lexicography and etymology. All the great Qur'anic commentators also had to be greatly skilled in these areas.

59   He spells it out plainly in his 'Prologue: The Goals and Methodology of This Work.' Goals one through four concern Muslims, but the fifth targets non-Muslims. He mentions in particular that non-Muslims 'believe that if Islam has any concern for love it is only beause of the Sufis, or perhaps certain Hadiths (whose authenticity they in any case doubt), and not in the Qur'an itself' (Ghazi 2013, 7).

60   See the Introduction chapter.

61   Ghazi 2013, xvi–xvii, emphasis mine. I certainly recognize the Christian discourse Nasr castigates in this quote, and it has likely been present in Christian-Muslim encounters from the beginning. But one also has to say that this kind of emphasis on God's love that he praises in Ghazi's book is, to my knowledge at least, rare outside of Sufi circles. Nevertheless, that does not make it any less sincere, or potentially influential.

62   Ghazi 2013, 26, emphasis his.

63   Still in the introductory part of the book, xix–xxxiv.

64   Ghazi 2013, xxi–xxii. He groups those verses by similar theme. But altogether, I counted 20 instances of God not loving people whose character he approves and 21 instances of God loving those who are evil doers in some way.

65   See for instance 21:47 and 7:8-9.

66   The eleventh-century scholar who wrote the most authoritative lexical work on the Qur'an, *al-Mufradāt fī Gharīb al-Qur'ān* ('The Vocabulary in the Mysterious Qur'an').

67   Ghazi 2013, 259.

68   When he had quoted this verse on page 26, he had translated *husban* as 'reckoning,' which does not have the same connotation in English.

69   Ghazi 2013, 260.

70   Ghazi 2013, 261.

71   Ghazi 2013, 262.

72   This is taken from Q. 9:7, which he quotes in full (Ghazi 2013, 115).

73   Ghazi 2013, 118.

74   Ghazi 2013, 120. The phrase, 'and God knows best,' for those not familiar with Islamic literature is ubiquitous, and particularly in Qur'anic commentaries.

7

Justice and Love: Christian Perspectives

Imam Gamal Fouda stood at his minbar for the khutba (Friday sermon) at the Al Noor Mosque in Christchurch, New Zealand on March 15, 2019. A self-declared white supremacist barged in with an assault riffle and began slaughtering those in attendance. A week later in his next khutba, the imam said, 'I saw the hatred and the rage in the eyes of the terrorist.' He then paid tribute to the love millions around the world had shown his congregation and the Muslim community in particular. But Imam Fouda also had this warning and challenge:

> Islamophobia KILLS. Muslims have felt its pain for many years. It has killed before in Canada and its brutality was used against teens in Norway and against innocent Muslims in the UK, USA and other countries around the world.
>
> Islamophobia is REAL. It is a targeted campaign to influence people to dehumanize and irrationally fear Muslims.[1]

Following that short sermon, that mosque's call to prayer was broadcast live all over New Zealand on that day.

I begin this last chapter by circling back to the second one, in which I examined anti-black racism in the United States, except that in this instance I will tie it to Islamophobia. My guide here is Khaled A. Beydoun, a native of Detroit and Associate Professor of Law at the University of Detroit Mercy School of Law. Beydoun is also a leading young Muslim scholar activist in America.[2] In his 2018 book, *American Islamophobia: Understanding the Roots and Rise of Fear*,[3] Beydoun defines Islamophobia as 'the presumption that Islam is inherently violent, alien, and unassimilable, a presumption driven by the belief that expressions of Muslim identity correlate with a propensity for terrorism.'[4] He also differentiates between 'private Islamophobia' (harassment and violence perpetrated by private actors against Muslims based on this belief); 'structural Islamophobia' ('the fear and suspicion of Muslims on the part of government institutions and actors');[5] 'dialectical Islamophobia' ('the process by which structural Islamophobia shapes, reshapes, and endorses views and attitudes about Islam and Muslim subjects inside and outside of America's borders').[6]

That third category is especially important because, as Beydoun explains it, Islamophobia feeds on itself to become more virulent through a kind of double feedback loop process. As the state feeds on popular stereotypes of Muslims as potential terrorists, it enacts laws and advances policies like President George W. Bush's Uniting and Strengthening America by Providing Appropriate Tools Required to Intercept and Obstruct Terrorism Act (USA PATRIOT Act) and the National Security Entry and Exit Registration (NSEERS), which in turn reinforce non-Muslim Americans' perception of Muslims as a danger to the state, and thereby increasing the potential for hate and violent acting out against Muslim individuals. In other words, the 'deviant' character of Craig Hick's 2015 murder of three Muslim students in their apartment in Chapel Hill, North Carolina, is better understood as part of a wider context in which 'the state's repeated message that Muslim identity alone is grounds for suspicion that justifies vigilante action by private citizens.'[7] Naturally this is further reinforced by television, print and social media, and Hollywood films which mostly paint Muslims in this light.[8]

Yet in the aftermath of the 9/11 attacks of 2001, the policies of President Bush were only the first wave. Beydoun devotes more than a chapter to the additional structural Islamophobia put into place by President Barack Obama. Surprisingly perhaps, because of his June 2009 speech in Cairo which promised 'a new beginning' in America's relationship with Muslims, in August 2011, launched the Countering Violent Extremism (CVE) policing program, which sought the help of the Muslim community to identify young people suspected of being radicalized and to prevent them from committing acts of terror. This strategy of counter-radicalization sounds benign on paper, but it spelled trouble for the Muslim community in several ways. First, though 'extremism' was framed in neutral terms and could theoretically involve white supremacist groups, 'it is disproportionately if not entirely focused on 'ideas' and behavioral 'processes' linked to Islam and expressions of Muslim identity.'[9] Second, in practice it ensures that any young man who begins to practice his faith more seriously is likely to be flagged as a potential terror suspect – a 'bad Muslim' versus a 'good Muslim' who foregoes outward signs of religiosity.

The final reason Obama's CVE program 'ranks among the most destructive forms of structural Islamophobia' is that it intentionally set out to divide the Muslim community. Not only did it pit Sunnis against Shia, and the like, but it also pitted those individuals and organizations that accepted large grants in return for cooperation with the state against those who felt this was a direct attack on their civil rights and freedoms, and worse yet, an internalizing of the principles underpinning Islamophobia in the first place. These government 'informants', Beydoun observes, have done much damage to the cohesion and health of the Muslim community in the long run.

If Obama's CVE policy represented the second phase of modern structual Islamophobia, President Trump's Muslim bans 1, 2, and 3, and his overt use of Islamophobic slurs both in his speeches as candidate and as president represent the third phase. While under Presidents Bush and Obama laws and policies were enacted on the presumption that Muslims were terror suspects, 'Trump peddled and mainstreamed an outwardly explicit Islamophobia to match it.'[10] What his victory and his consistent approval ratings demonstrate is that Islamophobia resonates with a large proportion of Americans, mostly in the Republican Party, but also among Democrats.[11]

Unfortunately, Islamophobia has a long pedigree in the United States. We saw in the first chapter how a large proportion of the African slaves forcibly imported was Muslim but over generations under duress lost their connection to Islam. Beydoun starts there as well and then tells us of a second phase of Muslim erasure, a stark example of structural Islamophobia. For over a century and a half Muslims were banned by law from becoming American citizens. He notes, 'Trump's ban proposal, which he advanced by way of three executive orders, was driven by the same discourse and stereotypes that prohibited Muslims from becoming US citizens from 1790 to 1944.'[12] This period dubbed by historians as the 'naturalization era' was one in which Muslims were deemed 'an enemy race,' as people 'fundamentally different and unassimilable.'

The word 'race' above, as in 'enemy race,' is appropriate for two reasons. First, during the naturalization era courts only allowed 'free white persons' to attain American nationality. Being 'Muslim' was incompatible with being 'white' by law. The Naturalization Act of 1790, therefore, dissuaded many Muslims from ever attempting to migrate to the United States. But remember that those who were already there, were slaves whose involuntary labors and suffering helped to build the infrastructure and prosperity of this new nation. The sad paradox is that the specifically American construction of the 'black' race also served to demonize, or at least to erase, the Muslim identity of so many of them.

A second reason for the role of racialization in American Islamophobia has to do with eighteenth and nineteenth century Orientalism, which pigeonholed Muslims as Arab Middle Easterners.[13] Orientalism as a concept was the brainchild of influential Palestinian-American thinker Edward Said (1935–2003).[14] He spent most of his career analyzing Western literature about the 'Orient' (in fact the Middle East) and demonstrating how this discourse about the Oriental 'other' was laced with disdain mixed with fear. It was the gaze of a colonial master who deemed these mostly Muslim inhabitants to be 'inferior and subhuman, unassimilable and savage, violent and warmongering.'[15] Although he never used the term 'Islamophobia,' already in his 1981 book, titled *Covering Islam,* Said specifically critiqued the role of the American media played during and after the Iran hostage crisis in filling the minds of viewers and readers with a distorted image of Islam and Muslims which in turn justified the American imperial designs on the Middle East. Orientalism, in other words, *is* Islamophobia.

The convergence of Orientalism and Islamophobia can be seen in two particular twentieth-century court cases. In 1909 George Shishim, born in the Mount Lebanon Province of the Ottoman Empire (Lebanon today), was a California resident serving as a policeman in Los Angeles. He was in court petitioning for American citizenship. As mentioned above, whiteness was a sine qua non of citizenship. Judge George H. Hutton denied Shishim's request on the grounds that, being an Arab, which is synonymous with Muslim, he 'did not meet the legal mandate for whiteness.'[16] In a desperate, 'Hail Mary plea,' as Beydoun puts it, Shishim stood up with his LAPD badge shining on his lapel and said, 'If I am a Mongolian, then so was Jesus, because we came from the same land.' Put otherwise, if Jesus was white, then he was too. Shishim knew well that Christianity in the US was a condition for whiteness and he was a Christian. He had the judge cornered, or at least the judge in this case allowed himself to be convinced. The petition was granted.

Shishim's accession to American citizenship was the first of several cases in which Arab Christians would be deemed 'white,' not on the basis of their 'race' but because of their religion. Beydoun observes, 'American whiteness, therefore, was very much a social construction, endorsed by law and subject to revision.'[17] But the first time a Muslim was granted citizenship was because US geopolitical interests in the Middle East were now focused on oil. In 1944 Mohammed Mohriez, a Saudi national, stood in a Massachussetts court asking for American citizenship. Eleven years earlier President Herbert Hoover had agreed with the king of Saudi Arabia to form the Arabian American Oil Company (ARAMCO). Now America stood on the edge of a second world war. The judge granted the obviously Arab and Muslim petitioner his request and thus not only opened the door for Muslims to be admitted into America as citizens, but also established the precedent for the contemporary designation of Middle Easterners as legally 'white.'

Khaled Beydoun's book ends with a plea for all groups struggling to be treated with the dignity they deserve as human beings to come together to form new coalitions. The increased Islamophobia of the Trump era has already challenged non-black American Muslims to recognize their own racial prejudices inherited from their homelands and perhaps exacerbated by their own striving to be recognized as 'white' in the halls of American political power.[18] But that is beginning to change, he writes. After 9/11, in coalition-building meetings in Los Angeles, Detroit, New York and many other places, Beydoun remembers activists saying, 'Where were the Arabs and Muslims when profiling was a black and Mexican issue?[19] That was the truth, however painful it seemed at the time. The Muslim community, apart from the black Muslims and a few others, was not willing to work with other progressives until they felt the sting of discrimination themselves.

That collaborative spirit of the younger Muslim leadership represented by Beydoun himself is in full evidence today and, as he notes, the bulk of its most infuential thinkers and communicators are women. None, however, has a higher profile than Brooklyn Palestinian American, mother of three, Linda Sarsour. This quote from Beydoun summarizes best what he and others see is the best strategy for fighting today's Islamophobia, both private and structural:

> Sarsour was already a fixture, widely known to black and brown, straight and LGBTQ, Muslim and non-Muslim activists, occupying a platform that few Muslim Americans, let alone women, held before her. She was hardly a new commodity in social justice circles, but an activist who had earned her stripes in her native New York City and later emerged as one of the most forthright voices against sexism, racism, and anti-blackness within the broader Muslim American community. She symbolizes the new face and voice of Muslim America – the coalitional spirit of her generation, and the generations following, are championing.[20]

I would simply add that both justice and love are calling us together as human beings to speak out prophetically against laws that marginalize any group and against hate which divides us and robs us all of the wealth of human friendship and peace. As I hope was evident in this brief excursion into American Islamophobia, granting one's neighbor her rights to respect and love is both an individual effort and one undertaken by a government through public policies that level as much as possible the playing field for all. In that spirit I seek to wrap up Nicholas Wolterstorff's discussion of justice and love.

Wolterstorff's *Justice in Love*

Although I cannot do justice to a book so carefully argued step by step, I nevertheless offer the main points that relate to the issues touching this project. Nor can I hope to give the reader more than a glimpse of the vast literature over the ages on how justice and love might relate. Wolterstorff notes that both concepts have long been 'prominent in the moral culture of the West,' such that we find it difficult to imagine a society in which people think only about love, or one in which people think only in terms of justice.[21] To the contrary, our collective memory holds 'two comprehensive imperatives issued by the writers of antiquity':

> One is the imperative to do justice, coming to us from both the Athens-Rome strand of our heritage and the Jerusalem strand. "Do justice," said the prophet Micah in a well-known passage.[22] The ancient Roman jurist Ulpian said that we are to render to each person his or her *right* or *due* (*ius*). The other imperative comes to us only from the Jerusalem strand: love your neighbor as yourself, even if that neighbor is an enemy. Do not return evil for evil, said Jesus. The ancient Greek writers praised *eros*-love and *philia*-love. Jesus, quoting the Torah, enjoined *agape*-love.[23]

The three Greek words in the above quote are virtual synonyms for 'love,' with *eros* emphasizing desire directed toward beauty (as mentioned by Ghazi in his definition of love); with *philia* pointing particularly to friendship; and with *agape* as a more self-sacrificing kind of love, used in the Greek translation of the Hebrew Bible during the third century BCE, called the Septuagint,[24] and in the Greek text of the New Testament. But whatever the word chosen, the literature over the centuries that examined the relationship between love and justice was mostly characterized by tension – to follow one imperative means one cannot follow the other, or at least to some extent, compromises will have to be made. And besides 'incidents of unjust love and incidents of unloving justice,' we tend to assume that as we act out of love it will not be necessarily a just act; that as we act justly it may be unloving at the same time.

Wolterstorff says from the outset that his goal is to show that 'when these two imperatives are rightly understood, they are not in conflict.'[25] The task, however, is made more complex by the fact that, though no one has ever stated that doing justice is the be-all-end-all of ethical living, many have in fact asserted that love sums up every other virtue. That ethical orientation since the last century is called 'agapism' (from the Septuagint and New Testament Greek word for 'love,' *agape*).[26]

Modern Day Agapism and Its Limits

Within the modern agapist movement, particularly Protestants, says Wolterstorff, one would have to cite such luminaries as Karl Barth, Reinhold Niebuhr and Paul Ramsey, but the foundational texts go to the Dane, Soren Kierkegaard (d. 1855, *Works of Love*)[27] and the Swede, Bishop Anders Nygren (d. 1978, *Agape and Eros*).[28] The following summary is a useful introduction to this section:

> All modern day agapists held that agapic love is a species of that sort of love which consists of seeking to promote the good of someone as an end to itself, provided one does not do so because justice requires it. Such love, when the recipient is someone other than oneself, is *benevolence*, or *generosity*; apagic love for the other is a species of benevolence. Those who held that one should not include oneself among the recipients of one's agapic love often described it as *self-sacrificial* love. As Barth was fond of saying, agape is *being for* the other.[29]

Central to Kierkegaard's discussion of agapic love was how it is contrasted to other kinds of human love – romantic love, love of country, family, friends, and the like. Agapic love, by contrast, has nothing to do with emotional attachment. It is a Christian duty, which must be disinterested in the sense that it is not calculated in any way, or sparked by a particular emotion. Nygren agrees, but says that all other human loves stem from *eros*, which contains some desire from within the person who is loving. So what could move one to love even one's enemy? Nygren replies that it can only be a deep heart-felt response to God's forgiveness in Christ, which is the supreme model of agapic love. Its motive cannot come from the object loved, nor from some ulterior purpose, except to obey and emulate the God who sacrificed his Son for us.

Justice in this discourse is nowhere to be found. Wolterstorff does find one interesting clue, however, in a passage of Kierkegaard's *Works of Love*, which speaks to the 'inner glory of equality' in all human persons. Could he mean that we intuitively respond to the image of God in each person we encounter? But the idea is nowhere developed, and certainly not connected directly to the idea of love – that would be to provide an intellectual reason for loving one's neighbor, or so Wolterstorff conjectures. Still, the question remains, what if I act out of spontaneous and gratuitous agapic love and, without trying to, I fulfill a requirement of justice? Kierkegaard doesn't answer this question, but Nygren does. His rather extreme position is that the legal requirements of the Old Testament subsumed under the Greek word *nomos* (law) are completely obsolete in the New Testament scheme.[30] Justice has been superseded by love.

This point, it turns out, is useful for Wolterstorff's own explanation, because it involves two parables of Jesus, which have often been used to disassociate love from justice. The first is that of the workers in the vineyard (Mt. 20:1-16). Here, the owner hires day laborers at the crack of dawn promising them a day's wage. During the day he hires others who sit by the road, hoping for work, and even one batch of laborers an hour before the day's end. The parable then tells of the owner at day's end giving all the laborers the wage promised to the first ones hired. The latter, of course, grumbled. The owner told one of them, 'Friend, am I not allowed to do what I choose with what belongs to me? Or are you envious because I am generous?'[31] Nygren concludes that from a justice point of view the owner acted unfairly, but that Jesus was pointing to love as generosity over and beyond the scales of justice.[32]

Nygren, along with other proponents of modern agapism, sees the parable of the prodigal son in the same light (Lk 15:11-32). The younger of two sons uses his share of his father's inheritance to live a life of self-indulgence in a far away country. But in time the squandered wealth runs out and, to make things worse, famine struck the land. This poor Jewish boy finds himself feeding pigs just to survive. But then 'he comes to his senses' and determines to go back home, confess his sin to his father and beg him to take him in as one of his servants. Yet this was not to be, because the father, seeing him come from a distance, was 'full of compassion and love' and chose to celebrate his return with a great banquet for the whole village. Naturally, his older brother found it difficult to celebrate, and that's where the story ends. Nygren concludes once more that the elder brother, angry as he is that his father never threw a party like this for him, is right

– here he was, the hard-working, faithful son, who never left his father's side. Justice was not served; the father demonstrated 'unjust love.'[33]

But this kind of interpretation leaves Wolterstorff baffled. To him, Nygren's reading of the two parables is 'an almost-willful misinterpretation.'[34] There is nothing unfair at all in the way the landowner treated the workers in his vineyard, he retorts. The owner of the vineyard challenges the grumbler with these words, 'Friend, I am not treating you unjustly (*adikos*); did you not agree with me for a denarius? Take what belongs to you, and go. I choose to give to this last as I gave to you.'[35] In the same way, Nygren sees the father admitting to the older son he is unfair, but that since his younger brother was lost and is now found, he had to throw a party for him, even if in doing so he is wronging him. Wolterstorff objects. What the father actually says in the text is different: 'Look dear son, you have always stayed by me, and everything I have is yours. We had to celebrate this happy day. For your brother was dead and has come back to life! He was lost, but now is found!'[36]

Wolterstorff points out that the older brother still inherits everything that remains in the father's estate. He isn't wronged in any way. Perhaps, he adds, the older son is thinking about justice as 'a reciprocity code': his brother's shameful behavior deserved a punishment, not a party! He's the one deserving a party! But I agree with Wolterstorff who sees the father deliberately rejecting that code: 'Yes, the behavior of the younger son was bad; but he has returned penitent, so now is the time for a feast of forgiveness. Justice does not require that he be punished.'[37] Agapic love has *not* caused injustice in either of the two parables. For Wolterstorff this illustrates well the conundrum that modern day agapists are left with: to love people sometimes causes injustice. But if this is so, then a loving act would cause one to violate one's neighbor's 'right not to be so treated.' As you read his explanation, recall the discussion about justice as rights in Chapter 3:

> And if he has a right not to be so treated by me, then I ought not to treat him that way. In general it's true that if someone has a right against me to my not treating him than way, then I have a correlative obligation toward him not to treat him thus. The position of the agapist implies that I am sometimes permitted to do what I ought not to do; sometimes it is even the case that I *should* do what I ought not to do. That cannot be right. Something has to give in the classical version of modern day agapism.[38]

The other modern day agapist who devoted the most energy to this question of justice and love was Reinhold Niebuhr. Wolterstorff calls his view 'non-classical agapism.'[39] That is so, because for Niebuhr, justice is for this age, while love in its fullest dimension belongs to the age to come after Jesus returns. An American public theologian greatly influential in the 1950s and 1960s, Niebuhr was known for his theological and political realism. As human beings, he taught, we are incurably self-centered and incapable of resolving our interpersonal conflicts in any meaningful way. Jesus' ethic is uncompromising and idealistic – it is not designed for a world in which struggles between people and factions are pervasive and even violent. To love one's neighbor in the way Jesus demonstrated is to suffer what came to him – victimization and grief. Although in some fashion justice points to love, it does so as a distant 'echo' of love's ideal, and particularly in its call for equality. A democratic society which promotes the basic rights to life and property, and, even more so, calls for laws to enshrine 'moral rights and obligations' is 'a closer approximation of the law of love.'[40]

That idea of 'approximation,' of course is a very different position from that espoused by Nygren. As Wolterstorff puts it, there is 'a certain structural affinity between justice and the ideal of love.' 'True justice,' he explains, 'requires that everybody's rights be honored equally.' This is where I want to inject a thread of our previous conversation between Muslims and Christians. For Muslims, Shari'a is precisely that ideal that informs the nitty-gritty of human laws so as to provide a bullwark against the strong seeking to take advantage of the weak. As we have seen, Majid Khaddury ably chronicled how the issue of justice was debated among Muslims over time, and how it grew out of the interaction of the sacred texts and the intense political struggles emerging from the Prophet's succession and subsequent dynasties and states.

It is the same ardent search today by believers on a spectrum that runs from the puritanical Salafi-jihadis of the Islamic State who in the name of Shari'a justice conquered territories and executed apostates and enemies alike; to a variety of islamist groups, including the ruling Justice and Development Party of Turkey that long ago made its peace with a secular constitution; and finally, to a growing number of scholars and intellectuals who believe that Shari'a as an Islamic ideal has to be rethought for the present context. Certainly Tariq Ramadan would be one representative of this group. I have recently examined the works of three other influential Muslim scholars who have wrestled with the need to adapt Islamic law to the urgent task of incorporating human rights discourse – Khaled Abou El Fadl, Abdulaziz Sachedina and Abdullahi An-Na'im.[41]

So with that background conversation in mind, here is what Niebuhr argued in the 1950s, emphasizing the value of justice and the idea of 'natural law':

> The ideal of equality is a part of the natural law which transcends existence, but is more immediately relevant to social and economic problems because it is an ideal law, and as law presupposes a recalcitrant nature which must be brought into submission to it. The ideal of love, on the other hand, transcends all law... It is impossible to construct a social ethic out of the ideal of love in its pure form, because the ideal presupposes the resolution of the conflict of life with life, which is the concern of law to mitigate and restrain. For this reason Christianity really had no social ethic until it appropriated the Stoic ethic.[42]

For Niebuhr, justice, which is rendering to each person what is due, is a process that cannot be carried out in society without a certain amount of coercive force. Thus justice in this world automatically falls short of the ideal of love. And justice for him is useful only in conflict situations. With the coming of the eschaton (the 'new age' inaugurated by Jesus' return), justice will no longer be needed; love will rule unopposed, asserts Niebuhr. As with Nygren's view of justice and love, Wolterstorff concludes that 'here too we are confronted with an interpretation that has gone wrong.'[43] We have need for a theory that incorporates justice within love.

Wolterstorff's Care Agapism

Wolterstorff discredited 'modern day agapism' for running roughshod over justice. What is needed, he says, is a new definition of love. Yes, love does 'seek to promote the good in someone's life as an end in itself,' but it must also seek to treat the other in a just way. Justice in love here means ensuring that we treat our neighbor 'in a way that befits her worth,' or such that her rights are honored. He explains,

> The understanding that we need, if agapism is to be plausible as an ethical system, is an understanding of love as seeking both to promote the good in a person's life and to secure that she be treated as befits her worth. To treat her as one does because justice requires it is to love her. Of course, that to which she has a right is itself a good in her life, not something in addition, and so too for being treated as befits her worth. So the more precise way of putting the point is that we need an understanding of love such that seeking

to secure for someone the good of being treated as befits her worth is an example of love for her.[44]

It is precisely this aspect of love as recognizing worth in one's neighbor that leads Wolterstorff to say that it is also akin to eros, or 'attraction-love.'[45] At the very least, this attraction to the inherent worth of the other will lead us to consider how to treat him in a way that respects his rights. It is in that sense that he writes, 'Agape incorporates eros.'[46]

Another definition Wolterstorff makes in the following chapters and that must be cited here is his definition of love as 'care,' and not simply 'benevolence' or 'benefaction.'[47] He argues that the English word that best combines seeking the good of the other and securing the other's rights is the word 'care.' Of course, when love inadvertantly causes injustice in the other's life, we must admit that it was 'malformed care.' But the intention presumably was to seek that person's wellbeing in accordance with her rights. The word 'benevolence,' by contrast, contains the notion of care for someone's welfare, but it does not necessarily focus on respecting her rights. The other reason he chooses 'care' is that both the golden rule ('do unto others as you would have them to unto you,' Mt. 7:12) and the commandment to love one's neighbor ('love your neighbor as yourself,' Lev. 19:18, Mk 12:31 and parallels) presuppose that in the first place one has a healthy dose of self-esteem.[48] Benevolence toward oneself does not fit in this case, whereas care for one's own wellbeing is a sign of mental health and a necessary prerequisite for loving others.

Wolterstorff in his Chapter 14 ('Love, Justice, and the Good') brings the discussion back to human rights, and in so doing, points to God's love. The problem with twentieth-century agapism is that it limits God's love to forgiveness with the cross as its symbol. That is crucial for Christians of course, but Christians are united with their Jewish and Muslims brothers and sisters in proclaiming God's infinite benevolence in creating the world and humanity, and in caring for this creation on a daily basis. God's love is both benefaction and care. The Genesis one creation narrative contains six times the refrain 'God saw that it was good.' Wolterstorff observes that this 'litany culminates with the declaration, upon the creation of human beings, that "God saw everything that God had made, and inded, it was very good."'[49] This offers us a distinction, he writes, between benefaction (bringing about some good) and 'acknowledging a good already there.'[50] This is an example of attraction-love, the eros-type of love Plato discusses in his *Symposium*.

God's acknowledgment of human worth at creation, then, serves as a bridge between love as benefaction and love as a just rendering of humanity's worth. Of course, one would think immediately of the qur'anic parallel: 'We have honoured the sons of Adam and carried them by land and sea; We have provided good sustenance for them and favored them specially above many of those We have created.' (Q. 17:70). Notice how this thought leads Wolterstorff in the direction of human rights:

> To treat the other justly is to advance her life-good in some respect; that is benefaction. It is also to to pay her what due respect for her worth requires; that is acknowledgment. In doing justice, benefaction and acknowledgment are united. And because care incorporates acting justly, care likewise unites benefaction with acknowledgment.[51]

This leads us to his discussion of 'divine love and human rights.' As Wolterstorff argued in *Justice: Rights and Wrongs*, God's love for each and every human being provides a grounding for the human rights paradigm that was worked out in the wake of two horrific world wars in 1948 – the Universal Declaration of Human Rights (UDHR). There is nothing wrong with the common understanding of human rights, he declares. It does not matter what our nationality or ethnic background or social class or religious belonging might be; simply belonging to the human race qualifies us as bearers of human rights. Certainly some of these rights overlap with animal rights (like the right to be treated in a humane way),[52] but most human rights are specific to human beings. That said, not all human rights are universal. The right to being protected by a police force does not apply to people living in areas without a police force. So in that sense, they are 'not wronged on account of not being protected by police.'[53] So even though our *status* as human beings qualifies us for a long list of 'human rights' (as listed in the UDHR and following covenants), our circumstances may disqualify us from certain ones.

Yet despite the discussions and disagreements on any particular list of human rights, Wolterstorff endorses the mainstream view that they are 'grounded in the dignity of the rights-holders.'[54] In his words,

> Because of the equal, ineradicable, and animal-transcending dignity each human being has *qua* human being, none may be carved up for stew, none may be shot and tossed into a dumpster for waste management to haul away, none may be deposited on a mountainside to die, none may be tortured for the vengeance or the pleasure of the torturer.[55]

But how does that 'animal-transcending dignity' come to be attached to human beings?[56] That is the relationship that has vexed human rights theoreticians ever since the promulgation of the UDHR in 1948. How does one ground human rights? This excellence and worth 'does not settle on things willy-nilly.' What is it that gives humanity its worth? Almost all secular accounts of human worth following Kant are predicated on some quality that humans possess, and it is usually rational capacity. The great legal philosopher Richard Dworkin disagrees. This dignity, he argues, can only supervene 'on the way in which human beings are created.'[57]

This is a crucial point, Wolterstorff notes. Otherwise, if rational capacity or even moral agency are grounds of human worth, infants and adults suffering from dementia would be automatically disqualified. In *Justice: Rights and Wrongs*, Wolterstorff had argued that it was human nature's quality of *resembling* God (creation in God's image) that qualified every human being as a bearer of human rights. Even more, God loves every human being, and that is what bestows worth on any and every human being, even the dementia patient who has lost all awareness of himself and the world around him. And this is where Worlterstorff cites John Calvin's (d. 1564) commentary on Genesis 9:6, 'Whoever sheds the blood of a human, by a human shall that person's blood be shed, for in his own image God made humankind.' Here's Calvin's commentary, which, surprisingly perhaps, nicely furthers his own argument:

> Men are indeed unworthy of God's care, if respect be had only to themselves; but since they bear the image of God engraven on them, he deems himself violated in their person. Thus, although they have nothing of their own by which they obtain the favour of God, he looks upon his own gifts in them, and is thereby excited to love and care for them. This doctrine, however, is to be carefully observed, that no one can be injurious to his brother without wounding God himself. Were this doctrine deeply fixed in our minds, we should be much more reluctant than we are to inflict injuries.[58]

It is precisely because God is 'excited to love and to care' for people, then, that injuring a fellow human being is to injure her Creator. Wolterstorff sees this love as God's attachment to that person, by virtue of his recognizing his own image in her. This makes sense, he adds, because out of all creatures only humans are capable of friendship. He could have cited the Genesis passage which recounts the aftermath of Adam and Eve's disobedience. Look at this part of the Hebrew narrative in the light of our present discussion:

⁸When the cool evening breezes were blowing, the man and his wife heard the Lᴏʀᴅ Gᴏᴅ ᴡᴀʟᴋɪɴɢ ᴀʙᴏᴜᴛ ɪɴ ᴛʜᴇ ɢᴀʀᴅᴇɴ. Sᴏ ᴛʜᴇʏ ʜɪᴅ ғʀᴏᴍ ᴛʜᴇ Lᴏʀᴅ Gᴏᴅ ᴀᴍᴏɴɢ ᴛʜᴇ ᴛʀᴇᴇꜱ. ⁹Then the Lᴏʀᴅ Gᴏᴅ ᴄᴀʟʟᴇᴅ ᴛᴏ ᴛʜᴇ ᴍᴀɴ, 'Wʜᴇʀᴇ ᴀʀᴇ ʏᴏᴜ?'

¹⁰He replied, 'I heard you walking in the garden, so I hid. I was afraid because I was naked' (Gen. 3:8-10).

The story line is clear in its implication that God often would come to spend time with his two creatures, Adam and Eve. God's question is both natural and surprising. God is by definition omniscient and would have seen every detail of what had transpired. And God is spirit, not corporeal, and his 'walking about in the garden' makes no theological sense, much less it being something than can be heard. But that's the genius of this narrative. With these concrete, if surely symbolic, details, the writer tells the reader that God enjoyed his friendship with Adam and Eve; that it involved a rhythm of daily walks together (perhaps); that their sudden hiding spelled an ominous change in that idyllic relationship.

Jesus, Paul, and Justice

I end this account of Wolterstorff's thesis⁵⁹ with the particularly Christian expression of 'justice in love,' both from the last chapter of this book and then with his discussion of Jesus and Paul and justice in *Justice: Rights and Wrongs*. We have to start, he would urge, with the notion that the Bible is God's story that begins with the creation narrative in Genesis, whereby God, having honored his human creatures by wanting to be their friend devises a plan that will in the end restore that friendship. It was a plan that involved choosing one man, Abraham, with whom he could make a covenant of friendship (Abraham in the Islamic tradition is called *khalīl Allāh* – 'God's friend') that will involve his descendants who are to become 'a blessing to all nations' (Gen. 12:3) and 'a light to the nations' (Isa. 42:6; 51:4; Lk 2:32). Yet, although the Israelites later received the covenant more formally through Moses at Mount Sinai, they were not able in the end to stay obedient to its injunctions. As a result of their consistent ignoring of the many warnings brought to them by the prophets, they were sent into exile. And although some did come back in time to the land of Israel, in Jesus' day they were suffering under Roman occupation.

This is the point at which Wolterstorff discusses Paul's message of 'justification,' mostly from his letter to the Romans. In chapter 2 Paul upbraids the Jews who pass judgment on non-Jews (or Gentiles), 'because you who pass judgment do the same things' (2:1). But someday God's 'righteous [or just, in the Greek] judgment will be revealed.' He explains:

> God "will repay each person according to what they have done."[60] To those who by persistence in doing good seek glory, honor and immortality, he will give eternal life. But for those who are self-seeking and who reject the truth and follow evil, there will be wrath and anger. There will be trouble and distress for every human being who does evil: first for the Jew, then for the Gentile; but glory, honor and peace for everyone who does good: first for the Jew, then for the Gentile. For God does not show favoritism (Rom. 2:6-11, NIV).

So for the Jews who say, 'we have the law,' Paul demonstrates that no one is able to obey the law in full, because 'Jews and Gentiles alike are all under the power of sin' (Rom. 3:9). But in God's unfolding story the crucial climax has just taken place in the person of Jesus the Messiah. Here's how Paul explains this:

> But now apart from the law the righteousness of God has been made known, to which the Law and the Prophets testify. This righteousness is given through faith in Jesus Christ to all who believe. There is no difference between Jew and Gentile, for all have sinned and fall short of the glory of God, and all are justified freely by his grace through the redemption that came by Christ Jesus. God presented Christ as a sacrifice of atonement, through the shedding of his blood – to be received by faith. He did this to demonstrate his righteousness, because in his forbearance he had left the sins committed beforehand unpunished – he did it to demonstrate his righteousness at the present time, so as to be just and the one who justifies those who have faith in Jesus (Rom. 3:21-26 NIV).

Any English translation will struggle to render Paul's wordplays with the term translated here by 'righteousness' (*dikaiosune*). It also means 'justice,' and its cognate word *dikaiosis* is the word Paul uses for 'justification.' This only underscores the importance of Paul's last sentence, or the conclusion of this part of his argument: the way in which God deals with his human creatures displays at once his justice (all are treated in the same way, with faith as the only condition) and his love (he provided redemption through Jesus' atonement on the cross).

But, you might ask, what is the connection between the two quotations above from Romans? In the first one those who 'persist in doing good' (Jews or Gentiles) obtain eternal life. In the second one, the condition is faith in Christ's work of redemption. Is this a contradiction? Paul comes to this in the next chapter and he uses Abraham as his example (Rom. 4:3-11). He begins with Gen. 15:6, 22, which reads, '[Abraham's] faith was reckoned to him as *dikaiosune*,' which for Paul also means 'he was justified by faith.' The common Protestant understanding of this is that 'God imputes innocence to Abraham, reckons him as innocent, knowing all the while that he is not.'[61] But that cannot be. Paul nowhere says that God declared Abraham *dikaios* ('righteous,' or 'innocent'). What he does mean is that as Abraham stands before the divine Judge, although his actions condemn him as guilty and therefore the judge cannot acquit him on account of his works, the Judge nevertheless reckoned his faith as righteousness. That is what makes him *dikaios* and allows the Judge to clear all charges against him. As Paul later says in Rom. 8:1, 'There is now no condemnation for those who are in Christ Jesus.' It is pure grace, a gift from God because of Jesus' sacrifice. In effect, faith in that sacrifice allows Christ's righteousness to cover our sins.

But, you might object, Abraham had no knowledge of Jesus, who came a couple millennia after him. True, Paul answers, but the God Abraham trusted, the One in whom he believed, is the God who promised to bless all nations through him (Gen. 12:3) and who fulfilled that promise by sending Jesus as the Messiah to save all people from their sin. So the two principles come together. As Wolterstorff argues later, faith is no 'add-on,' not something extra but one's whole 'life orientation.' He explains,

> To have faith in God requires repenting of all the ways in which one has wronged God and neighbor. The reason God justifies those who have faith and not some other set of human beings is that it with these that God can become friends. How can God become friends with those who reject him?[62]

So the phrase in chapter 2, 'To those who by persistence in doing good seek glory, honor and immortality, he will give eternal life' has to be paired with 'This righteousness is given through faith in Jesus Christ to all who believe' (Rom. 3:12). Those to whom God gives eternal life on the Last Day will be those who, looking back, realize that their faith was placed in the God who judges them through the righteousness of Jesus. They were friends of God.

But as noted above, the story of Jesus and justice would be terribly incomplete without recalling what led to the cross, the focal point of all four gospel narratives. The one called by God to inaugurate his reign of justice falls victim to a perverse travesty of justice himself. This story is best told by University of Pennsylvania law professor David Skeel.

David Skeel and the Crucifixion

Skeel departed from his usual publications on bankruptcy laws and the like to publish a book defending Christianity as the thought system that best deals with the complexities of human life.[63] He sets up what he calls five paradoxes and shows how the Christian faith arguably explains them in the most satisfactory way: consciousness (why do we humans seemingly have to explain our place in the universe?); beauty (why do we see beauty as both transcendent and yet fleeting and compromised?); suffering (why do we struggle to see something everywhere in nature as also wrong?); death and the afterlife (why do we seem compelled to create afterlife scenarios?). The fifth paradox is the one about justice: 'Why do the advocates of each new system of justice believe they can devise legal codes that will achieve a fully just social order, even though every previous system of justice has failed?'[64] I will come to his answer to this in the Conclusion, but for now I will just comment on Jesus' experience of injustice.

Betrayed by Judas, Israel's religious leaders arrest Jesus and bring him to trial during the night. Considering that they had several times attempted to assassinate him, it is likely that they had decided that due to Jesus' popularity, a murder would turn the people against them. So the wiser course of action was to conjure up the legitimacy of a trial according to the injunctions of the Mosaic law and its later elaboration by the jurists. But the decision to try Jesus secretely and at night likely robbed the proceedings of any legal standing from the beginning.[65]

Still, the law called for the agreement of two witnesses. That condition, however, proved to be difficult, if not impossible to fulfill. This led to the biggest breach of the Jewish law, as Skeel explains:

> The impasse was broken only after the high priest interjected himself into the proceedings and asked Jesus, "Are you the Christ, the Son of the Blessed?" (Mark 14:61). When Jesus stated that he was indeed both Christ and the Son of God, the high priest immediately ended the trial, declaring Jesus guilty of blasphemy for having equated himself with God. The high priest's intervention was illegal, because he was forbidden by Jewish law from participating in a capital trial prior to the vote on the verdict.[66]

The matter, however, could not end there, because the Jews were militarily occupied by the Romans whose law stipulated that only Rome could execute a capital punishment. So they came to Pontius Pilate, the Roman governor, early in the morning building up the best case for Jesus' death that they could muster. Note that this second trial began very differently from the first. The Jewish leaders set out to put Jesus to death, but Pilate will not condemn without formal charges. Knowing that a blasphemy would not pass muster with the Roman official, they accuse Jesus of sedition. Jesus, they charge, has proclaimed himself king, over and against the Roman emperor.

Undeterred, Pilate believes that Jesus is innocent and only framed for reasons of jealousy by the Sanhedrin. So he looks for legal technicalities. Is Jesus from Galilee, he asks? Then let Herod try him. But Herod promptly sent him back. Then Pilate tries to persuade Jesus to defend himself – to no avail. Still, he thinks, there is one more solution. Surely the people gathered here have seen all the good that this man Jesus has done and if given the choice between freeing Jesus and Barabbas, a known criminal, they will surely choose Jesus. This last resort also failed. The crowd, in fact, had gathered for an execution. Encouraged by the religious leaders, they cried out for Jesus' crucifixion.

Summing up the lessons learned from these two trials, Skeel concludes that the two best legal systems of the day, the Jewish law and the Roman law, failed on that day. But that is the exact point. This illustrates well the justice paradox: a) we believe a good legal code can create a just society; b) in fact all codes, when put in place, fail miserably. He explains: 'the Jesus story shows that even two legal systems working together and potentially correcting one another cannot ensure a just outcome. The justice paradox is at the heart of the Christian story.'[67]

At the end of our discussion of justice and love with Wolterstorff and now Skeel as guides, my Muslim readers likely feel excluded from the conversation, although I hope they benefited from learning a bit more about the Christian perspective. Jesus and his teaching offers much common ground for Muslims and Christians, but his crucifixion likely does not. Allow me to briefly suggest, however, that Jesus and the cross are a potentially fruitful area of Muslim-Christian dialogue. This is certainly what Lebanese American scholar Mahmoud Ayoub demonstrated in one of his finest essays.[68]

Mahmoud Ayoub on Islam and the Crucifixion

I will only touch on a couple of points which also have a bearing on our central issue of justice in Ayoub's essay, 'The Death of Jesus, Reality or Delusion – A Study of the Death of Jesus in Tafsir Literature.' It centers on the Qur'anic phrase, 'it was made to appear like that to them,' from the wider context:

> [The Jews] said, "We have killed the Messiah, Jesus, son of Mary, the Messenger of God." (They did not kill him, nor did they crucify him, though it was made to appear like that to them; those that disagreed about him are full of doubt, with no knowledge to follow, only supposition: they certainly did not kill him – No! God raised him up to Himself. God is almighty and wise) (Q. 4:157-8).

The standard Muslim belief is that God 'raised [Jesus] up to Himself' before the crucifixion and that he changed the likeness of another person to look like Jesus who then was crucified in his place. Some versions offer a candidate who volunteers; others point to someone who deserves punishment, like Judas Iscariot. Ayoub comes through a variety of 'subtitutionist' versions over the centuries, but adds that this line of thinking creates two problems, both of which touch on injustice. First, God makes one person suffer in the place of another.[69] Second, 'what would the implications of this confusion of identities by God be for social norms and the credibility of historical testimony?'[70] This was the objection made by commentator Fakh al-Din al-Razi (d. 1209), which led him to reject the substitutionist hypothesis. To follow this view, he argued, would gravely unsettle social norms such as marriage or property ownership. What is even worse, it would undermine historical research, and in particular the cardinal rule of what makes a chain of historical transmission of hadiths reliable, that is, *tawātur*. Razi listed several other views but did not commit to any particular one. As Ayoub then comments, 'Razi was more concerned with the understanding of Christ, the spirit of God and His Word.'[71]

The Qur'an, argues Ayoub, 'presents Jesus as a challenge not only to human folly and unbelief (*kufr*) but equally to human ignorance and the reliance on mere conjecture.'[72] Right after it states, 'it was made to appear like that to them,' it warns that those who disagreed 'are full of doubt,' basing their reasoning on 'conjecture,' or 'supposition.' Yet the verse is far from clear. Ayoub agrees with other scholars that the Qur'an plainly affirms that Jesus died, although not necessarily on the cross.[73] He quotes the first great commentator al-Tabari who himself quotes Ka'ab al-Ahbar, the Jewish chief rabbi, as saying, 'Thus, when Jesus saw the small number of those who accepted him and the multitude of those who rejected him, he complained to God. Then God revealed to him, 'Surely I am receiving you (*mutawaffika*) and lifting you up to me. For the one who I take up to Me is not dead.'[74] Thus several early commentators offered various schemes whereby Jesus died a natural death before being taken up to heaven, since that is the literal meaning of *mutawaffika* (I will cause you to die).

For Razi, centuries later, there had to be more to these verses. He understood *mutawaffika* metaphorically: 'I [God] shall render you [Jesus] as though you are dead,' and somehow God took him up to heaven both in body and spirit. In a similar way, notes Ayoub, the Sufis emphasize the importance of this fact: 'The significance of Christ's life in heaven is his example as a favored human being who has rise[n] beyond this world of material existence to the divine presence.' And heaven, as al-Hasan al-Basri believed, 'is the locus of the grace (*karamah*) of God and the dwelling place of His angels.' Through his presence, they will 'attain his grace (*barakah*), because he is the Word of God and his Spirit.'[75]

After examining several modern scholars' views on the crucifixion, Ayoub concludes that 'Muslim commentators have not been able convincingly to disprove the crucifixion. Rather, they have compounded the problem by adding the conclusion of their substitutionary theories.'[76] So what position can a Muslim take that is both faithful to the theology of the Qur'an and yet open to further conversation with Christians about Jesus? It would definitely not be the position of Rashid Rida (d. 1935), contends Ayoub. Like his mentor Muhammad Abduh (d. 1905) and other modernists in the early twentieth century, reason became the arbiter of truth. Furthermore, the context was Christian polemics about Islam. So Rida categorically stated that God through the cross could not have reconciled justice and mercy. In fact, the crucifixion 'nullifies' them both.[77] Jesus, after all, is an innocent man allegedly suffering for the sins of others. But this is to miss the meaning of the wider theological panorama, retorts Ayoub. When the Qur'an says that the Jews didn't kill Jesus, it is not a factual statement about a historical event (Jesus was not crucified) but rather a theological one. It is 'a denial of the power of human beings to vanquish and destroy the divine Word, which is forever victorious.' The phrase 'it was made to appear like that to them' is God's judgment against human arrogant and ignorant schemes.

I will quote below his concluding paragraph, which is unique to him and certainly not representative of any known current in contemporary Islam. Yet like Prince Ghazi of Jordan in penning the Common Word letter, Mahmoud Ayoub (b. 1935) is seeking to build bridges. He has spent his entire career working on interfaith dialogue, and with Christians in particular. Both sides will need to make efforts to learn from each other. In the following statement, I find Ayoub intriguingly perceptive. And even though nothing is said of justice and love, he is opening a theological space wherein the Creator has invested his glory in his human creatures in a way that is remarkably resonant with Wolterstorff's discussion of the inherent worth and dignity of all human beings as an object of God's love:

> Christianity has insisted, and with equally uncompromising seriousness, on "letting God be man" in order for "man to be divine." The gap between an extreme Islamic and an extreme Christian position on this point is admittedly vast. The difference is, I believe, one of theological terminology rather than intent. The final purpose for the two communities of faith is one: let God be God, not only in His vast creation but in our little lives as well. Then and only then could man be truly man, and the light of God would shine with perfect splendor in our mouths and hearts.[78]

Conclusion

We began this chapter with the complex web of injustice woven into American Islamophobia. We saw how interwoven justice and love are in Wolterstorff's understanding of justice as rights grounded in God's love for every human being he created. In the next and final chapter I attempt to pull together all the different strands of this book in order to put forward a vision of justice and love that both Muslims and Christians can embrace.

Endnotes

1   'Friday sermon by the imam of New Zealand mosque attacked by gunman,' Reuters (March 22, 2019), online, https://www.reuters.com/article/us-newzealand-shootout-sermon-text-idUSKCN1R30G2.

2   In 2017, he was named both the American Arab Anti-Discrimination Committee Advocate of the Year and the Arab-American Association of New York's Community Champion of the Year.

3   Beydoun 2018.

4   Beydoun 2018, 28.

5   Beydoun 2018, 36. Further he explains, 'Structual Islamophobia is manifested by historic policy and state action against Islam and Muslims, and most visibly today, by the abundant laws, policies, and programs enacted to police Muslims during the protracted war on terror,' (Beydoun 2018, 37).

6   Beydoun 2018, 40.

7   Beydoun tells this story in detail as an introduction to this chapter on defining Islamophobia (Beydoun 2018, 23–27). For another analysis of this event, see also Johnston 2015b, 'Islamophobia Sows Fear,' http://www.humantrustees.org/blogs/religion-and-global-society/item/138-islamophobia-sows-fear.

8   See for instance, 'Same Hate, New Target: Islamophobia and Its Impact on the United States,' Council on American-Islamic Relations (CAIR) and The Center for Race & Gender at the University of California, Berkeley; available as a pdf document, http://pluralism.org/document/same-hate-new-target-islamophobia-and-its-impact-in-the-united-states/.

9   Beydoun 2018, 136. Since 9/11, white supremacist killings in the US have significantly outnumbered Islamic-inspired ones. The Anti-Defamation League revealed that in 2018 '[r]ight-wing extremists were linked to at least 50 murders last year, a 35 percent increase over 2017.' Kelly Kohen, 'Trump doesn't think white nationalism is a threat – but the data say otherwise', see Kohen, 2019, online, https://www.vox.com/identities/2019/3/16/18268856/new-zealand-shooter-white-nationalism-united-states.

10   Beydoun 2018, 191.

11   A 2015 Bloomberg poll found that over two-thirds of likely Republican voters said they 'strongly supported[ed] the ban' while '25 percent of likely Democratic voters either supported the ban or were unsure'. Beydoun points to other figures that show a good deal of Islamophobia on the left, though a bit less than on the right.

12   Beydoun 2018, 47.

13   Notice this other side of the above paradox: 'If black meant property and slave, and Muslim meant Arab or Middle Eastern, then black Muslim was a legally impossible and contradictory identity in early American history' (Beydoun 2018, 49).

14   It is based on his classic book, *Orientalism*, see Said 1979.

15   Beydoun 2018, 51.

16   Beydoun 2018, 60.

17   Beydoun 2018, 61.

18   Beydoun in his chapter 'Anti-Black Racism and Islamophobia' highlights the irony of Muhammad Ali and Malcolm X being so popular among American Muslims, yet the non-Black majority is not open to discussing the correlation between Islamophobia and anti-black racism. As a result, 'Racism within the Muslim American community, combined with the broader dis-indentification of African Muslims as bona fide Muslims, is a reality black Muslims continually grapple with' (Beydoun 2018, 169).

19   Beydoun 2018, 179.

20   Beydoun 2018, 187.

21   Wolterstorff 2011, Preface, vii.

22   Cf. the first page of this chapter.

23   Wolterstorff 2011, Preface, vii.

24   The distinction between the three words becomes important in the following discussion, as the Christian conversation about love in the twentieth century is called 'Agapism.'

25   Wolterstorff 2011, 1.

26   Wolterstorff uses this term for all the discussions among Christians on this issue since at least Augustine in the fourth century, but he does note that the conversation took a specific turn in the twentieth century, which he calls 'modern day agapism' (the title of his Chapter 2).

27   Kierkegaard 1995.
28   Nygren 1953. Wolterstorff chooses this work despite its well-known lacunae in biblical interpretation, its questionable philosophy, and its anti-Semitic overtones, because it was systematic in a way that was 'wonderful to behold' and became influential for that reason (Wolterstorff 2011, 21–22).
29   Wolterstorff 2011.
30   Wolterstorff 2011, 46.
31   Wolterstorff 2011, 48.
32   Wolterstorff quotes another famous Protestant theologian who writes, 'The substance of the parable is not the justitia civilis but the justitia evangelica which consists precisely in the cessation of all deserving, in the denial of all lawful claims, and is hence the antithesis of the law of worldly justice' (Brunner 1945, 111).
33   Wolterstorff 2011, 49.
34   Wolterstorff 2011, 60.
35   Wolterstorff 2011, This is Wolterstorff quoting Mt. 20:13-14 in the NRSV, a more literal translation than the NIV, and especially the NLT. Wolterstorff takes up the question of just and unjust generosity in Chapter 18.
36   Lk 15:31-32.
37   Wolterstorff 2011, 60.
38   Wolterstorff 2011, 61, emphasis his.
39   He devotes an entire chapter to him using that as his title (Wolterstorff 2011, 62–72).
40   Wolterstorff 2011, 68, quoting from Niebuhr 1957, 110.
41   Johnston 2015, 113–48.
42   Wolterstorff 2011, 68-9, quoting from Niebuhr 1957, 149–50. 'Christianity really has no social ethic' – that is a statement many Christians would disagree with. Roman Catholicism since at least Pope Leo VIII's 1891 encyclical *Rerum Novarum* has developed a strong social ethic. See for instance the statement issued by the United States Conference of Catholic Bishops, 'Seven Themes of Catholic Social Teaching,' available online at: http://www.usccb.org/beliefs-and-teachings/what-we-believe/catholic-social-teaching/seven-themes-of-catholic-social-teaching.cfm accessed July 30, 2018.
43   Wolterstorff 2011, 72.
44   Wolterstorff 2011, 93. The phrase 'if agapism is to be plausible as an ethical system' calls up material from his book, *Justice : Rights and Wrongs*, which he summarizes in his Introduction here. I do not have the space here to detail his ethical theory, but suffice it to say that he examines *egoism* (my only obligation is to promote the good in my own life), *eudaimonism* (the majority view of the Greeks, whereby I seek to promote the good in someone else's life in so far as it promises to enhance my own wellbeing) and *utilitarianism* (when deciding about what to do, I should take into account the wellbeing of all who might be affected by this action and I should choose that course of action that maximizes net utility). In the course of his examination, he finds all three of these theories wanting, and this is what leads him to examine agapism, a position rarely discussed in the philosophical literature because of its religious background, but which he avers should be on offer – hence his book.

45 Ghazi (2013:13) puts a good deal of emphasis on eros – love as attraction to beauty – in his own exposition of love.

46 Wolterstorff 2011, 93.

47 He devotes Chapter 9 to this issue, 'Love as Care' (101–109).

48 See Wolterstorff's discussion of this, Wolterstorff 2011, 94–97.

49 Wolterstorff 2011, 143.

50 Wolterstorff 2011, 143, emphasis his.

51 Wolterstorff 2011, 144.

52 My comment, not his. But I think that is what he meant.

53 Wolterstorff 2011, 146. A good example of a universal human right is 'the right not to be tortured for the pleasure of the torturer.' No matter the circumstance, this should be recognized as the right of every person anywhere and at any time.

54 Wolterstorff 2011, 147.

55 Wolterstorff 2011.

56 Wolterstorff uses the more technical term: how does that dignity 'supervene' on human beings?

57 Wolterstorff 2011, 148.

58 Wolterstorff 2011, 153. Wolterstorff does not offer the reference to this passage in Calvin's commentary.

59 I am choosing to bypass Part Three of his book, 'Just and Unjust Love,' which deals with the three foremost candidates of unjust love: forgiveness, generosity and paternalism. Of the three, I regret that I have no space to give justice to Wolterstorff's treatment of forgiveness. For the reader interested in his excellent presentation (chapters 15–17) read them alongside Russel Powell's 'Forgiveness in Islamic Ethics and Jurisprudence' (2012). Now I move to this last chapter, which is the second of two chapters in Part Four, 'The Justice of God's Love.' I have skipped the first chapter, a discussion of the Apostle Paul's view of God's generosity in his letter to the Romans, and will end with a few comments in his last chapter, 'What Is Justification and Is It Just?'

60 The footnote in the NIV says this is a quotation from Ps. 62:12 and Prov. 24:12.

61 Wolterstorff 2011, 263.

62 Wolterstorff 2011, 276.

63 Skeel 2014.

64 Skeel 2014, 10.

65 Skeel 2014, 123.

66 Skeel 2014.

67 Skeel 2014, 126.

68 Ayoub was Director of Islamic Studies at the Department of Religion at Temple University (1988–2008) and is now Faculty Associate of Shi'ite and Christian-Muslim Relations and Co-Director of the Duncan Black MacDonald Center for the Study of Islam and Muslim-Christian Studies at Hartford Seminary in Hartford, CT.

69 Later he says this, 'The substitutionist theory will not do, regarless of its form or purpose. First, it makes a mockery of divine justice and the primordial covenant of God with humanity to guide human history to its final fulfillment (Q. 7:172; 2:38). Would it be in consonance with God's covenant, his mercy and justice, to deceive humanity for so many centuries?' (Ayoub 2007, 166–167).

70   Ayoub 2007, 160.
71   Ayoub 2007, 164. Ayoub is referring to Q. 3:45: 'The angels said, "Mary, God gives you news of a Word from Him, whose name will be the Messiah, Jesus, son of Mary, who will be held in honour in this world and the next, who will be one brought near to God."' Also Q. 4:71: 'The Messiah, Jesus, son of Mary, was nothing more than a messenger of God, His word directed to Mary, and a spirit from Him.'
72   Ayoub 2007, 166.
73   E.g., Q. 3:55; 5:117; 19:33. In the first two instances it is the same verb (*mutawaffa*) which literally means 'cause to die' and which is usually translated in these passage 'take him up.' Commentators knew this was the literal meaning and debated these verses accordingly.
74   Ayoub 2007, 169.
75   Ayoub 2007, 170.
76   Ayoub 2007, 176.
77   Ayoub 2007, 175.
78   Ayoub 2007, 176.

Conclusion

Justice and Love: Muslim-Christian Synergy

I will sing of your love and justice;
to you, LORD, I will sing praise (Ps. 101:1 NIV).1

God commands justice, doing good, and generosity (Q. 16:90)

But you must return to your God;
maintain love and justice,
and wait for your God always (Hosea 12:6 NIV)

We decreed to the Children of Israel that if anyone kills a person ... it is as if
he kills all mankind, while if any saves a life it is as if he saves the lives of all
mankind (Q. 5:32)

He has shown you, O mortal, what is good.
And what does the LORD REQUIRE OF YOU?
To act justly and to love mercy
and to walk humbly with your God (Micah 6:8 NIV)

None of you has faith until you love for your brother what you love for yourself.
(Hadith found in Sahih Bukhari and Sahih Muslim)

As I conclude the book as a whole, I invite you to reconsider justice and love
as two sides of the same coin in the common revelation of the Abrahamic
traditions. Following Nicholas Wolterstorff, we have examined what justice is at its roots – granting each human being his or her intrinsic rights.
So justice begins on an individual level as an endeavor to treat every person we come across in a just manner. Naturally, this does not guarantee
that love is included in that interaction, but as we saw from the Common
Word letter, Christianity and Islam (and Judaism, by extension) enjoin us

to love our neighbor in all circumstances. So naturally in the context of our everyday dealings with others, we are to act both justly and lovingly.

Yet justice must be also translated into just laws and good governance, as we have seen in our case studies, from racism and Islamophobia in the United States, to the poor treatment of minorities in Pakistan and Egypt, to the oppression of the Palestinians in the Occupied Territories and the historical tensions between Muslims and Christians in Nigeria. This was also driven home to me as I translated the book that the Tunisian islamist leader Rached Ghannouchi mostly wrote in prison in the 1980s, *The Public Freedoms of the Islamic State*.[2] Here was a man who entered politics in order to shape a more righteous and just society in the name of Islam, but who found himself on the receiving end of a 'Muslim' despotic ruler. In his book he forcefully argues for a democratic state in which the rights of every citizen are respected, although he does see some limits for non-Muslims.

After 22 years of exile in London, and after his party, Ennahada, had won the most votes in the parliamentary elections following the 'Jasmine Revolution', Ghannouchi had the chance to see some of his ideas implemented. But with neighboring Libya falling into chaos and the resulting rise of terrorism in his own nation, including the asssassination of two prominent liberal politicians, he pulled his party out of power and cooperated with various factions of the Tunisian political class and civil society to draw up a new constitution.[3] In the end, Ennahda still plays a junior role in the current government and Ghannouchi, reelected to the premiership of his party at Ennahda's Tenth Congress in 2016, declared in his opening speech that 'political Islam' was no longer needed in Tunisia.[4] His thinking about justice in society had not changed, but he saw things very differently as the political climate in Tunisia itself had changed.

Ghannouchi would be the first to say, however, that justice through governance is best approximated by a political system that separates executive, legislative and judicial powers; that allows for a rotation of power through the ballot box, and that crafts a host of other practical, common sense measures which can be adapted to each context and tweaked as needed over time. But justice is also about families, neighborhoods, local institutions, and civil society at large, all seeking the common good of society. And this is where grassroots conversations among people of different communities are so important, bridging their differences, putting behind past animosities, and vowing to keep talking to each other and finding common solutions.

Yet justice, even at the level of the state, will be better served if it is tied to human rights. As we learned from Wolterstorff, primary justice as right order, whether in its ancient Greek form or in the writings of recent theorists, sees human rights as only a subcategory of a just legal order. In that perspective, human beings do not bear rights *qua* human beings, as opposed to the claim made by the modern human rights paradigm, as first set out in the 1948 Universal Declaration of Human Rights (UDHR). But it is also the doctrine taught by the three monotheistic faiths by virtue of God's creation. Intrinsic human dignity is also the central affirmation of the Parliament of the World's Religions, as I have written elsewhere.[5] In the monotheistic perspective, the dignity of the human person is rooted in God's special favor conferred on the human race from the beginning. The texts of both the Qur'an and the Bible point to God's empowering humans to serve him as his trustees, stewards or deputies on earth, yet it is not this honor which confers upon them that dignity.[6] I agreed with Wolterstorff that it is God's love for his image-bearing creatures that endows them with that inalienable worth.[7] The mandate to manage the earth in his stead flows out of this love; and with it, naturally, comes accountability to our Creator on the Last Day.

Hence, this project was about *both* justice and love. Wolterstorff taught us that despite the vast literature accumulated since the Greeks which found these two concepts mostly incompatible – and despite the well-worn cliché that Islam is about justice and Christianity is about love, the best definition of love includes both seeking 'to promote the good in someone's life as an end in itself' and treating our neighbor 'in a way that befits her worth.'[8] Such a view could not be further from the avidly self-focused western liberal stance on 'rights,' which has led to a society wracked by frivolous law suits. 'Justice in love,' by contrast, links reponsibility with rights.[9] By definition, it is other-focused, with people doing their very best to avoid harming others, to actively seek their benefit as well as their own, and what is more, to seek reconciliation and healing when distrust, conflict and wounds have long been festering.

Before I launch into my conclusion in a more activist mode, allow me to say here what I hope this book will do for scholars working from different disciplinary pathways on the wider topic of Muslim-Christian relations. Here I have drawn from Islamic studies, theology, law, biblical and qur'anic studies, history, philosophy and social ethics. More of this interdisciplinary work will need to be done in order to uncover different facets of the issues touching on justice and love for these two communities, and for interfaith relations in general. Yet my adding a variety of case studies was to remind the reader that injustice has roots in the human heart in the form of prejudice and racism – all of which manifest their ugly outworkings in discriminatory policies, hate speech in the social media, and at times in acts of violence. Each context has its special combination of historical, ethnic, class, sociopolitical and economic factors.

In that respect, one element lacking here is the contribution of the social sciences. I teach a course on the sociology and anthropology of Islam at Fuller Seminary and I have come to see these as tools to tease out a variety of dynamics at play under the cover of 'religion.' Such studies must also be consulted in both Muslim and non-Muslim social contexts, as they will no doubt offer hope on the one hand, as we document shared cultural values and interfaith projects that bring Muslims and Christians into collaboration.[10] On the other hand, other studies could lay bare economic, social and political factors that pull these communities apart. Justice and love touch on much more than theoretical concerns of ethics, theology, and the readings of sacred texts.

Justice, Love, the Common Word and our Common Planet

I have to end this book with a nod to our central theme – justice subsumed under God's command to love him with all our heart, soul and strength, and our neighbor as ourself. Providentially, as I see it, Prince Ghazi of Jordan called our attention to this truth as also central to the Islamic tradition and thereby set in motion a flurry of initiatives, dialogues, and writings bringing Muslims and Christians together as never before. By the late 1990s it was this vision that drew me to the idea of the human trusteeship or custodianship. I have no doubt that love of God and neighbor is the most succinct formulation of the divine mandate for us to steward the earth – caring for one another, our planet and all of its creatures. This is because loving neighbor and caring for our common planet are indelibly linked.

Arguably the Dean of Muslim American scholars of Islam, Sayyid Hossein Nasr, was one of the first American theologians in the 1960s to sound the alarm about the impending ecological crisis and parse it in theological terms.[11] Years later, Nasr contributed a chapter to an edited book of papers on the Common Word by both Christian and Muslim scholars.[12] In it, after dealing with some of the 'irreducible differences' between the two faiths, Nasr points to the commonalities, like belief 'in the transcendent God who is above and beyond all change and becoming, who creates, loves, and has Mercy for His creatures.'[13] Moreover, 'For both of us, although God is ultimately the Godhead, the ground of being, the Urgrund, *al-Ḥaqq*, or *Huwa*, He is also the Person who addresses and whom we can address as Thou.'

This common ground, then, has social implications: 'As Christians and Muslims, we both believe in the ethical character of human life on earth. We hold firm to the reality of divine justice and see justice as well in the social order.' He then touches on Catholic social teaching and mentions a recent papal encyclical that picks apart 'unbridled capitalism.' How can Muslims not agree with that, he asks? Then he urges all of us to take on a more active role as partners: 'Why can we not sit together and devise a new economic philosophy based on our mutual understanding of human nature in its full reality and our sense of justice that is a reflection of a divine quality in human life?'

We both believe in human rights, continues Nasr, but only as 'combined with human responsibility toward God, human society, and the natural environment.' Then this profound statement that effortlessly summarizes much of the impulse behind this present book:

> Rather than criticizing each other's understanding of this issue, we can come together in the realization of the consequences for human beings 'made in the image of God,' of the substitution of the 'Kingdom of Man' for the 'Kingdom of God,' and the absolutization of the rights of man reduced to a merely terrestrial being with total indifference to the rights of God and other creatures. We could render the greatest service not only to our own communities, but also to the whole of humanity, by bringing the full weight of our traditions together to bear upon this crucial issue.

Coming Together

I would answer 'yes' to Nasr's proposal, in full agreement with Wolterstorff, Ghazi, and many others whose voices we have heard in this book. God loves justice. He himself acts with justice and he 'works to bring it about that human beings treat each other justly.'[14] More, 'God is love' (I John 4:8), or, as the Qur'an has it, 'Your Lord has taken it on Himself to be merciful' (6:54). The rights that each one of us possesses and which justice requires all of us to honor are grounded in the infinite love of God who elevated us to become his friends. For Christians this fact is sealed by God's Messiah dying on a cross to redeem us from our sins; for Muslims it is God's gracious, life-giving path (Shari'a) open to believers to follow. By faith in both cases, believers throw themselves on God's mercy and love, and commit to living out this love fully in daily, practical ways. In doing so, they love their neighbors by treating them as befits their worth and according to their rights as bearing God's image; and thereby they seek to set the world right, along with all other people of good will.

One venue showcases the newfound passion for social justice among American evangelicals, and mostly of the millennial generation. Started in 2010 by Ken Wytsma, the Justice Conference organizes bi-yearly gatherings.[15] Around 6,000 attended the third conference in Philadelphia (2013), in which Wolterstorff participated.[16] As of this writing, spin-off conferences have been held on several continents. Hundreds of charitable societies, advocacy groups, artists (both in the visual arts and music) come together to explore this vision:

> The **Justice Conference** was birthed out of a simple idea and a compelling paradox - true life is found when we give our lives away on behalf of others. What if Christians truly lived out the message of Jesus and transformed their communities through their love and the practice of authentic justice?[17]

What if this initiative were to spin off interfaith branches in different parts of the world, joining others who are already at work doing this kind work on behalf of the poor, oppressed, addicted or enslaved? Certainly Eboo Patel's Interfaith Youth Core, started in Chicago and now with branches in several US cities, is an inspiring example of young Muslims, Jews, Christians, Buddhists and others committing to work together to address issues of injustice in their communities.[18] Also, joint ventures between Muslims and Christians like Peace Catalyst International to fight Islamophobia and create understanding, love, and common service projects, are going a long way to further God's justice and love in the US and Europe.[19]

In the course of our conversation we've looked at several sample cases of injustice, all involving in some way the weakest and most vulnerable of our fellow humans. In the end, though I've only scratched the surface of this issue of justice and love and what it means for Muslims and Christians today, my hope is that this conversation will continue. It may be in the shadow of the Common Word initiative or in other venues; in academic settings or in local interfaith projects. For my part, the Common Word warning that global peace cannot happen without Muslims and Christians joining hands is no exaggeration, particularly with the rise of various nationalisms and the spread of authoritarian regimes. In a world which seems to be losing the cooperative spirit which led nations after WWII to draw up the Universal Declaration of Human Rights and the many conventions that followed, may together we find ways, beyond the niceties of official dialogues, to demonstrate love and justice on this earth, make things right and implement more than just a taste of King's 'beloved community.'

So now, come back to your God.
Act with love and justice,
and always depend on him. (Hosea 12:6)

Endnotes

1   The Bible, New International Version 2011.
2   A forthcoming book published by Yale University Press in their World Thought in Translation series in May 2020.
3   This enabled the famous Tunisian National Dialogue Quartet which made all of this happen to receive the 2015 Nobel Peace Prize.
4   See the full text of that speech online, http://d19cgyi5s8w5eh.cloud-front.net/eml/Z3MRep5sSxWcE6LJfAnytA?e=wtaylor@usip.org&a=6bl_JhdOTLqCbi6c3lWxAg&f=&t=1 accessed July 25, 2018. The following two books offer a good deal of material on Ghannouchi: Cesari 2014; and Esposito et al., 2015. Also see two series of three blog posts I did on Ghannouchi, online, http://www.humantrustees.org/blogs/religion-and-human-rights?start=6.
5   Under the section, 'The Ethics of Trusteeship,' I explained how Hans Küng had drafted a declaration ahead of the meeting of the Parliament of the World's Religions, which in its third draft 'remained virtually unchanged throughout the discussions by the 200 plus delegates from all the major religious groups of the globe in Chicago from August 28 to September 4, 1993' (Johnston 2010a: 475-476). The declaration turned the UDHR's affirmation of human rights into an ethic: 'the full realization of the intrinsic dignity of the human person, the inalienable freedom and equality of all humans, and the necessary solidarity and interdependence of all humans with each other' (Johnston 2010a: 475).
6   Here is one representative quote from Ghannouchi on this, from his Ch. 2, 'The Islamic Perspective on Freedom and Human Rights': 'Islam is not content to declare the human person's right to life, freedom and personal integrity; it considers that a sacred duty enjoined upon the community and the individual. The human being is appointed as God's trustee, that is, his deputy charged with the responsibility to judge among his creatures with justice. Thus anyone who sets out to obey God and judge his creatures aright is God's trustee.'
7   After quoting Calvin and unpacking some of his statements, he writes, 'Let's add what seems to be implied: God's love for human beings is God's attachment to them, the attachment being evoked by God's 'discerning' that they image God: God's care for human beings is then evoked by God's attachment to them' (Wolterstorff 2011a, 154).
8   Wolterstorff 2011a, 93.

9　So-called communitarian philosophers and theologians like Alaisdair MacIntyre and Stanley Hauerwas also see rights as emanating from a just society and not inherent theologically in humanity. For more on this, see a paper I delivered to the Society of Vineyard Scholars in 2014, 'The Church, the Kingdom of God, and Human Solidarity: Stanley Hauerwas, Steven L. Carter, and Pope Francis,' online, http://www.humantrustees.org/resources/item/184-hauerwas-and-pope-francis.

10　Heather J. Sharkey, who has written several books on Christian missionary involvement in the MENA region, has more recently published a pathbreaking historical study of the late Ottoman Empire and the dynamics of Muslim, Jewish and Christian relations, see Sharkey 2017. She highlights the role of religion but also the limits of religion in these relations, which vary greatly from region to region and over time. By bringing to light articles of clothing, art, foods and sounds, she is able to weave a narrative of shared culture, communal harmony, as well as the economic disparities and political decisions that led to increased tension and, leading up to World War I, catastrophic violence.

11　In 2010, on the tenth anniversary of the Earth Charter, I organized a panel discussion on Islam and Ecology at the American Academy of Religion. My own presentation, which highlighted Nasr's pioneering role, was later published in a volume dedicated to this issue which I co-edited under the title, 'Intra-Muslim Debates on Ecology: Is Shari'a Still Relevant?' See Johnston 2012: 218-238.

12　Sayyid Hossein Nasr, "A Common Word' Initiative: Theoria and Praxis,' in El-Ansary and Linnan 2010, 21-28.

13　El-Ansary and Linnan 2010, 23.

14　Wolterstorff 2011a, 89.

15　See their website at http://www.thejusticeconference.com/. Wytsma is a creative adviser for World Relief (which plays a major role in this network), president of Kilns College School of Theology and Mission in Oregon, and lead pastor of Antioch Church in Bend, Oregon.

16　You can watch Wolterstorff's presentation ('What Is Justice?') online at https://vimeo.com/20325071.

17　From their website https://www.thejusticeconference.com/about/.

18　See the Interfaith Youth Core website at http://www.ifyc.org/. See also my blog on Patel's journey, available online at http://www.humantrustees.org/blogs/religion-and-global-society/item/110-jefferson-patel-pluralism.

19　See https://www.peacecatalyst.org/.

Bibliography

A Common Word Website. 2007. A Common Word between Us and You. Available at: https://www.acommonword.com/publications/

Ahmed, Idris Nassery, and Muna Tatari, eds. 2018. *The Objectives of Islamic Law: The Promises and Challenges of Maqasid al-Shari'a*. Lanham, MD: Lexington Books, 285–296.

al-Banna, Jamal. 1986. *Judging by the Qur'an and the Issue of Applying the Shari'a (Al-Ḥukm bi-l-Qur'ān wa-qaḍiyyat taṭbīq al-sharī'a)*. Cairo: Dār al-Fikr al-Islāmī.

al-Banna, Jamal. 1994a. *Faith in God in the Noble Qur'an and According to the First Generations, the Mu'tazilites and the Moderns (al-Imān bi-l-allāh fī al-qur'ān al-karīm wa-ladā al-salaf wa-l-mu'tazila wa-l-mu'āṣirīn)*. Cairo: Dār al-Fikr al-Islāmī.

al-Banna, Jamal. 1994b. *The Responsibility for the Failure of the Islamic State in the Modern Era: And Other Essays (Mas'ūliyyat fashal al-dawla al-islāmiyya fī al-'aṣr al-ḥadīth: wa-buḥūth ukhrā)*. Cairo: Dār al-Fikr al-Islāmī.

al-Banna, Jamal. 1995a. *Towards a New Jurisprudence (Naḥwa fiqh jadīd)*, vol. 1. Cairo: Dār al-Fikr al-Islāmī.

al-Banna, Jamal. 1995b. *The Theory of Justice in European and Islamic Though (Naẓariyyāt al-'adl fī-l-fikr al-urūbbī wa-l-fikr al-Islāmī)*. Cairo: Dār al-Fikr al-Islāmī.

al-Banna, Jamal. 2003a. *Interpretation of the Noble Qur'an: Revelation to Ancients and Moderns (Tafsīr al-qur'ān al-karīm bayān al-qudamā' wa-l-muḥdithīn)*. Cairo: Dār al-Fikr al-Islāmī.

al-Banna, Jamal. 2003b. *Islam as Religion and Umma and Not as Religion and State (al-Islām dīn wa-umma wa-laysa dīnan wa-dawla)*. Cairo: Dār al-Fikr al-Islāmī.

al-Banna, Jamal. 2003c. *Our Position on Secularism, Nationalism and Socialism (Mawqifnā min al-'ilmāniyya, al-qawmiyya, al-ishtirākiyya)*. Cairo: Dār al-Fikr al-Islāmī.

al-Banna, Jamal. 2004. Concluding Statement. Islamic Reform Conference, Cairo, Oct. 5–6, 2004. The Saban Center for Middle East Policy at the Brookings Institution and the Ibn Khaldun Center for Developmental Studies, in association with the Center for the Study of Islam and Democracy (Washington) and the Islamic Dialogue Forum (London). Available at: https://www.brookings.edu/wp-content/uploads/2012/04/cairoclosing.pdf

al-Banna, Jamal. 2005. *The Renewal of Islam and the Reestablishment of Islamic Institutions of Learning* (*Tajdīd al-Islām wa-iʿādat taʾsīs manẓumāt al-maʿrifa al-Islāmiyya*). Cairo: Dār al-Fikr al-Islāmī.

al-Hilali, Muhammad Tagi-ud-Din, and Muhammad Muhsin Khan (trans). 1999. Interpretation of the Meanings of the Noble Qur'an in the English Language: A Summarized Version of At-Tabari, Al-Qurtubi and Ibn Kathir with comments from Salih Al-Bukhari Riyad, Saudi Arabia: Dar-us-Salam Publications.

Al Jazeera News. 2012. Qatari Emir in Historic Gaza Visit. No author given. Available at: https://www.aljazeera.com/news/middleeast/2012/10/2012102353137370247. html

al-Qaradawi, Yusuf. 1977. *The Islamic Solution: Both a Duty and a Necessity* (*al-Ḥall al-islāmī farīda wa-ḍarūra*). Cairo: Maktabat al-Wahba.

al-Qaradawi, Yusuf. 1979. *Contemporary Fatwas* (*Fatāwa muʿāṣira*). 3 vols. Cairo & Kuwait City: Dār al-Qalam.

al-Qaradawi, Yusuf. 1993. *Madkhal li-dirāsat al-sharīʿa al-islāmiyya*. Beirut: MuŒassat al-Risāla.

al-Qaradawi, Yusuf. 2001. Introduction to the Study of the Islamic Shari'a (*Madkhal li-dirāsat al-sharīʿa al-islāmiyya*). Cairo: Maktabat Wahda.

al-Qaradawi, Yusuf. 2006. *A Study of the Jurisprudence of the Shari'a's Purposes: Between the General Purposes and the Specific Texts* (*Dirāsa fī maqāṣid al-sharīʿa: bayn al-maqāṣid al-kulliyya wa-l-nuṣūṣ al-juzʾiyya*). Cairo: Dār al-Shurūq.

al-Qaradawi, Yusuf. 2011. The Khutbah (Sermon) of Yusuf al-Qaradawi in Tahrir Square. Trans. Yahya Michot and Samy Metwally. *Beliefnet*, https://www. beliefnet.com/columnists/cityofbrass/2011/03/the-khutbah-sermon-of-yusuf-al.html

al-Qaradawi, Yusuf. 2012. The 25 January 2011 Revolution of the People: Shaykh Qaradawi and the Egyptian Revolution [Declarations, Sermons, Fatwas, Articles and Pictures] (*25 yanāʾir sanat 2011 thawrat shaʿab: al-shaykh al-Qaraḍāwī wa-l-thawra al-miṣriyya* [*Bayanāt wa-khutab wa-fatāwa wa-maqalāt wa-suwar*]). Cairo: Maktabat Wahba.

Akwagyiram, Alexis. 2018. Nigeria grazing violence kills many more than Boko Haram, poses serious threat-think tank. Reuters. Published July 26, 2018. Available at: https://af.reuters.com/article/topNews/idAFKBN1KG18X-OZATP

Alexander, Paul. 2013. Raced as White. *Prism.* Published July 1, 2013. Available at: http://prismmagazine.org/raced-as-white/

Alford, Terry. 2007. *Prince Among Slaves.* New York & Oxford: Oxford University Press.

Amanat, Abbas and Frank Griffel, eds. 2007. *Sharia: Islamic Law in the Contemporary Context.* Stanford, CA: Stanford University Press, 62–82.

Amnesty International Website. 2018. Qatar: Partial Abolition of 'Exit Permit' Lifts Travel Restrictions for Most Migrant Workers. Available at: https://www. amnesty.org/en/latest/news/2018/09/qatar-exit-system-reform-first-step/

Arkoun, Mohammed. 1984. *Toward a Critique of Islamic Reason* (Pour une critique de la raison islamique). Paris: Maisonneuve et Larose.

Ateek, Naim Stifan. 1989. *Justice and Only Justice: A Palestinian Theology of Liberation.* Maryknoll, NY: Orbis.

Ateek, Naim Stifan. 2008. *A Palestinian Cry for Reconciliation.* Maryknoll, NY: Orbis.

Ayoub, Mahmoud 2007. 'Toward an Islamic Christology II – The Death of Jesus, Reality or Delusion,' in *A Muslim View of Christianity: Essays on Dialogue by Mahmoud Ayoub,* ed. Irfan a. Omar (Maryknoll, NY: Orbis).

Azad, Hasan. 2014. Tariq Ramadan and the Reconfiguration of Islamic Authority on Web 2.0. *Al-Jazeera Online.* Published September 2, 2014. Available at: http://www.aljazeera.com/indepth/opinion/2014/09/tariq-ramadan-reconfiguration-is-20149214173222672.html

Barzegar, Abbas. 2011. Discourse, Identity, and Community: Problems and Prospects of the Study of Islam in America. *The Muslim World* 101(2): 511–38. Available at: https://doi.org/10.1111/j.1478-1913.2010.01394.x

BBC. 2004. Yusuf al-Qaradawi Tells BBC Newsnight that Islam Justifies Suicide Bombings. BBC Press Release. Published July 7, 2004. Available at: http://www.bbc.co.uk/pressoffice/pressreleases/stories/2004/07_july/07/newsnight.shtml

BBC. 2006. Muslim Clerics Reach Out to the Pope. Published October 16, 2006. Available at: http://news.bbc.co.uk/2/hi/europe/6050156.stm

Benedict, Pope Benedict XVI. 2006a. Full Text of Pope Benedict XVI's Regensburg Lecture. The Catholic Church in England and Wales. Published September 18, 2009. Available at: http://www.catholic-ew.org.uk/Home/News/2006/2006-Offline/Full-Text-of-the-Pope-Benedict-XVI-s-Regensburg-Lecture/(language)/eng-GB

Beydoun, Khaled A. 2018. *American Islamophobia: Understanding the Roots and Rise of Fear.* Oakland, CA: University of California Press. https://doi.org/10.1525/9780520970007

Benedict, Pope Benedict XVI. 2006b. Address of His Holiness Benedict XVI to the Ambassadors of Countries with a Muslim Majority and to Representatives of Muslim Communities in Italy. Vatican website. Published September 25, 2006. Available at: http://w2.vatican.va/content/benedict-xvi/en/speeches/2006/september/documents/hf_ben-xvi_spe_20060925_ambasciatori-paesi-arabi.html

Benhabib, Seyla. 1992. *Situating the Self: Gender, Community and Postmodernism in Contemporary Ethics.* New York & London: Routledge.

Ben Menachem, Yoni. 2018. Muslim Brotherhood Religious Authority Resigns. *Jerusalem Center for Public Affairs.* Published November 15, 2018. Available at: http://jcpa.org/muslim-brotherhood-religious-authority-resigns/

Black Lives Matter Website. Healing Justice. Available at: https://blacklivesmatter.com/healingjustice/

B'Tselem Website. 2019. Fake Justice: The Responsibility Israel's High Court Justice Bear for the Demolition of Palestinian Homes and the Dispossession of Palestinians. Available at: https://www.btselem.org/publications/summaries/201902_fake_justice

Brown, Daniel. 1999. Islamic Ethics in Comparative Perspective. *The Muslim World* 89(2): 181–92. https://doi.org/10.1111/j.1478-1913.1999.tb03677.x

Brueggemann, Walter. 1997. *Theology of the Old Testament*. Minneapolis, MN: Fortress Press.

Brunner Emil, *Justice and the Social Order*, New York: Harper & Brothers, 1945, 111.

Caeiro, Alexandre, and Mahmoud al-Saify. 2009. Qaradawi in Europe, Europe in Qaradawi? The Global Mufti's European Politics. In *Global Mufti: The Phenomenon of Yusuf al-Qaradawi*, edited by Bettina Gräf and Jacob Skovgaard-Petersen, 109–148. New York: Columbia University Press.

Cairo Institute for Human Rights Studies. 2003. Paris Declaration. On Means of Renewing Religious Discourse, n.p.

CBN News. 2015. www.cbn.com/cbnnews/world/2015/July/Pakistan-Court-Overturns-Asia-Bibis-Death-Sentence/

Cesari, Jocelyne. 2014. *The Awakening of Muslim Democracy*. Cambridge, UK: Cambridge University Press. https://doi.org/10.1017/CBO9781107359871

Chapman, Colin. 2015. *Whose Promised Land? The Continuing Crisis over Israel and Palestine*. 5th rev. ed. Oxford: Lion Hudson.

Cross, Alan. 2014. *When Heaven and Earth Collide: Racism, Southern Evangelicals, and the Better Way of Jesus*. Montgomery, AL: NewSouth Books.

Chrysostom, St. John. 1984. *St. John Chrysostom: On Wealth and Poverty*, trans. Catharine Roth. Crestwood, NY: Vladimir Press.

Council on American-Islamic Relations (CAIR) and The Center for Race & Gender at the University of California Berkeley. 2011. Same Hate, New Target: Islamophobia and Its Impact on the United States. Available at: https://www.crg.berkeley.edu/crg-publications/same-hate-new-target-islamophobia-and-its-impact-in-the-united-states-2011/

Culzac, Natasha. 2014. Israel-Gaza Crisis: Reconstruction of Flattened Gaza Will Cost $8 Billion, Palestinian Officials Say. *The Independent*. Published Sept. 5, 2014. Available at: http://www.independent.co.uk/news/world/middle-east/israelgazacrisis-reconstruction-of-flattened-gaza-will-cost-5billion-palestinian-officials-say-9713905.html

Cumming-Bruce, Nick. 2018. Taking Migrant Children from Parents is Illegal, U.N. Tells U.S. *New York Times*. Published June 5, 2018. Available at: https://www.nytimes.com/2018/06/05/world/americas/us-un-migrantchildren-families.html

Curtis, Edward E. IV. 2002. *Islam in Black America: Identity, Liberation, and Difference in African American Islamic Thought*. Albany, NY: State University of New York.

Dorsey, James M. 2018. Will the Real Pakistan Stand Up, Please! *The Turbulent World of Middle East Soccer* (blog). Available at: https://mideastsoccer.blogspot.sg/2018/03/will-real-pakistan-stand-up-please.html.

Duderija, Adis, ed. 2014. *Maqasid al-Shari'a and Contemporary Muslim Reformist Thought*. New York: Palgrave Macmillan. https://doi.org/10.1057/9781137319418

Dunning, Tristan. 2018. Yemen, the 'Worst Humanitarian Crisis in the World,' Continues. Research Paper Series 2018–2019, *Parliamentary Library* (Australia), published December 6, 2018. Available at: https://www.aph.gov.au/About_Parliament/Parliamentary_Departments/Parliamentary_Library/pubs/rp/rp1819/Yemen.

Dworkin, Ronald. 2011. *Justice for Hedgehogs*. Cambridge, MA: The Belknap Press. https://doi.org/10.2307/j.ctvjf9vkt

El Feglery, Moataz. 2017. Taking Beliefs to Court: Blasphemy and Heresy, and Freedom of Expression under Islamic Law. In 'Islam and Human Rights: Key Issues for Our Time,' a report published by the *Atlantic Council*, Geneive Abdo, ed. Available at: https://www.atlanticcouncil.org/publications/reports/islam-and-human-rights-key-issues-for-our-times.

Equal Justice Initiative Website. 2015. Lynching in America: Confronting the Legacy of Racial Terror. Published Feb. 2015. Available at: https://lynchinginamerica.eji.org/report/

Emon, Anver. 2018. Epilogue. In *The Objectives of Islamic Law: The Promises and Challenges of Maqasid al-Shari'a*, edited by Rumee Ahmed, Idris Nassery, and Muna Tatari, 285–296. Lanham, MD: Lexington Books.

Evans, Malcolm. 2009. Human Rights and the Freedom of Religion. In *Justice & Rights: Christian and Muslim Perspectives*, edited by Michael Ipgrave, 109–116. Washington, DC: Georgetown University Press.

Esack, Farid. 1997. *Qur'an, Liberation and Pluralism: An Islamic Perspective on Interreligious Solidarity against Oppression*. Oxford: Oneworld.

Fadel, Mohammad H. 2007. Public Reason as a Strategy for Principled Reconciliation: The Case of Islamic Law and International Human Rights Law. *Chicago Journal of International Law* 8(1): 1–20.

Fakhry, Majid. 1991. *Ethical Theories in Islam*. Leiden: Brill.

Fea, John. 2018. *Believe Me: The Evangelical Road to Donald Trump*. Grand Rapids, MI: Eerdmans.

Feldman, Noah. 2007. Shari'a and Islamic Democracy in the Age of Al Jazeera. In *Sharia': Islamic Law in the Contemporary Context*, edited by Abbas Amanat and Frank Griffel, 104–119. Stanford, CA: Stanford University Press.

Galtun, Johann. 1969. Violence, Peace, and Peace Research. *Journal of Peace Research* 6(3): 167–91. https://doi.org/10.1177/002234336900600301

Gamal El-Din, El-Sayed. 2016. Egyptian writer Fatima Naoot sentenced to 3 years in jail for 'contempt of religion.' *Ahramonline*. Published January 26, 2016. Available at: http://english.ahram.org.eg/NewsContent/1/64/185963/Egypt/Politics-/Egyptian-writer-Fatima-Naootsentenced-to--years-i.aspx

Gamal El-Din, El-Sayed. 1990. Cultural Violence. *Journal of Peace Research* 27(3): 291–305. https://doi.org/10.1177/0022343390027003005

Ghazi, Prince Ghazi bin Muhammad. 2013. *Love in the Holy Qur'an*. 7th ed. Cambridge, UK: The Islamic Texts Society.

Gräf, Bettina, and Jacob Skovgaard-Petersen, eds. 2009. *Global Mufti: The Phenomenon of Yusuf al-Qaradawi*. New York: Columbia University Press.

Gräf, Bettina. 2007. The Concept of *wasatiyya* in the Work of Yusuf al-Qaradawi. In *Global Mufti: The Phenomenon of Yusuf al-Qaradawi*, edited by Bettina Gräf and Jacob Skovgaard-Petersen, 213–238. New York: Columbia University Press.

Guyinn, Jessica, and Monica Rohr. 2019. Blackface: Digging at the Roots of Racism. *USA Today*. Published Feb. 11, 2019, 3A.

Hallaq, Wael. 1999. *A History of Islamic Legal Studies: An Introduction to Sunni Uṣūl al-Fiqh*. Cambridge: Cambridge University Press.

Hallaq, Wael B. 2005. *The Origins and Evolution of Islamic Law*. Cambridge: Cambridge University Press.

Haley, Alex. 2016. *Roots: The Saga of an American Family*, Media Tie In ed. Boston: Da Capo Press.

Haley, Alex and Atallah Shabazz Malcolm X. 1987. *The Autobiography of Malcolm X*. New York: Ballantine Books.

Hart, H. L. A. 2012 [1961]. *The Concept of Law*, 3rd ed. with introduction and notes by L. Green, and postscript by J. Raz and A. Bulloch. Oxford: Clarendon Press.

Hart, Marion. 2018. 'UNICEF Report: 900,000 Rohingya Struggle for a Future.' Published by UNICEF Aug. 22, 2018. Available at: https://www.unicefusa. org/stories/unicef-report-900000-rohingya-refugees-struggle-future/34680. https://doi.org/10.1093/he/9780199644704.001.0001

Hauerwas, Stanley. 2011. *War and the American Difference: Theological Reflections on Violence and National Identity*. Ada, MI: Baker Academic.

Hershkind, Charles. 2009. *The Ethical Soundscape: Cassette Sermons and Islamic Counterpublics*. New York: Columbia University Press.

Hourani, Albert. 1985. *Reason and Tradition in Islamic Ethics*. Cambridge: Cambridge University Press. https://doi.org/10.1017/CBO9780511570780

Inner-City Muslim Action Network Website (IMAN), http://www.mana-net.org/, accessed June 17, 2019.

Ghārib l-Iṣfahānī, Abū al-Qāsim al-Ḥussayn Ibn Muḥammad. 1907. *The Vocabulary in the Mysterious Qur'an (al-Mufradāt fī al-gharīb al-qur'an)*. Cairo: Muṣṭafā al-Bābī al-Ḥalabī.

Interfaith Youth Core Website. Available at: http://www.ifyc.org/

Jackson, Sherman A. 2011. *Islam and the Blackamerican: Looking toward the Third Resurrection*. Oxford & New York: Oxford University Press.

Johnston, David L. 2004. A Turn in the Epistemology and Hermeneutics of *Usul al-Fiqh*. *Islamic Law and Society* 11(2): 233–282. https://doi.org/10.1163/156851904323178764

Johnston, David L. 2007a. Maqasid al-Shari'a: Epistemology and Hermeneutics of Muslim Theologies of Human Rights. *Die Welt des Islams* 47(2): 149–187. https://doi.org/10.1163/157006007781569936

Johnston, David L. 2007b. 'Allal al-Fasi: Shari'a as Blueprint for Righteous Global Citizenship. In *Sharia': Islamic Law in the Contemporary Context*, edited by Abbas Amanat and Frank Griffel, 83–103. Stanford, CA: Stanford University Press.

Johnston, David L. 2010a. *Earth, Empire and Sacred Text: Muslims and Christians as Trustees of Creation*. Sheffield: Equinox.

Johnston, David L. 2010b. *Evolving Muslim Theologies of Justice: Jamal al-Banna, Mohammad Hashim Kamali and Khaled Abou El Fadl*. Penang, Malaysia: CenPRIS and Universiti Sains Malaysia.

Johnston, David L. 2012. Intra-Muslim Debates about Ecology: Is Shari'a Still Relevant? *Worldviews: Global Religions, Culture and Ecology* 11(2): 218–238. https://doi.org/10.1163/15685357-01603003

Johnston, David L. 2013. 'America's First Muslim Celebrity'. Available at: http://www.humantrustees.org/blogs/muslim-christian-dialog/item/105-princeamongslaves

Johnston, David L. 2014a. A Muslim and Christian Orientation to Human Rights: Human Dignity and Solidarity. *Indiana International & Comparative Law Review* 24(4): 899–920. https://doi.org/10.18060/18264

Johnston, David L. 2014b. Yusuf al-Qaradawi's Purposeful Fiqh: Promoting or Demoting the Future Role of the Ulama? In *Maqasid Al Shari'a and Contemporary Muslim Reformist Thought*, edited by Adis Duderija. New York: Palgrave Macmillan.

Johnston, David L. 2015a. Islam and Human Rights: A Growing Rapprochement? *American Journal of Economics and Sociology* 74(1): 113–148. https://doi.org/10.1111/ajes.12085

Johnston, David L. 2015b. Islamophobia Sows Fear. Personal website. Available at: http://www.humantrustees.org/blogs/religion-and-global-society/item/138-islamophobia-sows-fear.

Johnston, David L. 2019a. Nigeria: A Brief History of Muslim-Christian Relations. Personal website. http://www.humantrustees.org/resources/item/183-nigeria-case-study.

Johnston, David L. 2019b. Human Rights and Solidarity: Stanley Hauerwas, Steven L. Carter, and Pope Francis. Personal website. Available at: http://www.humantrustees.org/resources/item/184-hauerwas-and-pope-francis.

The Justice Conference Website. Available at: http://www.thejusticeconference.com/

Justinian. 1985. *The Digest of Justinian*. Philadelphia, PA: University of Pennsylvania Press.

Kabha, Mustafa, and Haggai Ehrlich. 2006. Al-Ahbash and Wahhabiyya: Interpretations of Islam. *International Journal of Middle East Studies* 38(4): 519–38. https://doi.org/10.1017/S0020743806412459

Kamali, Mohammad Hashim. 1989. Source, Nature, and Objectives of Shari'ah. *The Islamic Quarterly* 33(4): 215–235.

Kamali, Mohammad Hashim. 2001. *Freedom, Justice, and Equality in Islam*. Cambridge, UK: Islamic Texts Society.

Kamali, Mohammad Hashim. 2002. Issues in the Understanding of Jihād and Ijtihād. *Islamic Studies* 41(4): 617–634.

Kamali, Mohammad Hashim. 2008. *Shari'ah Law: An Introduction*. London: Oneworld.

Kamali, Mohammad Hashim. 2009. The Ruler and the Ruled in Islam: A Brief Analysis of the Sources. In *Justice & Rights: Christian and Muslim Perspectives*, edited by Michael Ipgrave, 3–13. Washington, DC: Georgetown University Press.

Kecia, Ali. 2015. The Truth About Islam and Sex Slavery Is More Complicated Than You Think. *Huffington Post*. Published Aug. 19, 2015. http://www.huffingtonpost.com/kecia-ali/islam-sex-slavery_b_8004824.html

Kohen, Kelly. 2019. Trump Doesn't Think White Nationalism Is a Threat – But the Data Say Otherwise. *Vox*. Published March 16, 2019. Available at: https://www.vox.com/identities/2019/3/16/18268856/new-zealand-shooter-white-nationalism-united-states

Khadduri, Majid. 1984. *The Islamic Conception of Justice*. Baltimore and London: The Johns Hopkins University Press.

Khalfaoui, Mouez. 2018. *Maqāṣid al-Sharīʿa* as Legitimization for the Muslim Minorities Law. In *The Objectives of Islamic Law: The Promises and Challenges of Maqasid al-Shari'a*, edited by Rumee Ahmed, Idris Nassery, and Muna Tatari, 271–284. Lanham, MD: Lexington Books.

Khan-Cullors, Patrisse. 2016. We Didn't Start a Movement. We Started a Network. Personal website. Published Feb. 22, 2016. Available at: https://medium.com/@patrissemariecullorsbrignac/we-didn-t-start-a-movement-we-started-anetwork-90f9b5717668.

Kirkpatrick, David C. 2011. After Long Exile, Sunni Cleric Takes Role in Egypt. *New York Times*. Published February 18, 2011. Available at: https://www.nytimes.com/2011/02/19/world/middleeast/19egypt.html?pagewanted=all. https://doi.org/10.1016/S0262-1762(11)70137-7

Kirkpatrick, David C. 2019. *A Gospel for the Poor: Global Social Christianity and the Latin American Evangelical Left*. Philadelphia, PA: University of Pennsylvania Press. https://doi.org/10.9783/9780812296051

Kurz, Lester R. 2017. 'Women's Rights, Human Rights, and Duties: From Domination to Partnership,' *Interdisciplinary Journal of Partnership Studies* 4(1): Art. 6. https://doi.org/10.24926/ijps.v4i1.152

Kuruvilla, Carol. 2018. This Diverse Group of Evangelicals Is Trying to Take Back the Faith. *Huffington Post*. Published Oct. 3, 2018. Available at: https://www.huffingtonpost.com/entry/diverse-evangelicals-take-backfaith_us_5bb4fdf5e4b028e1fe3a0dbd.

Labberton, Mark, and Shane Claiborne, eds. 2018. *Still Evangelical? Insiders Reconsider Political, Social, and Theological Meaning*. Downers Grove, IL: IVP.

Lorritz, Bryan, and John Ortberg. 2018. Insider Outsider: My Journey as a Stranger in White Evangelicalism and My Hope Us All. Grand Rapids, MI: Zondervan.

Ludwig, Frieder. 2008. Christian-Muslim Relations in Nigeria Since the Introduction of Shari'ah in 1999. *Journal of the American Academy of Religion* 76(3). https://doi.org/10.1093/jaarel/lfn058

MacIntyre, Alastair. 1981. *After Virtue: A Study in Moral Theory*. Notre Dame, IN: University of Notre Dame Press.

Makdisi, George. 1983. 'Ethics in Islamic Traditionalist Doctrine,' in *Ethics in Islam*, edited by Richard G. Hovannisian, 50-61. Malibu, CA: Undena Publications.

Madden, David. 2014. As Murder Rate Skyrockets in Chester, Officials Promise Crime Crackdown. *CBS Philly.* Published May 6, 2014. Available at: http://philadelphia.cbslocal.com/2014/05/06/ as-murder-rateskyrockets-in-chester-officials-promise-crime-crackdown/

Masud, Muhammad Khalid. 1989. *Islamic Legal Philosophy: A Study of Abu Ishaq al-Shatibi's Life and Thought.* Delhi: International Islamic Publishers.

M'Bokolo, Ilikia. 1998. 'The Impact of Slavery in Africa,' *Le Monde Diplomatique.* Published April 1998. Available at: https://mondediplo.com/1998/04/02africa

McEvoy, Kaeley. 2014. Protecting God's Children: How Gun Violence Impacts America's Youth. *Sojourners.* Published Oct. 20, 2014. Available at: http:// sojo.net/blogs/2014/10/20/protecting-god%E2%80%99s-childrenhow-gun-violence-impacts-america%E2%80%99s-youth

Meijer, Roel, ed. 2009. *Global Salafism: Islam's New Religious Movement.* Oxford & New York: Oxford University Press.

Michael Paulson. 2014. US Religious Leaders Embrace Cause of Immigrant Children. *The New York Times.* Published July 23, 2014. Available at: https:// www.nytimes.com/2014/07/24/us/us-religious-leaders-embrace-cause-ofimmigrant-children.html

Moosa, Ebrahim. 2002. The Poetics and Politics of Law after Empire: Reading Women's Rights in the Contestation of Law. *UCLA Journal of Islamic and Near Eastern Law* 11 (Fall/Winter 2001-2002): 1–46.

Moosa, Ebrahim. 2003. The Debts and Burdens of Critical Islam. In *Progressive Muslims: On Justice, Gender and Pluralism,* edited by Omid Safi, 118–127. Oxford: Oneworld.

Moosa, Ebrahim. 2012. Muslim Political Theology: Defamation, Apostasy, and Anathema. Series on 'Cartoons and Minarets: Reflections on Muslim-Western Encounters,' Heinrich Böll Stiftung, Middle East Office, 1–10. Available at: https://lb.boell.org/en/2012/08/15/muslim-political-theology-defamation-apostasy-and-anathema

Mulder, Mark T. 2015. *Shades of White Flight: Evangelical Congregations and Urban Departure.* New Brunswick, NJ: Rutgers University Press.

Murdoch, Lindsay. 2017. Dalai Lama adds Voice to the Pope's in Calling for the Persecution of Rohingya to End. *The Sydney Morning Herald.* Published March 3, 2017. Available at: https://www.smh.com.au/world/dalai-lama-adds-voice-topopes-in-calling-for-the-persecution-of-rohingya-to-end-20170303-gupz06.html

Nasr, Sayyid Hossein. A Common Word Initiative: Theoria and Praxis. In *Muslim and Christian Understanding: Theory and Application of 'A Common Word,'* edited by Waleed El-Ansary and David K., 21–28. Linnan. New York: Palgrave Macmillan. https://doi.org/10.1057/9780230114401_3

Nebehay, Stephanie. 2018. Executions, Torture and Slave Markets Persist in Libya. *Reuters.* Published March 21, 2018. Available at: https://www.reuters.com/article/us-libya-securityrights/ executions-torture-and-slave-markets-persist-in-libya-u-n-idUSKBN1GX1JY

News.com.au. 2009. Gunmen Slay Italian Nun in Somali Capital. Published March 17, 2009. Available at: https://www.news.com.au/national/gunmen-slay-italian-nun-in-somali-capital/news-story/59282bf4be5b3ab86fb335d175143ee7

Niebuhr, Reinhold. 1957. *Love and Justice: Selections from the Shorter Writings of Reinhold Niebuhr*, edited by D. B. Robertson. Philadelphia, PA: Westminster Press.

Novak, David. 1998. *Natural Law in Judaism*. Cambridge: Cambridge University Press, 41.

O'Donovan, Oliver. 1996. *The Desire of Nations*. Cambridge: Cambridge University Press.

Opwis, Felicitas. 2007. Islamic Law and Legal Change: The Concept of Maslaha in Classical and Contemporary Islamic Legal Theory, in *Sharia': Islamic Law in the Contemporary Context*, edited by Abbas Amanat and Frank Griffel, 62–82. Stanford, CA: Stanford University Press.

Paden, John N. 2008. *Faith and Politics in Nigeria: Nigeria as a Pivotal State in the Muslim World*. Washington, DC: United States Institute of Peace.

Peace Catalyst International Website. Available at: http://www.ifyc.org/

Philpott, Daniel and Timothy Samuel Shah (eds.) 2018. *Under Caesar's Sword: How Christians Respond to Persecution*. Cambridge: Cambridge University Press.

Raheb, Mitri. 2014. *Faith in the Face of Empire: The Bible through Palestinian Eyes*. Maryknoll, NY: Orbis.

Ramadan, Tariq. 2005. An International Call for a Moratorium on Corporal Punishment, Stoning and the Death Penalty in the Islamic World. Personal website, published April 5, 2005. Available at: https://tariqramadan.com/an-international-call-for-moratorium-on-corporal-punishment-stoning-and-the-death-penalty-in-the-islamic-world/

Ramadan, Tariq. 2006. A struggle over Europe's religious identity – Editorials and Commentary, International Herald Tribune. *New York Times*. Published Sept. 20, 2006, accessed June 19, 2019, https://www.nytimes.com/2006/09/20/opinion/20iht-edramadan.2876272.html

Ramadan, Tariq. 2009a. A Call for a Moratorium on Corporal Punishment: The Debate in Review. In *New Directions in Islamic Thought and Practice: Exploring Reform and Muslim Tradition*, edited by Kari Vogt, Lena Larsen and Christian Moe, 163–174. London & New York: I.B. Tauris.

Ramadan, Tariq. 2009b. *Radical Reform: Islamic Ethics and Liberation*. Oxford & New York: Oxford University Press.

Ramadan, Tariq. 2012. *Islam and the Arab Awakening*. Oxford & New York: Oxford University Press.

Rawls, John. 1999 [1971]. *A Theory of Justice*, rev. ed. Cambridge, MA: The Belknap Press.

Rawls, John. 2005 [1993]. *Political Liberalism*, 2nd ed., Columbia Classics in Philosophy. New York: Columbia University Press.

Reid, Charles J., Jr. 1991. The Canonistic Contribution to the Western Rights Tradition: An Historical Inquiry. *Boston College Law Review* 33(1): 37–92.

Reinhart, Kevin A. 1995. *Before Revelation: The Boundaries of Muslim Moral Thought.* Syracuse, NY: State University of New York Press.

Reuters. 2019. Friday Sermon by the Imam of the New Zealand Mosque Attacked by Gunman. Published March 22, 2019. Available at: https://www.reuters.com/article/us-newzealand-shootout-sermon-text-idUSKCN1R30G2

Rida, Rashid. 1984. The Ease of Islam and the Foundations of General Legislation (*Yusr al-islām wa-uṣūl al-tashrīʿ al-ʿāmm*). Cairo: Maktabat al-Salām al-ʾĀlamiyya.

Rumee, Ahmed, Idris Nassery, and Muna Tatari, eds. 2018. *The Objectives of Islamic Law: The Promises and Challenges of Maqasid al-Shari'a.* Lanham, MD: Lexington Books.

Saeed, Abdullah. 2002. The Charge of Distortion of Jewish and Christian Scriptures. *The Muslim World* 92(3): 419–436. https://doi.org/10.1111/j.1478-1913.2002.tb03751.x

Said, Edward W. 1979. *Orientalism.* New York: Vintage.

Said, Edward W. 1997. *Covering Islam: How the Media and the Experts Determine How We See the Rest of the World.* Rev. ed. New York: Vintage.

Saleh, Fakhri. 2009. Arab Reactions to the Pope's Visit: Signs of Hope. Quantara. de website. Published October 30, 2009. Available at: https://en.qantara.de/content/arab-reactions-to-the-popes-visit-signs-of-hope

Sanusi, Lamido Sanusi. 2007. Politics and Sharia in Northern Nigeria. In *Islam and Politics in Africa*, edited by Benjamin F. Soares and René Otayek, 177–188. New York: Palgrave Macmillan. https://doi.org/10.1057/9780230607101_10

Sharkey, Heather J. 2017. *A History of Muslims, Christians and Jews in the Middle East.* Cambridge: Cambridge University Press. https://doi.org/10.1017/9781139028455

Singha, Sara. 2018. Christians in Pakistan and Afghanistan: Responses to Marginalization from the Peripheries. In *Under Caesar's Sword: How Christians Respond to Persecution*, edited by Daniel Philpott and Timothy Samuel Shah, 229–258. Law and Christianity Series, edited by John Witte, Jr., Cambridge: Cambridge University Press. https://doi.org/10.1017/9781108348331.008

Sizer, Stephen. 2005. *Christian Zionism: Roadmap to Armageddon?* Downers Grove, IL: IVP Academic, 2005.

Skeel, David. 2014. *True Paradox: How Christianity Makes Sense of Our Complex World* (Downer's Grove, IL: IVP Books).

Solomon, Noah. 2016. *For Love of the Prophet: An Ethnography of Sudan's Islamic State.* Princeton, NJ: Princeton University Press.

Stassen, Glen H. 1992. *Just Peacemaking: Transforming Initiatives for Justice and Peace.* Louisville, KY: Westminster John Knox Press.

Stassen, Glen, ed. 2008. *Just Peacemaking: A New Paradigm for the Ethics of Peace and War.* Boston, MA: Pilgrim Press.

Stassen, Glen H., and David P. Gushee. 2017. *Kingdom Ethics: Following Jesus in the Contemporary Context*, 2nd ed. Grand Rapids, MI: Eerdmans.

Tammam, Husam. 2007. Yusuf al-Qaradawi and the Muslim Brothers: The Nature of a Special Relationship. In *Global Mufti: The Phenomenon of Yusuf al-Qaradawi*, edited by Bettina Gräf and Jacob Skovgaard-Petersen, 55–84. New York: Columbia University Press.

Theodorou, Angelina E. 2016. Which countries still outlaw apostasy and blasphemy? *Pew Research Center*. Published July 29, 2016. Available at: https://www.pewresearch.org/fact-tank/2016/07/29/ which-countries-still-outlaw-apostasy-and-blasphemy/

Tierney, Brian. 2006. *God's Joust and God's Justice: Law and Politics in the Western Tradition*. Grand Rapids, MI: Eerdmans.

United States Institute of Peace (staff). 2017. Nigeria's Imam and Pastor: Faith at the Front (Video). Published September 29, 2017. Available at: https://www. usip.org/publications/2017/09/nigerias-imam-and-pastor-faith-front-video

United Nations. 1979. UN General Assembly Session 34/90B. Published Dec. 12, 1979. Available at: http://www.un.org/en/ga/search/view_doc.asp?symbol=A/ RES/34/90

United States Conference of Bishops. 2005. Seven Themes of Catholic Social Teaching. Available at: http://www.usccb.org/beliefs-and-teachings/what-we-believe/ catholic-social-teaching/seven-themes-of-catholic-social-teaching.cfm

Van Dam, Andrew. 2018. The Surprising Way Gun Violence is Dividing America. *The Washington Post*. Published May 31, 2018. Available at: https://www. washingtonpost.com/news/wonk/wp/2018/05/31/the-surprising-way-gun-violence-is-dividing-america/?utm_term=.e3e2c0e082b6

Vaughan, Olufemi. 2016. *Religion and the Making of Nigeria*. Durham NC & London: Duke University Press.

Volf, Miroslav, Ghazi bin Mohammad and Melissa Yarrington, eds. 2010. *A Common Word: Muslims and Christians on Loving God and Neighbor*. Foreword by Tony Blair. Grand Rapids, MI: Eerdmans.

Wacks, Raymond. 2014. *Philosophy of Law: A Very Short Introduction*, 2nd ed. Oxford & New York: Oxford University Press. https://doi.org/10.1093/actrade/9780199687008.001.0001

Wallis, Jim. 2013. *On God's Side: What Religion Forgets and Politics Hasn't Learned about Serving the Common Good*. Grand Rapids, MI: Brazos Press.

Wallis, Jim. *America's Original Sin: Racism, White Privilege, and the Bridge to a New America* Grand Rapids, MI: Brazos Press, 2017.

Waltz, Susan. 2004. Universal Human Rights: The Contribution of Muslim States. *Human Rights Quarterly* 26: 799-844. https://doi.org/10.1353/hrq.2004.0059

Wikipedia. 'Black Lives Matter', accessed July 18, 2018. Available at: https:// en.wikipedia.org/wiki/Black_Lives_Matter#Internet_and_social_media

Wilson-Hartgrove, Jonathan. 2018. *Reconstructing the Gospel: Finding Freedom from Slaveholder Religion*. Downers Grove, IL: IVP.

Wolterstorff, Nicholas. *Justice: Rights and Wrongs*. Princeton and Oxford: Princeton University Press, 2008. https://doi.org/10.1515/9781400828715

Wolterstorff, Nicholas. 2011a. *Justice in Love*. Grand Rapids, MI, and Cambridge, UK: Eerdmans.

Wolterstorff. Nicholas. 2011b. What Is Justice? *The Justice Conference* (video, 42:35 min.). Available at: https://vimeo.com/20325071

Yamani, Sheikh Ahmad Zaki. Founder's Introduction. Al Furqān website. Available at: https://www.al-furqan.com/en/al-furqan-foundation/al-maqasid/chairmans-introduction

Yerkes, Sarah. 2016. What Egypt under Sissi Is Really Like for Coptic Christians. Brookings. Published June 20, 2016. Available at: https://www.brookings.edu/blog/markaz/2016/06/20/what-egypt-under-sissi-is-really-like-for-coptic-christians/

Zaqzuq, Mahmud Hamdi, ed. 2012. The Objectives of the Islamic Shari'a and Contemporary Issues: Research and Realities (*Maqāṣid al-sharīʿa al-islāmiyya wa-qaḍāyā al-ʾaṣr: buḥūth waw wa-qāʾiʿ*). The 22nd General Conference of the Supreme Council of Islamic Affairs, Cairo, February 22–25, 2010. Cairo: *Al-Majlis al-Aʿlā li-l-Shuʿūn al-Islāmiyya, Wizārat al-Awqāf, Jumhuriyya Maṣr al-ʾArabiyya*.

Index

Biblical References

Qur'anic References

Lightning Source UK Ltd.
Milton Keynes UK
UKHW020847230320
360730UK00003B/26